GLOBAL FRAGMENTS

GLOBAL FRAGMENTS

Latinamericanisms, Globalizations, and Critical Theory

EDUARDO MENDIETA

STATE UNIVERSITY OF NEW YORK PRESS

Cover Artwork by Craig Mueller.

Published by
State University of New York Press, Albany

For information, contact State University of New York Press, Albany, NY
www.sunypress.com

Production by Ryan Morris
Marketing by Michael Campochiaro

Library of Congress of Cataloging-in-Publication Data

Mendieta, Eduardo.
Global fragments : globalizations, Latinamericanisms, and critical theory / Eduardo Mendieta.
p. cm.
Includes bibliographical references and index.
ISBN 978-0-7914-7257-6 (hardcover : alk. paper)
ISBN 978-0-7914-7258-3 (pbk. : alk. paper)
1. Globalization. 2. Globalization—Philosophy. 3. Globalization—Social Aspects—Latin America. 4. Latin America—Foreign relations—1980– 5. Civilization, Modern—21st century. 6. Critical theory. I. Title.

JZ1318.M46 2007
303.48'201—dc22

2007005486

10 9 8 7 6 5 4 3 2 1

CONTENTS

ACKNOWLEDGMENTS

This book was conceived as a whole, made up of parts, parts that would be written as time allowed. The parts have taken longer to compile and write than I intended. I must first of all thank Jane Bunker, editor-in-chief at State University of New York Press Press, for taking this project under her wing. I also want to thank the State University of New York Press editorial board, which reviews all the reader's reports and manuscripts and approves, rejects, or requests revisions of every book the press publishes. I am extremely honored and proud that my work has undergone this important and thorough vetting. I also want to express my deepest gratitude to the three anonymous readers who made invaluable suggestions for revisions, which I have to the best of my ability incorporated in the final version of the manuscript. The book is the better because of their incisive criticisms. If I did not do everything they requested and recommended, I have provided philosophical justification for holding my own position. Even then, they speak through me. Obviously, the failures are mine, and the success of the book is ours to share jointly. Over the years I have been extremely fortunate to have colleagues invite me to contribute to projects they were working on. Their invitations provided the impetus and alibi to write some of the chapters that are here printed, in seriously expanded and revised forms. David Ingram, George Yancy, Alfonso del Toro, and Manfred Steger were extremely judicious, thorough, and generous editors. Alexei Lalo, from Minsk, Belarus, and then faculty member at the European Humanities University, invited me to offer some graduate courses on globalization, postcolonialism, and border theory, which proved invaluable to my thinking through some of the central issues in this book. Teaching students from all over the former Soviet Union was an incredibly enlightening experience that I doubt will be replicated. Bob Catterall, editor-in-chief of *City: Analysis of Urban Trends, Culture, Theory, Policy and Action*, has been a wonderful friend, supportive editor, and encouraging critic. Chapter 2 of this book I owe to him and his prodding. Mario Sàenz read an early version of the manuscript and made substantive suggestions, many of which saved me from scholarly embarrassments. Linda Martín Alcoff has been a coeditor on several projects, but most importantly she has been an incomparable and dependable philosophical friend, even when we do not see eye to eye on questions epistemological and ontological. The support, encouragement, criticism, and exhortation by Jorge Gracia have been extremely important in my work. His trust, above all, has been sustaining as I have encountered resistance to some of my work from more orthodox colleagues (*philodoxers*, as Plato calls them in the *Republic*) in the field. My colleagues at the University of San Francisco, where I taught for seven years and where I began this book, were extremely supportive: David Batstone, Pedro Lange-Churión, Lois Ann Lorentzen. Associate Provost, Gerardo Marin made it possible for me to pursue the research that resulted in this book. My students Martin Woessner, Azucena Cruz, and Chad Kautzer were extremely judicious research assistants, proofreaders, and digitizers. Their help was indispensable. Special thanks go to Enrique Dussel and Cornel West, for their generosity and support of my work. Dussel actually hosted me and my family in his house during a research leave and has granted me complete access to his archives. West has also been extremely supportive and generous with his time. What is here published on him is neither the only thing nor the last thing I have to say about his philosophical contributions to dialogical cosmopolitanism. Finally, I want to express my gratitude to Professor Habermas, who hosted me in Germany, allowed me to translate some of his work, accepted my invitation to work on two interviews, and in turn invited me to challenge him on his views on religion. This book, and all the others of course, have been enabled and supported by the tolerance, patience, love, and companionship of my friend and wife, Jen. This book is dedicated to Emily and Callum, may they grow up to be as ecumenical and eclectic in their interests and friends as this book sought to be without apologies and shame.

Introduction

Epistemic Hubris and Dialogical Cosmopolitanism

How Not to Know

Globalization is to many pure ideology, and it is an ideology that operates at different levels, with different degrees of effectiveness, to the evident benefit of a very few. To many, globalization helps describe and name a new societal situation that is different not just in degree but also in kind from what preceded it, even if a precise dateline is not forthcoming. To many others, it is certainly a conceptual and theoretical utopia. The term is used as a noun although it is a verb, but it can also be marshaled as both an adjective and an adverb. The term is as versatile and seemingly innocuous as Martin Heidegger's *Sein*. Like Heidegger's *Sein*, it is complicit in concealing degrees of responsibility, deception, and self-delusion. It invites *Gelassenheit* and *Entschlossenheit*, letting be and resoluteness: Globalization will come of its own accord, or, alternatively, we must seize society and try to emulate the West and globalize—become global, globalize our modernity, and form part of globalization. In its uses and confusions, globalization resembles closely the other great word of contemporary social theory: modernity. I argue in this book that globalization has taken over the tasks that modernity used to perform. Like modernity, globalization is a term that helps us order societies in hierarchical and invidious ways that always put the United States and the so-called West, or Occident, in enviable and also unattainable positions. Like modernity, globalization is a theoretical grid that distorts the world, as it reveals aspects of it, while also distorting our place as epistemic subjects and objects. If modernity was the avant-garde position of the West—the European West—globalization is the avant-garde position of the United States, which has taken over the *mission civilisatrice* of the West. The United States is the latest, most forward point in a world-historical narrative and time line. This narrative and time line, which some have called a metanarrative, harkens back to the idea of divine history (*Heilsgeschichte*), which has as its underbelly a theodicy that exonerates humans of all culpability for their inequity and injustice. Today globalization is the name of this gospel. It promises salvation, but also the convenient alibi that globalization's devastating effects and exacting costs are both inevitable and, in the end, worth the sacrifice. Like God's salvation plan with its math of punishment and expiation, globalization offers wealth to some but a calculus of destitution, starvation and exclusion to far too many.[1]

Globalization is indeed ideology, part self-deluding fantasy, part distortion of reality, part epistemology in search of corroboration, part critical thought grappling with its own historicity and limits. Theodor W. Adorno's take on the concept of totality is instructive with respect to the ideological dimensions of globalization, and guides my analysis in this book. In *Negative Dialectics,* Adorno wrote: "Totality is to be opposed by convicting it of nonidentity with itself—of the nonidentity it denies, according to its own concept."[2] Indeed, the entire world is not globalized, does not form part of globalization, is not even actively globalizing. Furthermore and on the other hand, there are forms of globalization that are either elided or entirely negated by the type of globalization that gets the most press time in the West and the United States. Adorno also took a stand against "universal history." This history led from the sling shot to the atom bomb must be both "construed and denied."[3] This book operates under this kind of imperative, of having to construe, visualize, and represent a world that is conceptualized under this shibboleth "globalization" in order to convict it, to indict it, to deny it, because under its very conceptual light, the spreading darkness of its demise is concealed, negated, and dismissed. Under globalization, the world has become more fragmented as economic inequality shears continents and societies from each other as they grow more interdependent on the well-being of the planet. The other side of globalization, that celebrated by the West and the United States, is the cosmopolitan dimension of its political, ethical, and moral values. Human rights have become a global standard, even as the United States, to its own discredit, tramples them. Feminism and religious tolerance are also global standards. The rights of religious, ethnic minorities, and cultures on the brink of extinction are also a major global concern. The development of a global ecological movement and consciousness that is pushing regulation of multinationals, as well as fueling movements like the anti-GM foods and plants throughout the world, are part and parcel of this new global consciousness. Globalization has made it impossible to retreat behind the shields of nationalism, ethnic chauvinism, religious intolerance, and economic protectionism. Even, or some may say, especially, the United States cannot control the juggernaut of globalization. The Washington and Davos consensuses have to be countered with Porto Allegre, Seattle, and Beijing. The globalization from above has to be countered with a globalization from below. The globalization indexes of *Foreign Policy*, and the *New York Times*, have to be checkmated with the globalization indexes of Vandana Shiva's Research Foundation for Science,

Technology, and Natural Resources, the Worldwatch Institute, and Redefining Progress. In the language of my intellectual grandparents, we must think of globalization as both a normative and descriptive totality, which is both horizontal and vertical.[4] Globalization describes, but also evaluates or imposes normative standards. Similarly, it describes the world in terms of a pattern or process, but it also gives us snapshots, freeze-frame pictures of the state of the world at any given time. Globalization is not just about the growth in consumption, industrialization, and expansion of the car fleet; it is also about raising the living standards of more than half of the world population, about literacy, about gender equity, about the equitable and fair distribution and consumption of the planet's resources. There are many globalizations going on: one set, dreamed up and legislated from above, threatens to destroy the world; the other, fought from below, hopes to save the world and make sure that the world of globalization is a world of globalized political, economic, and cultural justice.[5]

The book is made up of fragments. It is about fragments, and about the fragmentation of the world in an age of globalization. The title *Global Fragments*, captures three central ideas that orient the book. First, one of the central ideas that is communicated by the title is that all theorizations, all images and imaginations of and about globalization are only fragmentary. I often make reference to Jorge Luis Borges's parables and metaphysical stories to illustrate this point. Borges was the master of the philosophical tale, and some of his classic stories have to do with libraries, Alephs, labyrinths, total books and inexhaustible encyclopedias, hyperrealistic maps, and ur-texts. In Borges's work, however, these total, totalizing, totalitarian accoutrements of utopian dreaming turn into their own nemesis. Even when viewing the impossible object, the Aleph, in which the whole world is captured and seen at once, like God's eye, can offer but a perspective. All that remains are the shreds, torn parchments, ruins, footnotes, fragments, and snapshots of a total but impossible *sub specie aternitatis* gaze. There can be no total perspective on the global world. Theories of globalization are at best epistemological fragments.

Another central idea that guides this book is that the fragments of society, of human consciousness, and even geohistorical units (whether we see them as fictions or actual geographic formations—that is, Latin America does not exist except in the geopolitical maps of nineteenth-century Imperial designs) are products of globalization, the process of globalizing the planet. This book argues, forcefully enough I hope, that as we have become more interdependent, entire regions of the world, but also sectors of society, within our own societies, have been torn from the fabric of civilization. Africa, for example, is plagued by AIDS, starvation, endless civil unrest, genocidal ethnic wars, and is sinking farther into what theologian Engelvert Mveng has called "anthropological poverty." Within the United States, we have our own types of fragments drifting away in seas of dehumanizing poverty, neglect, and ultimately, invisibility. African Americans, notwithstanding the minimal gains of a showcase black middle class, are caught in a vicious cycle of prisionization, criminalization, undereducation, social marginalization, and political disenfranchisements. Plantations, ghettos, hyperghettos, ethnoracial prisons, the death penalty—these are racial mappings, topographies of terror and exclusion.[6] They are the mechanism through which the United States sends adrift entire sections of its society into a sea of material destitution, despair, and hopelessness. Latin America is another global fragment, both theoretically and geopolitically. Continents and subcontinents do not exist.[7] They exist only in the imaginary maps of imperial designs. This is no less true of Latin America than it is of Europe, Africa, and Asia. Yet, even if they do not exist in actuality, these geopolitical markers matter profoundly, because they become the means by which sectors of society are precisely excluded and written out of history, from the web of human interdependence.

Finally, the third idea that is evoked in the title *Global Fragments* is that of biotheoretical fragments. The lives of ideas are linked to the ideas of the living, and the living give life to ideas in specific geohistorical contexts. It is not possible, after Giambattista Vico, G.W.F. Hegel, and José Ortega y Gasset, to say like Heidegger said of Aristotle, and I paraphrase: "That he lived, and what was important was his philosophy." The *bios-theoreticos* is a bios-historical. This book is oriented by a further qualification on the *bios-theoreticos*, that as a bios-historical it is also a fragment of geopolitical life. Ideas have historical lives, but these lives are geohistorical. In the age of globalization, ideas travel, either wittingly or unwittingly.[8] They are produced in local contexts, but have global effects, in different degrees, depending on where they are produced. Like commodities, ideas and the thinkers that produce them are caught in the rapacious grip of the global market of images, imaginaries, and imaginations.[9] In this book, however, I am interested in the theoretical fragments of systematic thinkers and how those fragments reflect the fragmentary character of a globalized world, and the way that globalization can only be conceptualized fragmentarily.

The book is therefore organized in three parts, each part dealing with three types, if you will, of fragments: epistemological fragments, geohistorical-political fragments, and biotheoretical fragments. The first part, "Globalizations," is made up of two of my fragments dealing with the different ways in which we have theorized globalization. I began writing the first chapter, "Philosophizing Globalizations," in the spring of 2002 when I taught a seminar on globalization and postcolonial theories at the European Humanities University in Minsk, Belarus. It has not previously been published. Like the second chapter, it outlines the philosophical project of developing a phenomenology of globalization from below. The assumption is that at very ontic and mundane levels we already have intuitions of what globalizations means. In this chapter I begin from below in a dual sense. I begin with those most poor, those excluded and exploited, the half of humanity that lives on less than two dollars a day in the megaslums of hyperurbanized humanity. But I also begin from the bottom of phenomenology, which claims that first philosophy is disclosedness.[10] The primacy of phenomenology is not a mark of obscurantism or philosophical purism. Thought begins with wonderment, and phenomenology begins with the wonder of human existence. In our case, it is the wonder, the outraged and aghast wonder at the poverty of human existence in an age of affluence and plenty. Philosophy can only be practiced responsibly today if it squats with living human beings in the squalor of a world so unequally shared and squandered.

The second part gathers fragments of what I called "Latinamericanisms," or, more precisely, the Latinamericanisms of globalization. These chapters are haunted by a tired but unconsumed nostalgia, the kind of mature but also bittersweet realization that we all seek to return to imaginary homelands—to use the felicitous expression by Salman Rushdie. In this age of easy identities, it is wonderful to be homeless and to yearn for something that is impossible. And to paraphrase Adorno, in the age of global mass culture, to be homeless, "not to be at home in one's own home," is perhaps one of the only traces left of ethics.[11] They are thus also haunted by the realization that "strategic essentialism" will not do, for it will continue to fuel an unhealthy nostalgia, the nostalgia for home, when home itself has succumbed to commodification. The chapters in the second part thus waver and quiver between the extremes of affirming that Latin America is but a geopolitical and imperial imaginary and affirming that there is a kind of Wittgensteinian family story that holds us together in the soothing embrace of the memory of suffering, with its ethical imperatives and moral duties. At least this is how I felt when I wrote them, although I also took them as occasions to educate myself about the philosophical struggles being waged in Latin America, Europe, and the United States about how to make sense of the relationship between theory and geopolitics. Still, while they are about Latin America, both real and imaginary, these chapters are also about the geohistorical chronology of master ideas and the idea of masters: modernity, postmodernity, and globalization. Each chapter offers, thus, a case study in the acculturation of ideas and the itinerary of traveling ideas and ideologies. However, insofar as these chapters all deal with different chronotopes—that is, ways of mapping time and temporalizing space—they are contributions to what I have called "chronotopology.[12]

The third part of *Global Fragments* gathers four chapters about three public intellectuals who have influenced, guided, and inspired my thought. In these chapters, I have tried to think with these titans of thought in unusual and unexpected ways. I have studied and read them from the standpoint of my own unusual location—but we all do that. I have deliberately sought to read these thinkers in tangential, although appositional ways.

Enrique Dussel, whom I have translated and edited for a long time, for instance, I read as contributing to a critical theory of globalization. I also seek to place him within a less nationalistic, Eurocentric, geopolitics of ideas. I think he is not just a Latin American philosopher. He is also a thinker of the West, of and against globalization. Dussel should be perhaps more aptly characterized as a post–Latin American and postoccidentalist philosopher.[13] This entire book labors under the shadow of his monumental *Ética de la Liberación en la edad de la globalización y de la exclusión.*[14]

I read Jürgen Habermas, another of my major influences, from the angle of religion and theology, and especially from the angle of how he inherits the central European Jewish roots of a critique of religion that still sees religion as a source of critical thought. For this tradition the critique of religion is also a religious critique of the world.[15] Indeed, Habermas, "the Jew and theologian," could have been the subtitle of my chapter on him in this volume. As preposterous as this may sound to some, Habermas has thought out of, with, and against this unfathomably generative tradition of Jewish romantic, messianic, prophetic, posttheological, and postphilosophical social critique. In fact, the chapter was first written for the introduction to a volume of Habermas's selected chapters on religion, theology, and rationality.[16] The volume, which was first published in Spanish with the more appropriate title of *Israel or Athens*,[17] gathered only a portion of the many chapters Habermas has written on these themes. With this edited volume I wanted to document Habermas's long involvement with the tradition and thematic of religious critique. Thus, Habermas is not a latecomer to the question of the relationship between religion, democracy, modernity, and now globalization. Nor is he an opportunistic philosemite. (And by the same token, he cannot be accused of antisemitism when he criticizes the United States for its disastrous policies in the Middle East.[18])

The final chapter is particularly dear to me because in grappling with Cornel West's relationship to pragmatism and the black traditions of critical thought in the United States, I come closest to my own philosophical and existential dilemmas.[19] Philosophically, Cornel West is quintessentially an "American" thinker: he combines skepticism of the mind with an optimism of the heart. He is the philosopher clearing the philosophical underbrush but also the religiously inspired visionary that can point in the direction of a better future. He is also confessedly and avowedly on the side of the poor. His philosophizing is always guided by a preferential option for the niggerized, ghettoized, and racialized in the United States and world society. Since I began work on this book, I began with the thought that the only way critical thinking, in the tradition of the Frankfurt School at the Institute for Social Research, can be responsibly carried on is if we combine the kind of thinking that these three figures metonymically embrace. Dussel, thinker of the underside of globalization and modernity; Habermas, thinker of the enlightenment to come and the power of discursive-communicative reason at work in quotidian existence; West, thinker of a political pragmatism that gives primacy to the empowerment of society's downtrodden. Their thinking is linked by their common preoccupation with the power of reason to break through fetishized social reality, with the promise and hope gathered in the compendium that is religion, and with the historical efficacy of historicized reason as it is plucked from the thorny bush of tortured reality by the engaged democratic praxis of cosmopolitan and ecumenical postnational, and postsecular, agents. Dussel, Habermas, and West, in my analysis (and this is what I argue within the last part of this book), are pivotal centers of thought in a new constellation of critical thought for the twenty-first century in the age of globalization and global fragments.

Cosmopolitanisms

This book, which so insistently defends and affirms the fragmentary, however, should not and cannot be read as condoning a frivolous and insouciant form of postmodernism. The affirmation of the fragmentary that is the mark of this text is an overt denunciation and challenge to all forms of epistemic hubris, which comes in the form of either closing knowledge claims to the claims of those who have been rendered voiceless and unworthy of recognition, or in the form of an epistemic neglect that would not consider the claims of the voiceless as worthy of consideration at all. Thus, it could be said that the critique of epistemic hubris entailed by the celebration of circumscribed and historicized knowledge claims is at the service of the recognition of the other. In all my work, here and elsewhere, the other is not some metaphysical specter. The other is neither pure alterity nor a metaphysical edge. The other is always historical, specific, and most importantly, suffering flesh and clamoring subjectivity. As with Adorno's critique of epistemology and positivistic sociology, which were recruited at the service of a negative moral philosophy,[20] my critique of epistemology, comprehensive theories of globalization, and the adverse effects of certain epistemic matrices are also at the service of an ethics that recognizes, affirms, and responds to other. Therefore, notwithstanding the seeming agnostic and nonaffirmative character of most of the chapters in this book, the thrust of my argumentation is to endorse what I call a "dialogic cosmopolitanism." I will now turn to a characterization of this form of cosmopolitanism, which opens up a horizon of encounter and response in space left decolonized and pacified by the work of epistemological critique.

In an essay published in the fall of 1994 in the *Boston Review*, Martha Nussbaum succinctly and eloquently elaborated and defended a form of civic cosmopolitanism, which she juxtaposed to parochial and jingoistic patriotism. The aim of the essay, however, was not just to defend cosmopolitanism and reject patriotism, but also to endorse cosmopolitanism as the focus of civic education. For Nussbaum, who has philosophized extensively on pedagogy, the relevance of the debate is determined by how it would impact the way we would educate citizens. Thus, for Nussbaum, cosmopolitanism is not an abstract, philosophical stance, but rather a very practical and result-oriented attitude. If we educate citizens to see themselves primarily as citizens of a world community, as opposed to members of narrow, special, chosen, and exceptional communities, then these citizens would be less likely to engage in the rituals of blood that are so indispensable to patriotism, and would instead be more responsive and engaged with the cultures and welfare of communities across the globe. In this essay, therefore, Nussbaum elaborates four arguments for why a cosmopolitan-oriented and -guided civic education is a greater benefit to the United States, and others as well, than patriotically oriented civic education. First, because "through cosmopolitan education, we learn more about ourselves." Second, we are better prepared to solve problems that "require international cooperation." Third, "we recognize moral obligations to the rest of the world that are real and that otherwise would go unrecognized." Fourth, we learn to "make consistent and coherent" arguments that we are prepared to defend intelligibly.[21] One can quickly unfurl myriad arguments against Nussbaum's defense of cosmopolitanism, which can easily be confused with a rootless form of universalism and abstract humanism (as several of the commentators on her original essay already have). Yet, it is difficult not to be sympathetic with the pedagogical aims of her defense of cosmopolitanism. While it is true that we are socialized and nurtured in local ethical communities, we are faced with global problems that command that we look to the world, even as we are indisputably rooted in specific ethical traditions. What I want to underscore and take from Nussbaum's four arguments in defense of a cosmopolitan-focused civic education is her fourth reason. Being educated to think as a member of global community raises the epistemic bar on what kinds of distinctions and arguments we are capable of making. What Nussbaum is pointing out, I think, is that cosmopolitanism is not just an emotive or affective stance toward the claims of others, but that it is also a theoretical and conceptual stance that commands us to assess the cogency of our claims from the standpoint of sometimes abstract others (but sometimes very concrete others) who happen to be on different continents. Cosmopolitanism is also an epistemic stance.

Kwame Anthony Appiah, who was one of the respondents to Nussbaum's chapter, published in 2006 a book entitled *Cosmopolitanism: Ethics in a World of Strangers*.[22] Appiah, who has written on questions of identity, multiculturalism, race, imperialism, and nationalism extensively, frames this book in terms of what is the proper rubric to use in order to confront the challenges of the modern world: globalization, multiculturalism, or cosmopolitanism? He settles on the last, although he notes that its meaning is contested and it can be argued that cosmopolitanism is both an ideal and a particular stance. Appiah, however, proceeds to profile two distinct "strands" within cosmopolitanism. One strand underscores the idea that we have "obligations" to others. The other strand affirms that we must "take seriously the value not just of human life but of particular human lives, which means taking an interest in the practices and beliefs that lend them significance."[23] Human difference, for this second strand, is an intrinsic good and must be preserved, celebrated, and most importantly, learned from. As with Nussbaum, for Appiah cosmopolitanism has eminently pedagogical benefits, and like her, he also thinks that cosmopolitanism entails a moral orientation. This moral orientation imposes on all certain duties and responsibilities. Much of what follows in this book is about profiling these duties and responsibilities, the contexts in which they become most evident, and what elements and forms of thinking and knowing obscure these obligations toward strangers. There is, however, an argument in Appiah's book that is implicit in his distinction between two strands within cosmopolitanism but that only becomes explicit much later in the book. In the chapter entitled "The Counter-Cosmopolitans," in which Appiah discusses the neofundamentalist, Christian, Muslim (etc.) reaction to the cosmopolitan challenge, he writes: "If cosmopolitanism is, in a slogan, universality plus difference, there is the possibility of another kind of enemy, one who rejects universality all together. 'Not everybody matters' would be their slogan."[24]

Indeed, whether you are a religious, market-economy, or American-supremacy *überalles* fundamentalist, and thus you think that there are a lot of others who do not matter and that their interests, knowledge claims, local histories, threatened traditions, and endangered forms of life are unimportant or worth our respect and concern, you're still within the space of reason. Appiah is clear about this: "Once you start offering reasons for ignoring the interests of others, however, reasoning itself will usually draw you into a kind of universality."[25] This is an extremely important insight, one that Appiah arrives at through a via negative—that is, when those who want to take a stance against cosmopolitanism draw up their reasons, they are unwittingly in the grip of universal reason. Yet, I would argue, not only the countercosmopolitan but also the avowed cosmopolitan is in the grip of some sort of "universality." Both are in the space of reason. Consequently, I can make the claim that cosmopolitanism is an ethical orientation that puts reason on call, on guard. Universality, consequently, must be rearticulated, defended, expanded, and made concrete. Cosmopolitanism must therefore entail a self-critique of one's prejudices, as well as a confession and disclosure as to one's own epistemic standpoint.

The reason of the cosmopolitan must be a cosmopolitan reason and yet-to-be-specified universality. For this reason, one can speak of a naïve, or ideological cosmopolitanism, the kind that makes communitarians and conservatives bristle with contempt but that also makes those critical of cultural imperialism impatient and highly critical of dehistoricized enunciations of universal reason. This type of cosmopolitanism, which refuses to submit its own universality claims to critique, to enter the space of reason in a symmetrical and egalitarian way with others who are at the table of cosmopolitanism, can turn into a form of epistemic arrogance that, like a fig leaf, barely conceals contemptuous disregard and brutal self-interest. Unfortunately, the history of the modern world furnishes plenty of examples of such forms of naivete, and in most cases, imperial cosmopolitanism. Neither Nussbaum nor Appiah are naive cosmopolitans. Nor can one accuse them of offering fodder for the canons of neoliberal globalism and Western neoimperialism. Their work on cosmopolitanism, absolutely indispensable, must be extended and supplemented.

The opposite of naive—and imperial—cosmopolitanism, it may be argued, would be a critical cosmopolitanism. Walter Mignolo has in fact defended and articulated such a form of cosmopolitanism. He has done so weaving in a magisterial way a critical history of Western colonialism with incisive insights into key philosophical figures in a decolonized philosophical canon. Since I discuss in greater detail Mignolo's work in the second part of this book, I want to abstain from extensive commentaries. In a brilliant chapter entitled "The Many Faces of Cosmo-polis: Border Thinking and Critical Cosmopolitanism,"[26] Mignolo illustrates in actu the virtues of a critical cosmopolitanism by distinguishing among three different global-imperial designs and what were their corresponding cosmopolitan projects. According to Mignolo, to the global designs of the Spanish and Portuguese empires from the sixteenth through the seventeenth century, corresponded the cosmopolitanism of the Christian mission—that is, cosmopolitanism as evangelization and Christianization of the pagan and heathens. To the French and English imperial designs during the eighteenth and nineteenth centuries corresponded the cosmopolitan mission of civilizing, that is, cosmopolitanism as civilizing the barbarians. To the United States, translational, global, and neocolonial imperial designs during the twentieth century, corresponded the cosmopolitan mission of modernizing, that is, cosmopolitanism as modernization, or globalization, of the premodern and traditional. One does not need to subscribe to this particular chronology or the corresponding organizing principles (missionizing, civilizing, modernizing) in order to recognize the validity of the critique of the ways in which certain embodiments of cosmopolitanism have, explicitly or implicitly, condoned, justified, and legitimated colonialism, imperialism, and neocolonialism. Mignolo's task, in this essay as well as in most of his work, is not just deconstructive and critical; it is also positive and constructive. The point of this critical cosmopolitanism is to open it up to other voices and others who challenge the reason of imperial and global designs that have resulted in so much inequality and human suffering. The task of critical cosmopolitanism, then, is to rescue, retrieve, and made audible and visible the voices of those local histories that have been rendered subaltern and silent by the imperial ethos that heeds the call of "you're either with us or against us," to use the language of George W. Bush's Manichean theodicy. As Mignolo put it "Critical and dialogic cosmopolitanism as a regulative principle demands yielding generously ("convivially" said Vitoria; "friendly" said Kant) toward diversity as a universal and cosmopolitan project in which everyone participates instead of "being participated."[27] Critical cosmopolitanism, therefore, is oriented to a form of universality that Mignolo calls "diversality," a combination of diversity and universality. To paraphrase what was written above, the reason and universality of critical cosmopolitanism is a cosmopolitan diversality and rationality, or more precisely diversal rationality. In Mignolo's words: "Diversality should be the relentless practice of critical and dialogical cosmopolitanism rather than the blueprint of a future and ideal society projected from a single point of view (that of abstract universality)."[28]

What Mignolo is noting is that cosmopolitanism is caught in what has been called by Karl-Otto Apel a "performative contradiction," that is to say, there is a way in which all cosmopolitan claims are defacto deferred and thus awaiting further specification by that in the name of which we are called to respect, celebrate, and heed: the claims of the others, the claims of strangers, as Appiah calls them. Interestingly, Judith Butler has made this exact point in her response to Martha Nussbaum's essay "Patriotism and Cosmopolitanism." Butler's response takes up the "performative contradiction" character of universality claims implied in cosmopolitan claims and argues for a universality that must be articulated by and through the challenges to "its existing formulation, and this challenge[s] emerge[s] from those who are not covered by it, who have not entitlement to occupy the place of the 'who,' but who nevertheless demand that the universal as such ought to be inclusive of them."[29] This universality that is always deferred and caught in its own insufficiency is what Mignolo has called "diversality." Both Mignolo and Butler agree on something far more important than on signaling that all cosmopolitan enunciations of universality demand that the universal itself be held in suspension, as an asymptotic horizon, a counterfactual, without which but also against which, we must engage in order to enable a proper response to the other. They agree more dramatically on the place of the other in this pedagogy of the universal, in the expansion and enlightenment of universality itself. Mignolo has argued that critical cosmopolitanism is sustained in its critical stance when it adopts what he calls the locus of enunciation of the subaltern.[30] Butler has argued that it is the "who" that is excluded from a given articulation of the universal that constitutes the "contingent limit of universalization." Both, in my view, are arguing that cosmopolitanism is made cosmopolitan by the diversality of the subaltern, the excluded other, the stranger, the marginalized. For this reason, one can speak of a cosmopolitanism from below, one that matches the sociopolitical effects of a globalization from below, as I argue in part one of this book. Mignolo and Butler give voice to what can be called the cosmopolitanism of the subaltern, and it is one that has been educating those in the metropolises of the West and who claim to speak univocally and unequivocally for the universal as such. I argue in the part three of this book that Dussel, West, and Habermas have been articulating this type of cosmopolitanism when they have sought to think from the standpoint of the voice of those hitherto silence, excluded, and niggerized.

I noted at the outset of this section that I take this book to be defending a form of dialogical cosmopolitanism. I sought to profile my position through engagement with the work of several thinkers who have influenced my thinking on the issue. The work of Nussbaum led me to think of cosmopolitanism as a practical pursuit, and above all as a pedagogical pursuit that would influence civic education, to educating "good citizens." Appiah led me to recognize that cosmopolitanism is both an attitude and ideal that valorizes difference. His work also led me to recognize the theoretical work this valorization entails. Mignolo led me to see the extreme dangers of a dehistoricized and delocalized cosmopolitanism. Butler articulated in language that is very familiar to people who have been trained in German critical theory the challenges Mignolo articulated in the language of Latin American cultural studies and what he has called the "colonial difference." All of these thinkers have helped me, and us collectively, to see how honest and disingenuous cosmopolitanism must be critical, from below, obsequious of the subaltern, and above all, always alert to its potential misappropriations. Critical cosmopolitanism requires that we acknowledge our epistemic locus, that is to say, our hermeneutical point of departure, which in some cases may be a point of epistemic privilege but in others may command epistemic humility. Cosmopolitanism, simply put, demands that we situate ourselves, for as Butler wrote in her essay in response to Nussbaum, "the meaning of 'the universal' proves to be culturally variable, and the specific cultural articulations of the universal work against its claim to transcultural status."[31] One can therefore speak of a *situated* cosmopolitanism, as Lorenzo Simpson has.

In fact, critical theorist Lorenzo Simpson has articulated eloquently what Mignolo and Butler have argued, using singly different terminology, which explicitly takes up the challenge of Rortyan fulminations against vacuous forms of universalism. I quote at length:

> A hermeneutically self-aware ethnocentrist, one aware of her transcendental ethnocentrism, would hold others up to the criteria that her lights reveal, but not in a way that dogmatically precludes the possibility (or desirability) that her standards may change, that she could learn from others. To be hermeneutically self-reflexive implies, for me, an openness and a willingness to take seriously the conjecture that there is a disjunction between one's own stand-

> point and the regulative ideal of the "good life." On the other hand, the postmodern relativist's refusal to judge can betray a refusal *to be judged*, a refusal both to make claims *on* others and to be claimed *by* those others. Our openness to the claims of the other places our identities in relief. And the critical renegotiation of identity can take place on both sides of the conversation table.[32]

Critical cosmopolitanism of the sort that Mignolo advocates is precisely the same thing that Simpson calls "hermeneutically self-aware ethnocentrism." This form of self-reflexive hermeneutics that implies entering the space of reason symmetrically and in an egalitarian way also implies that one be open to having to give reason for one's claim to universality and the claims to universality of those others with whom we share many hermeneutical differences. The hermeneutical self-reflexive position is neither arrogant nor blasé, for there is a way in which disregard and ersatz humility are as pugnacious and searing as blunt and unmasked arrogance can be. This is a point that Amartya Sen has made in several occasions and particularly when he wrote with respect to the project of the promotion of democracy across the world: "The apparent Western modesty that takes the form of a humble reluctance to promote 'Western ideas of democracy,' in the non-Western world includes an imperious appropriation of a global heritage as exclusively the West's own."[33] Hermeneutical humility must be matched by hermeneutical solicitude. For this reason, the giving and requesting of reason must be symmetrical and reversible. Simpson, therefore, calls his form of cosmopolitanism "situated," as it explicitly confesses the circumscribed hermeneutical horizon from which it is enunciated. By now it should have become clear why it is that I call the type of cosmopolitanism that I defend in this book "dialogical cosmopolitanism." I call it dialogical not out of disrespect to my colleagues, nor because I am in the grip of the anxiety of influence, nor because my position is fundamentally different from theirs and I want to trace a line on the horizon that separates us. In my view, dialogical cosmopolitanism encompasses within its adjective references to critical, situated, self-reflexive, and most importantly obsequiousness and solicitude toward the pedagogy of the oppressed and subaltern. Just because epistemic purity and completeness are the privilege of only gods and eternal minds does not mean that we cannot learn from others and with others, and most importantly, it does not mean that our moral duties toward others are suspended or unjustifiable. The absence of certitude is not the absence of responsibility. Dialogical cosmopolitanism situates us in our global fragments, but also turns our moral look to our global responsibilities and duties toward others.

Part 1

GLOBALIZATIONS

1

Philosophizing Globalizations

Philosophy may be understood as an attempt to think things in a unified way, either by getting at the root of things, or by trying to think the processes that link them. Philosophy is also history captured in thought, as Hegel put it, and thus, it is a particular historical period's portrait of itself, with all of its hopes and prejudices painted in philosophemes. Since Vico, and much later Hegel, we have not been able to escape the cul-de-sac into which this dual move of philosophy has corralled us: the quest for the absolute, but from a particular standpoint; the attempt to think the immutable, but seen through our narrow conceptual telescopes. We cannot escape our historical singularity. This singularity is in fact our only point of entry into the universal. We cannot jump over our historical shadow. Nor should we want to, for it is this historical singularity that grants us a unique insight into the universal, without which that universal would itself be the poorer. Globalization is one of these philosophemes with which we have attempted to paint our historical period, and by means of which we have tried to access something fundamental to the human experience. Several decades of research, writing, and debate, have resulted in a rich, variegated, and unwieldy literature on "globalization." As we have already suggested, globalization has become as important as, if not more important than the philosopheme of "modernity." In later chapters of this book, for instance, I will discuss the relationship between globalization, modernity, postmodernity, and postcolonialism. In this chapter, however, I will focus only on the questions of whether we can define globalization in a unified way and whether it has any philosophical relevance. The key affirmation in this chapter is that in order to think globalization from the standpoint of globalization—not as observers but as participants, not as unperturbed gazers but engaged and affected agents in and of globalization—we can only do it fragmentarily and by way of fragments. Globalization, like historicism, localizes us in space and time. For this reason, we must speak of globalizations in the plural. We must speak of globalizations in the sense of the plurality of processes and conditions that form part of this new planetary and human condition. We must also talk about it in the plural, for our view and insight into those processes can but only be local, circumscribed, and thus, plural and fragmentary. At any given time, as participants in globalization, we experience and witness only aspects of it. As agents conditioned by it, we may be acted upon by planetary forces and tensions, but differentially. The planet is globalized, indeed, but not all in the planet are globalized in the same way. Some are more globalized than others, some are affected more than others, and some are globalized adversely while others beneficially.[1] We are all globalized but under conditions not of our choosing and not to the same degrees.

Since we will trade in fragments, I will now lay out three large segments that in turn must be further fragmented. When we speak about globalizations, we face, at the very least, three main areas of contention and problematization. First, we face the problem area of *description*. If we are to differentiate globalization from other similar philosophemes, then at the very least we must offer some chronologies, or periodizations. When did globalization get to be inaugurated as a new global consciousness? As with all historical events, such periodizations can only be formulated postfacto. Perhaps we are not yet ready to look back and attempt to baptize the moment of inception. But this much is clear, so long as the very nature of globalization is under contest, that is, so long as we continue to debate whether it is primarily a political, economic, social, or technological event, then we will not be able to point to a historical juncture that served as the moment, or moments, of release, inauguration, or departure. Along with the issue about temporal descriptions comes the question of geography. History has a geography, both actual and imaginary, real and figurative.[2] Just as with modernity, which was about a geopolitics of knowledge and a putative teleology of history that localized all truly modern knowledge in Europe and that thus centered the historical vanguard of progress in the heartland of Europe, globalization also traces geopolitical maps.[3] A map of technological globalization, for instance, drawn by tracing the lines of internet links, will show how the world is hardly globalized: Africa, part of central Asia, and South America will figure in this map as dark regions, not lighted by the blinks of computers and cell phones. Yet, if we draw a map of the world in terms of epidemics, AIDS for instance, Africa and Central Asia, and parts of the American continents light up as through they were wired by the same circuits. Maps help us move around and find places we want to reach, but for that we need the right kind of maps and we need to know where it is that we are going. Still, chronological tables and global maps must be drawn up, then layered upon each other. Like a palimpsest, these spatiotemporal maps will give us a sense of the nonsynchronicity and unfathomable distance among societies on the same planet, which are all nonetheless held together by the grip of the same global embrace.

Second, we face the problem of what I will call inelegantly the *epistemological* challenges that globalization presents. When we think about globalization we must think about whether we are using a normative, and thus evaluative, category, or whether we are seeking to be merely descriptive. The issue concerns the nature of the cognitive, or epistemological, categories that we must use when theorizing the global condition. The parallels with the philosophemes of modernity and postmodernity are obvious and not to be circumvented. Modernity was used to describe, to evaluate, and to offer normative standards. In this way, it came to operate invidiously. To modernize was good, to be premodern was bad. Furthermore, as a normative standard, it fixated our attention on what were presented as exemplars of modernity, generally central European nation-states, and rarely non-Western societies. And while postmodern criticism sought to unmask this overt epistemological Eurocentrism, it reinscribed it by also localizing the origin of the crisis of modernity in the West. Postcolonial criticism has corrected much of the Eurocentrism and epistemological provincialism of the theorizing on both modernity and postmodernity. Today, to be globalized is good, and not to be is bad. But what are the standards and indexes of globalization? These are epistemological or conceptual questions that must be discussed prior and concurrently with the questions about how to describe the global condition. Epistemology is by no means the last bastion of philosophical naivete. On the contrary, it is one of the most contested dwellings of the philosophical edifice. At the most elemental level, we must acknowledge that knowledge is not just about what can be known, but also not known. Epistemology is simultaneously a positive and a negative science. Just as there are epistemologies of knowing, there are epistemologies of ignorance. The former is always parasitic on the latter, and thus there is an asymmetry. What is claimed to be known may draw on what is suppressed, but once we address how the unknown or unknoweable is rendered such, we will know more about knowledge itself. Standpoint epistemologies, such as feminist epistemologies, make this asymmetry productive.

Epistemology, furthermore, concerns knowing subjects and subjects that cannot know. Epistemology, thus, concerns the genealogies of epistemic subjects, or more precisely the genealogy of a type of subjection that enables a certain type of knowing while disallowing other forms of knowing. Globalization, as a philosopheme, is also rooted in these debates.[4] How does globalization aid or hinder our knowing the world? Who, or more precisely what type of epistemic subjects, and more generally what kinds of societies, are enabled or disallowed to make claims about the global condition? In the end, globalization is an epistemic matrix that maps the world in such a way that particularly placed agents can read that (mis)translated palimpsest that is the "global order." As ever, and ineluctably, the plural haunts us. Globalization is a conceptual matrix, made up of other matrices: *When* and *where* are you *in* global space/time? There are only globalizations.[5]

Third, the next problem area has to do with what I will call the question of *processes and conditions*. In this book I also refer to this problem area in terms of a *phenomenology of globalization*, by which I mean that insofar as we are already agents in and of globalization we have existential evidence of what it means to live the global condition. Globalization is a worldview, but also a way in which the lifeworld is structured in a particular way. Before we can discuss the obvious question of how this new structuring of the lifeworld conditions our worldview, we must discuss how the global lifeworld has been destructured and restructured by those processes that have given rise to new horizons of experience and expectation. In discussing these processes and conditions we face a challenge not unlike that Jorge Luis Borges sought to express with his parable of the *Aleph*—a point, sphere, a region in space, without dimensions, in which everything in the world could be seen at once. Not just a theory of globalization, but a phenomenology of globalization, would have to include all the processes and conditions arising from those processes, if it were to be in accordance with the global condition. But even when looking at Borges's *Aleph*, which like Leibniz's monad is a window into the entire cosmos, we can only look at it from where we stand. I will now discuss some processes that appeared to be distinctly unique to the global condition, processes in fact that have given rise to new existential conditions. The following ought to be conceived as portals to a phenomenology of the global condition.

Megaurbanization is without question one of the new processes and conditions of the global experience.[6] Over the last century we have finally crossed the threshold where more humans now live in cities than in the countryside. For most of its history humanity has been predominantly rural and agricultural. In the twentieth century, after two centuries of industrialization and the introduction of industrial and biotechnological techniques in agriculture, humans have for the most part ceased to be farmers. Yet this momentous shift in the human condition has taken place under different and differentiated conditions. If the twentieth century was the century of European and North American metropolis, the twenty-first century will be the century of the non-European metropolis. The largest metropolises in the world today are in what has been called the developing world.[7] By the year 2015 there will be at least 550 cities with a population over one million, in contrast to only 86 in 1950. Circa the dawn of the twenty-first century, 3.2 billion humans lived in cities, more than the total world population in the 1960s. By the year 2050, world population is projected to top at approximately 10 billion, with most of this growth being adsorbed by cities and urban centers. About 95 percent of this growth is projected to take place in the so-called developing world.[8] What this means in terms of social arrest, ecological crises, struggle for resources, and the demographic flows, as well as the exacerbation of global pandemics, cannot be discussed properly in this overview. Yet, there is one aspect to the megaurban dimension of the global condition that needs to be underscored, and that is the *detranscendentalization of alterity*. Cities are the place for the encounter with the other. It is the locus where all are strangers. Cities, indeed, are the locus for a phenomenology of the foreign and alien. Yet, insofar as all are strangers, alterity is deflated, and detranscendentalized.

Modernity, to establish a parallel, was the phenomenological and epistemological condition in which the other—as a religious, racial, sexual other—presented limits and challenges. This other was a transcendental other precisely because it remained so alien, so distant, so new, so unexpected. Globalization has reversed this condition: the other, the foreign, is the most intimate, the most immediate, the most frequent. If alterity is detranscendentalized, deflated, demetaphysicalized, then what happens to modernity's alibis? One of the possible consequences is that alterity will cease to be an epistemic and metaphysical condition and will become a function of regimes of the production of alterity. In other words, the global condition of megaurbanization will force upon humans the realization that since all are foreign and strangers in the megaurbe, we decide under what conditions difference is inscribed. The detranscendentalization of alterity turns into the productivity of difference. Detranscendentalized alterity is alterity routinized, and as routine, it becomes part of the regimes of quotidian existence.

The *acceleration* of space-time, leading to what some theorists have called the collapse or bridging of space-time, is certainly an undisputed dimension of the global condition.[9] The proliferation and increasing sophistication of telecommunication devices has lead to the experience of a global simultaneity. The almost global ubiquity of the television, the fax, the portable phone, and the internet has made simultaneous communication across the globe both inescapable and indispensable.[10] Global financial networks and markets would be unthinkable without the information and telecommunications revolution. Distances, both spatial and temporal, seem insignificant, and we appear to live in a perpetual now in which before, later, and tomorrow are just a matter of minutes and seconds, a click of the mouse. Revisionism is the order of the day, as events get written and rewritten in the span of minutes and hours. Most importantly, televisions and computer screens become windows into either the affluence of the few or the squalor of the many. The collapse of space-time, due to the simultaneity of information sharing and communication across the world, has made us more intimate, even as this intimacy does not translate into the equal sharing of the blessings and curses of globalization. Or rather, our "horizon of expectations"[11] are guided by the imaginary of an intimate proximity, while our "spaces of experience," the worlds we actually inhabit, are remote from each other, progressively slipping away in to unbridgeable distances.[12]

The *symbolic* deconstruction of time, partly a result of the information revolution discussed above, has lead to a rethinking of the differences among natural, historical, and social time.[13] Social time is the time in which and at which societies experience their lifeworld. Or rather, just as Henri Lefebvre spoke of the "social production of space," we must also speak of the "social production of time."[14] This socially produced time is social time; it is the time that punctuates the rhythms of social existence. This is the time that ticks at the sounds of seconds, minutes, hours, days, months. This is the time that keeps track of workdays, academic calendars, and leisure time. This time, however, is *timed* by clocks and timetables that have been arranged in terms of assumptions, beliefs, and ideologies about how much time constitutes a workday, a work week, how long should persons work in their lifetime, and so on.[15] Like maps, clocks clock only what they have been arranged to clock.[16] The rhythms of social existence, however, intersect with historical and natural time. Historical time has to do with the time in which historical events, forces, processes, and transformations take place. Historical time is the time in which societies and civilizations live and mark their transformations. Historical time, one may say, is punctuated by political revolutions, wars, elections, and technological revolutions that may have accelerated the rhythms of social time. Finally, natural time is the time of nature, of tectonic plates, of seas, of weather patterns, of draughts and floods, of freezing or melting polar ice caps, and other such forces that are punctuated in millennia, in cycles whose regularity or patterns are not discernable because their time span is beyond human time.

What is distinctive about the global condition, at the phenomenological level, is that these three times have began to merge, or seem to have collapsed into each other. Social time has accelerated to such an extent that it has caught up with historical time. Revolutions are lived within decades. Major social transformations occur where entire societies are uprooted and restructured in the blink of the eye. What took centuries, now takes decades, and sometimes a score of years. History is being televised at any given moment, even as its revisionism is aired and posted that same evening. By the same token, historical time seems to have caught up to natural time: The El Niño weather pattern is now part of pedestrian speak. The greenhouse effect is melting the ice caps, and sea levels are rising, regions are turning into desserts, while desserts are turning into irrigated gardens. The cumulative effect is that time has to be symbolically reconstituted. The self-assurance of Cartesian and Newtonian thought that operated on the dependability and seeming immutability of natural and world historical time have to be traded for a type of thinking that will set out from the social productivity of temporality.

The symbolic reconstitution of time has been accompanied by a parallel *symbolic reconstitution of space*. This reconstitution has been elaborated under the spatial turn of social theory. Indeed, there is an entire canon of thinkers who study the social production of space. The global condition, however, has unsettled the boundaries between many spaces, and in the process has made the very notion of space malleable. Personal, social, and natural space have been rearranged. "The personal is the political," and "the private is a matter of public concern," were watchwords of the sixties. In the age of telecommunications and almost complete transparency due to the digitization of personal identities, the private and the public, the personal and the public are now matters for daily negotiation. More than ever the boundaries between bodies and personal identities have been unsettled by the pervasiveness of electronic filters. We move as if through a digital matrix that registers and maps our every move. Personal space is not a matter of a space contained and demarked by inviolable boundaries, but a region or horizon within which mobility is allowed or disallowed. Personal space is not inert but a kinetic and expandable net. At a more macro level we find that while national boundaries exist, these are less important that we may at first expect. Nation-states are hooked up into global networks that make the notion of national boundaries almost risible. In any event, national territories, or national geographies demarked by political boundaries, were a function of the political will of political sovereignties.

If sovereignty changes, the political will changes, and with it, the way it inscribes itself on space. The elevation of human rights to a supreme standard for civilized nations, along with the globalization of financial capital, the strengthening of the legal power of multinationals vis-à-vis nation-states, the unintended consequences of centuries of colonialism, the ready availability of global travel, the routinization and commercialization of tourism, and a whole host of other similar trends that are the signature of the global condition have destabilized the fixedness of social and national spaces. If cultural identities have been uncoupled from place, as we will discuss later on, political sovereignty has been uncoupled from geography. This is certainly one way in which we can conceive the establishment of human rights as global standard of legality. Human rights are a form of legal and political sovereignty that is beyond or above space. Something similar has happened with the space of nature, or so-called natural space. The unprecedented growth in the agrochemical industry and the expanding industrialization of agriculture in general, led to what has been called the "green revolution." This green revolution was touted as a cornucopia that would extricate humanity from famine by means of a massive and complete biotechnologization of agricultural. The next step in this industrialization of the seed was already taken when genetically modified seeds were introduced and planted. This utopian green revolution, however, has now turned into the dystopia of ecological imperialism;[17] in other words, the imposition of a homogenizing trend that depletes local biodiversity of its vitality and resilience.[18] As the larger areas of the agricultural field become thoroughly biotechnologized, accelerating the homogenization of agricultural gene pools and exacerbating the risk of blights, genetic pollution, and depletion of biodiversity, there is a drive to preserve "hot spots" of biodiversity. The planet has become a greenhouse, in the sense that whether cultivated or left so-called virgin, nature is under the care, or rapacious voracity, of humans. What is noteworthy about this condition is that even uncultivated nature finds itself in the provisional state of being a reserve, a garden, a nature preserve whose very existence is predicated on there being certain boundaries around it. Nature, thus, is what has been deliberatly left untouched by humans, and as the untouched, it is already touched. It is not that nature pushes against the boundaries of civilization, as may have been true during most of the history of humankind. Now, human society pushes up against nature, draws a line, and says this will remain nature. This is not to suggest that this is the first time this has taken place. In fact, the encounters between the so-called Old World and the New World gave occasions for one of the most dramatic and intense biological exchanges in human history. The new world was transformed not just because its people were devastated by epidemics, but its flora and fauna were overtaken by the plants and animals introduced by the colonizers. And while there was an element of planning and deliberation in the reseeding and repopulating of the New World with new animal species, and the relocation of peoples, what we have witnessed in the twentieth century has been an intensely planned and orchestrated gardening of the American continent.[19] Wherever we go on the American, Eurasian, and to a certain extent the African and Australian continents, there is little that has not been touched by humans, and when it is untouched, it is because it has been cordoned off from human touch. The experience that all spaces, be they personal, social, national, or natural, have been touched by human technology and design has contributed to the recognition that all space is always socially constructed. In this way, we have gone from Cartesian and Kantian dual ontologies, for which space is inert, a mere receptacle, a tabula rasa, to a postmetaphysical perspective in which space is fluid and intricately entwined with temporality. From the space of ontological fixidity, we have moved to the space of flows, a dynamic metaphysics in which space temporalizes and time spatializes.[20]

The *collapse* of universal history has been one consequence of the symbolic restructuring of both time and space.[21] Universal history had already begun to be dismantled during the twentieth century, with the appearance of "world historians" such as Arnold J. Toynbee and William McNeill, who began to dislodge Europe from the center of world history. Universal history is the secular version of divine history. Both share in common the assumption that history has a telos, and that this telos can be discerned from the standpoint of those societies that are alleged to be at the vanguard of history, at the most forward point in historical time. Universal history, like divine history, assumes that history is driven by a logic, a logos.[22] Indeed, universal history is the manifestation of a logos, a logic of social existence. Again, some societies have been assumed to epitomize this logos, while others have failed to live up to it. Modernity may be thought of in terms of universal history, that is, as a twentieth-century version of it. Partly as a reaction to two world wars and the crisis of European societies induced by these wars, historians began to call into question the privileged place European societies have been accorded in universal history. In addition, history, as a discipline, has undergone many transformations that have led to the abandonment of universal history. Two new forms of historical research illustrate poignantly the ways in which universal history has become untenable. On the one hand we have the proliferation of social history, or what has been called *Alltagsgeschichte* (everyday history) with its attention to detail, to the everyday, the quotidian and mundane. This type of history focuses on microsocial agents: women, slaves, immigrants, workers, gays, and so on. On the other hand, we have the emergence of macrohistory, of the sort that the Annales School practiced. This type of history chronicled long-term processes, the *Longue Durée* of slow but decisive historical time. Thus, Annales historians kept track of farming policies, harvest productivity, mortality rates, land parceling, road building, the time it took to go from one village to the next, migrant worker routes, and so on. Between these two schools, the directionality and univocity of universal history was replaced by complexity and causal overdetermination. In this way, world history has come to the forefront, and with it a type of *dialogic cosmopolitanism* of the type that was discussed in the introduction has become indispensable. This type of cosmopolitanism not only demands respect and tolerance of others, but above all it cautions a type of humility about the accomplishments of one's culture. Evaluative and hierarchizing labels or constructs, such as medieval, premodern, postmodern, developed, underdeveloped, and globalized, have been replaced by more self-consciousness categories such as imaginaries or modernities, in the plural and without metaphysical baggage.

The obsolescence of universal history and, with it, the deconstruction of its supporting metaphysics of history has also led to *rethinking* of science, or what counts as science. The decoupling of science from an Augustinian-Hegelian-Kantian metaphysics of history, in which the evolution of societies is directly linked to an evolution of science, has lead to a rethinking of the unity of society.[23] Science, like societies, does not transform in incremental or progressive ways. Science, in fact, is not one but many, and like societies, it is deeply determined by its materiality. Already since Thomas Kuhn, we have been aware of the discontinuity and noncumulative aspects of scientific knowledge. Over the last two decades, science studies and the philosophy of technology have led to more variegated insights into scientific practices and the production of knowledge. Instead of talking about science, as though science were not touched by technology, and in parallel, talking about technology as though technology were not already a form of science, thinkers have been urging us to talk instead about "technoscience." The philosopher of science and technology, Peter Galison, has articulated masterfully the critique of the unity of science and the dependence of science on technology when he differentiated among the conditions of experimentality, scientificity, and instrumentality.[24] If we must make these differentiations in order to acknowledge the dependence of technoscience on the materiality of theory and scientific objects, then we must also acknowledge that a series of "intercalated periodizations" emerged that debunks "positivist periodization." In this way, all technoscience(s) does not move at the same rate or in the same direction, and one theory or scientific paradigm is not abandoned just because it has been refuted or its defenders have died off. Instead, at any given time many different theories and paradigms are in contestation. Factors internal and external, having to do with whether appropriate experiments can be conducted, whether enough theoretical work has been done that can help theorize that model, and whether what evidence could be adduced would count as forming part of science—all of these factors are at play in nonreductivist ways.

This blow to the mythology of the supremacy of Western science has been dealt not by political pundits, irascible critics of Eurocentrism, but scientists and philosophers of science, many of them from the West itself. The disunity of science partly contributed to the science wars of the nineties. But these wars have muted what may be more serious debates about the future of science in the globalized world. One major area of conflict has to do with biopiracy and the patenting of forms of life and genetically modified organisms. Claims to ownership and intellectual ownership of such entities and organisms is predicated on the univocity and stable understanding of what counts as science and technology. Yet, it is the very work by philosophers of science and technology that has so thoroughly dismantled this unified and stable understanding of science. Indeed, the more what is admitted as science increasingly depends on economic treaties and legal sanction, rather than on the merits of the science itself, the more the question about the political nature of science becomes a point of reflection and debate. As globalization augments the exchanges among cultures, what counts as knowledge, as opposed to mere folklore and local practice, becomes more pressing. In the end, the dissociation of technoscience from a metaphysics of history has lead to the realization that both science and technology are determined by a political economy of the production of knowledge. This political economy turns out to be a geopolitical economy, in which many agents, traditions, and forms of local knowledge enter in tension with global forces and agents. Science is no longer an alibi for the alleged superiority of one society over others. Technoscience contributes to the further dismantling of the ideology of universal history.

This abandonment of universal history and the rise of micro and macrohistories, has resulted in the *provincializing* of the West.[25] Postcolonial historiography and theory have contributed greatly to the task of dismantling the sacrificial totems of Occidentalism and Orientalism.[26] Edward Said taught us to unmask the myths about the Orient and how fundamental they were for the self-definition and self-presentation of the West. Orientalism, like Occidentalism, is an ideology that disfigures the other, while projecting mirages of an allegedly unified and developed Western world. Purported Western superiority and exceptionality is predicated on its derogation and denigration of other cultures. But to the extent that Orientalism disfigures others, Western societies and Western culture is also disfigured and misrepresented. Occidentalism is the myth that Western culture's others project upon the West, with the same goals, even if not with the same kind of effectiveness.[27] While Orientalism and Occidentalism operated on the basis of the same type of mystifying, distorting, occluding, and subalternizing matrix, there is an asymmetry between them. While Orientalism aided and legitimated Western imperial projects throughout the world, and in particular the Arab and Islamic worlds, Occidentalism has been a reactive mythical construction. Indeed, a more detailed analysis would reveal that Orientalism projects its own form of Occidentalism, one in which the West is seen as towering above all cultures. It is part and parcel of these differentiating and derogating ideologies to bolster the prestige and self-regard of one's culture. Ideologies seeking to counter these dual moves—of putting down the other and elevating oneself—would reverse the logic; what is a virtue turns into a vice, what is a value is a negative quality. Globalization, and in particular cultural globalization, which entails the abandonment of grand universal history narratives, has lead to the provincializing of the West and, concomitantly, to the deprovincializing of the East. But the historical and spatial provincializing of the West is not only a lesson about epistemological humility and cosmopolitan respect, it is also and perhaps primarily about the internal heterogeneity of the West that was concealed and denied by the need to project a flattering and imitable image of the West. Provincializing, thus, within the context of globalization, means respect for and solidarity with the difference of the other and the difference among ourselves.

If the nature of science has had to be rethought, so has the nature of nature. A central concept of Western thinking has been the binary nature and human, or nature and society. Nature is what is not social. The social is what is different from the natural—that is, what is learned and thus not instinctual, what is produced rather than found, what is engineered as opposed to uncreated, what is voluntary as opposed to inevitable. The social has been defined in contrast with that which is allegedly untouched, uncontaminated, and undetermined. Yet, the nature-versus-society dichotomy has begun to collapse not just because of the ways in which entire continents have been transformed through agriculture and the sustained intervention of urban and rural planning, but also because of the ways in which through biotechnology the boundaries between what is produced and what is merely found have began to blur. We already noted how in the age of globalization nature is not what is untouched but what has been deliberately marked as untouchable, as that which is not to be disturbed. In this way, what is natural is inscribed within the horizon of the social. Nature is not what is outside society, but rather what is dependent on society for it to be designated as such. Thus, regions labeled "hot spots" of biodiversity become preserves for the sake of future exploitation. In parallel, the growth in both preventive and enhancing medicine, the proliferation of lifesaving devices, the expansion of neurological and hormonal medication, has contributed to the expansion of the human lifespan. Another consequence has been the lowering of the threshold of what is acceptable as an illness or infirmity that must be corrected and eliminated. Pharmaceutical man (*homo pharmakon*), the figure of the medically transformed and enhanced human, has anticipated and overtaken the cyborg, or bionic man, the figure of the machine transformed and enhanced human. We have already touched on the growth of biotechnology and the transformation of agriculture, but as more and more of our produce as well as poultry, meat, and basic foodstuffs are made up of genetically modified organisms, and the more we continue to see genetic manipulations as a logical and necessary step in agriculture and animal husbandry, the less clear becomes where the line distinguishing negative from positive eugenics lies. When we look at the fauna and flora of the Old and New Worlds, we see the products of centuries of human intervention, or when we visit a park to be in contact with nature, nature that exists as if in a furlough from society, or when we take a drug that is produced by a genetically modified animal, we are witnessing the fading of the line between nature and society.[28] Nature, it turns out, is what is already produced, and if it is produced, then a certain political economy must guide its modes of production. The global condition that discloses the already produced character of nature places on a different level the task of preserving and cultivating the environment. This kind of reflexive environmental consciousness requires that we negotiate a path between the Scylla of new age, neopagan spiritualism and the Charybdis of neoliberal and corporatist instrumentalism. The end of nature may turn into the birth of a new democratic, reflexive, and deliberative environmental consciousness.[29]

Glocalization is the English transliteration of a term coined in Japanese to refer to the process of the local adaptation and acculturation of Western products.[30] But it serves well, even if inelegantly, to describe precisely the experience that is fundamental to all cultures—namely that all cultures are always in the process of being cultivated, processed, transformed, localized, and exported. Glocalization refers to the process in which global products and processes take on local characteristics and, conversely, how local products and practices are exported and circulated through the global markets of both commodities and ideas. Glocalization could also be the name for that experience in which culture ceases to be the property of one specific community of society and appears to belong to global humanity.[31] The appearance in every major global city of Starbucks, fast-food places, and brand-name clothing outlets, seems to have led to a homogenization of the lifeworld. But, with each thrust in this direction, there is a similar counterthrust. Local forces and cultures counter by rearticulating its distinctiveness, its own uniqueness and intimacy. In the face of the threat from global cultures, local cultures affirm their identities. In this process, however, what is local and autochthonous recreates itself. The native and original are invented, woven with the new and imported. In this way, a new cultural product emerges. Traditions and practices that may or may not have existed are unearthed, rescued, reactivated, or if necessary invented. Yet, traditions are not so much invented as negotiated in the encounter with global forces. All culture is always already artificial and synthetic, always already fabricated and invented. Glocalization is the name for a process that makes explicit what has been going on at least since humanity began to trade. Yet, there is also something that glocalization makes explicit, and that is that cultures get to be either renewed and transformed in accordance with the will and initiative of their corresponding communities, or they are colonized and deformed under conditions not of their choosing. Cultural imperialism has always accompanied economic, political, and military imperialism. Yet, under the new global condition, which asserts the rights of the local precisely as a twin aspect of globalization, such imperialism is proscribed and rejected. Instead, we speak about "soft power." This soft power is predicated on cultural persuasion and the ability of a global public sphere to facilitate a cultural dialogue that is not necessarily arbitrated solely by the West.

The *uncoupling* of identities from their localities has been a parallel consequence of globalization. If cultures are glocalized, that is uncoupled from their places of origins, identities, which are cultural markers on and of people, are de facto also uncoupled.[32] This uncoupling could also be referred to in the affirmative as "traveling identities." As mentioned above, one of the fundamental aspects of the global condition is the unprecedented "urbanization" of humanity. Part and parcel of this globalization is the massive demographic flow of peoples across the planet over the last two centuries. Peoples are moving from the rural areas into cities, and from cities to other cities. Indeed, nothing parallels the population shifts in the nineteenth and twentieth centuries, except perhaps the third- and fourth-century "barbarian invasions" from the Eurasian steppes that brought about the transformation of the Roman Empire. The comparison should not be allowed to suggest that population emigrations from the so-called underdeveloped and developing nations should be seen as "barbarian" invasions. In fact, over the last two centuries the primary beneficiaries of emigrations have been the British Isles and Europe.[33]

These massive migrations have not all been voluntary. Many have been occasioned by global conflicts, civil wars, ethnoracial genocide, and the growing destitution of societies in regions of the planet on the border of ecological disasters.[34] With the expansion of travel routes and the cheapening of the means to travel, migration has become easier. Furthermore, one of the unintended consequences of Western imperialism throughout the world was to have created economic, political, and cultural links with their colonies in such a way that the former colonial metropolises have become refuge and sanctuary to peoples displaced from the former colonies. The colonies are now in the center of the former empires. What is to be foregrounded for our purposes here is that these population flows also mean the move of cultural identities. Thus, at any given time, in any major global city, you will find numerous but also plural cultural enclaves: little Chinas, little Italies, Japan towns, and so on. Cultural enclaves and identities that were born somewhere else now find themselves either freed or marooned in a global city, at the crossroads where many other cultures meet. The phenomenological experience of this uncoupling of identity from place, culture from geography, translates into the political and legal challenge of multiculturalism. All societies now, and not just the West, or even the United States for that matter, face the challenge of the rights of minority cultures. For this reason, over the last two decades, almost in parallel with the development of globalization theory, political philosophy and political theory have turned to the question of citizenship and the rights of minority cultures. This interest has not been a fashion, or something driven by so-called political correctness. Instead, it is motivated by the undeniable fact that all cultures find themselves in constant interaction and exchange with other cultures, in their midst and on a daily basis. A discussion of what this means in terms of rights, both in terms of human and citizen's rights, is beyond our scope, even as we can be certain that the rights of other cultures has become a fundamental, and not just temporary and artificial, political-philosophical concern.[35] What is within our scope, however, is reflection on the condition and process of demographic flows: the quotidian encounter with other cultures and their valid claim to acknowledgment and respect, on the one hand, and the further uncoupling of cultural identities from their regions and places of origin, on the other.

There is no factor, element, or dynamic that determines the logic of globalizations in as fundamental a way as does the growth in global inequalities. This is one of the most glaring aspects of both the global condition and growing interdependence—namely the massive, catastrophic, and accelerating exclusion of many from the benefits of globalizations. But, before we proceed, let's do some numbers. According to the World Development Report 2000/2001: "The world has deep poverty amid plenty. Of the World's 6 billion people, 2.8 billion—almost half—live on less than $2 a day, and 1.2 billion—a fifth—live on less than $1 a day, with 44 percent living in South Asia." Or, to put it in terms of another index of comparison, "The average income in the richest 20 countries is 37 times the average in the poorest 20—*a gap that has doubled in the past 40 years.*"[36] The growth that has accompanied economic globalization has also been deceiving, and misrepresented. For instance, while in East Asia the number of people living on less than one dollar per day fell from 420 to 280 million in the decade between 1987 and 1998, in Latin America, South Asia, and sub-Saharan Africa the numbers reversed. In fact, a similar regression took place in former Soviet Union countries, where people living on less than one dollar per day rose by twentyfold.[37]

Over the next quarter of a century the population will grow by a third of the present population, but 97 percent of this growth will take place in the so-called developing world.[38] The *World Development Report 2003* continues to draw more bleak and despairing picture. As so-called developing countries find it increasingly difficult to compete in the world markets, and their economies of importation are taxed and pillaged by interest on loans and tariffs, their base economic infrastructures are dismantled and destroyed by civil wars and proxy wars. Thus, during the 1990s forty-six countries were involved in some sort of military conflict, primarily a civil wars. "These conflicts have very high costs, destroying past development gains and leaving a legacy of damaged assets and mistrust that impedes future gains."[39] The stress to their environments due to poor industrialization policies and decades of civil war, coupled with urban growth, has meant a concentration of poverty in regions on the border of ecological disaster and almost complete civil and political collapse. As the rural areas of these poor nations became less productive, the number of cities in these regions with populations greater than ten million went from zero to fifty, while in developed and industrialized nations, the change was from one to four.[40] As Mike Davis has shown eloquently, with the convergence of neoliberal policies imposed by the International Monetary Fund and the World Bank, combined with rapid demographic growth, civil wars, and ecological failure, most of the urbanization that has taken place in the last three decades has been a growth in shantytowns, favelas, and slums.[41] As Davis put it, we are turning into a planet of slums.[42]

Christopher Flavin, an analyst on staff at the Worldwatch Institute, which produces the *State of the World* reports, put it this way: "Per capita income has increased 3 percent annually in 40 countries since 1990, but more than 80 nations have per capita incomes that are lower than they were a decade ago. Within countries, the disparities are even more striking. In the United States, the top 10 percent of the population has six times the income of the lowest 20 percent; in Brazil, the ratio is 19 to 1. More than 10 percent of the people living in 'rich' countries are still below the poverty line, and in many, inequality has grown over the last two decades."[43] Still, as of 2004, the rich nations of the world, which constitute less than 15 percent of the world population, accounted for almost 80 percent of the world's income. This inequality becomes even more stark if we articulate from below: while 2.6 billion people in middle-income countries share 17 pecent of the world's income, 2.4 billion share in less than 3.5 percent of that global income![44] These two inverse pyramids are the sacrificial pyramids of the affluent world that globalization has produced.

The costs of such global inequalities become even more stark and grotesque when we look at the actual effects on the environment. This is not to suggest that human poverty is not as catastrophic as the destruction of habitats. Rather, the point is to put in perspective the fact that this poverty is not only growing but can only continue to grow precisely because environments are being exploited beyond their ability to regenerate. In this way, poverty is not temporary but structural, with a long history and a long future. Citizens of the so-called first world not only consume the most but they consume the most at the expense of the future generations and the ability of other nations to ever extract themselves from cycles of enduring and entrenched poverty. One way in which these grotesque disparities of consumption are measured is by trying to index the ecological footprint of different societies. I will illustrate only four. (See Table 1.1.)

Table 1.1 Some Ecological Footprints in 1995.[45]

Country	Available Ecological Capacity	Ecological Footprint	Ecological Deficit (capacity minus footprint)
Netherlands	1.2	5.9	–4.7
United States	6.7	10.9	–4.2
Japan	0.8	4.7	–3.9
Israel	0.3	3.7	–3.5

Table 1.2 Some Ecological Footprints, With Their Ecological Deficits, in 2001.[46]

Country	Ecological Footprint in Global Acres	Biocapacity in Global Acres	Domestic Ecological Deficit/Remainder in Global Acres
Netherlands	11.9	2.0	–9.9
United States	24.0	13.0	–10.9
Japan	11.8	1.7	–10.0
Israel	11.0	1.4	–9.5
Kuwait	19.1	1.0	–18.2
United Arab Emirates	25.0	3.1	–21.9

In the November 2001 updated report by the Redefining Progress's Sustainability Program, the ecological footprints for some of the same countries, with two more additions, document some of the most egregious deficits in global acreage of biocapacity. But of course, this ecological deficit can only be sustained if some other society or nations are forced to underwrite it.

Still, we must look at these ecological footprints, with their insulting ecological deficits, in light of another major contradiction of the global world: the growing scarcity of water at the moment when the ice caps are melting and the level of the seas are rising. I quote from Vandana Shiva's recent book *Water Wars*: "The war crisis is the most pervasive, most severe, and most invisible dimension of the ecological devastation of the earth. In 1998, 28 countries experienced water stress or scarcity. This number is expected to rise to 56 by 2025. Between 1990 and 2025 the number of people living in countries without adequate water is projected to rise from 131 to 817 million [about 10% of the world population]"[47] Waterborne diseases are among the top ten global health risks, according to the World Health Organization. Approximately 1.2 billion people (one in every five, half of them in the so-called developing world) have no access to potable water. In addition, approximately 2.4 billion have no access to sanitation facilities. According to Peter Gleick of the Pacific Institute for Studies in Development, Environment, and Security, it was projected in 2002 that by 2020 more than a one hundred million people would die due to some sort of waterborne disease.[48]

The growing scarcity of potable water, rising populations and decreasing arable lands is matched by what has turned out to be one of the most disastrous agricultural policies in world history. I am referring to the so-called *green revolution*.[49] This revolution was touted as the answer to the population explosion and, above all, as a way to deal with the recurring famines in Africa and Asia. Yet, over the last five decades, all it has accomplished is the depletion of global biodiversity, the diminishment of the ability of developing societies to rely on their local biota, and just as importantly, has contributed to concealing the exorbitant costs of industrialized and biotechnologized agriculture. This so-called green revolution has made the world more dependent on megacorporations and has signaled the triumph of technocracy. Socially, it has driven potentially self-sufficient farmers from lands into cities, accelerating the rate of urbanization, and exacerbating the growth of urban poverty. Above all, it has dug a swath of biogeographically untenable monocultures that threaten the food basket of the world.[50] The green revolution—with its deluxe version in the biotech revolution of the last two decades—was predicated on a gamble that, once analyzed, discloses the staggering costs at which these revolutions have been enacted.[51] The swaths of corn, wheat, and rice, sustained on a kind of biochemical bombing through the use of fertilizer, pesticides, and water, have been predicated on the availability of water and oil.[52] In the end, however, these seeming technological wonders of the green revolution "result only 25 percent as efficient as hand-and-hoe agriculture, and half as efficient as ox-and-plow farming. Indeed—notes J. R. McNeill—modern U.S. farming burns far more calories than it produces when one factors in the energy requirements of making fertilizer."[53] If this is not clear enough, let me put it in Peter Manning's terms: "All together the food-processing industry in the United States uses about ten calories of fossil-fuel energy for every calorie of food energy it produces."[54] This type of energy deficit, which is accompanied by overconsumption, is sustained by subsidies, protectionist policies, and direct military interventions. Growing impoverishment, ecological decline, with asymmetrical consumption and waste, are two sides of the same growing global interdependence. Globalization has its promises, as well as its terrors. Thus far, most of the planet has been exposed to only the inhuman and rapacious face of globalization. It remains for us to make sure that the promises of globalization are realized and not squandered. For the moment, however, it is clear that the poverty of the world is not matched by the poverty of theory. There is a plethora of theorizing and philosophizing about globalization, but most of it is blinded by its own methodological hubris and insouciance. The world is one, but we have barely begun to make sense of what this means, when most humanity is not even sharing in or benefiting from the most minimal gains and promises of globalization.

2

Invisible Cities

A Phenomenology of Globalization *from Below*

> "I have also thought of a model city from which I deduce all others," Marco answered. "It is a city made only of exceptions, exclusions, incongruities, contradictions. If such a city is the most improbable, by reducing the number of abnormal elements, we increase the probability that the city really exists. So I have only to subtract exceptions from my model, and in whatever direction I proceed, I will arrive at one of the cities which, always as an exception, exist. But I cannot force my operation beyond a certain limit: I would achieve cities too probable to be real."
>
> —Italo Calvino, *Invisible Cities*

Introduction

There are many who think globalization to be the latest intellectual fashion, devoid of content, rich in rhetoric and vitriol. The polarization of positions concerning the meaning of globalization betrays less a substantive grasp of the issues in question and more a penchant to use this word as a stand-in for favorite strawman positions. Nonetheless, we can say that globalization concerns the fundamental issue whether our experience as well as representation and conceptualization of the world have radically altered in a way that neither "modernity" nor "postmodernity" can any longer grasp or hope to render legible and intelligible. At the core of the shift from the debate about modernity versus postmodernity to the debate about the whence and the whither of globalization, is the question concerning the extent to which our *Weltanschuung*, our conceptual gestalt of the planet, of what we can also call the *saeculum*, that is the horizon of human life and history, has already shifted so irreversibly and radically as to require a new lexicon, cartography, and even imaginary. Those who denounce globalization for justifiable reasons do so blinding themselves to a new set of forces and even new conceptual horizons, which if not discerned, make their criticisms vacuous and naive. Those who defend and blithely celebrate globalization do so only because they pay attention to one or two privileged and favorite aspects of the process of global integration, without regard or concern for its other aspects. In this way, these latter turn into spokespersons for the worst aspects of this new world order. There is either too much indeterminacy, vague notions about what constitutes globalization, or too much one-dimensionality, privileging of one or two areas of society as the catalysts of globalization.[1] This situation, however, is being masterfully remedied by the recent work of Held, McGrew, Goldblatt, and Perraton, which synthesizes erudite analyses and masterful summaries. They have also gathered in a volume a wide-spanning and heterogenous reading list of the different positions, theories, and analyses of globalization.[2]

The following reflections hope to navigate a middle path between the Charybdis of euphoric and celebratory pronouncements about the ineluctability of globalization by what many take to be the new apologists of a *pax americana*, and the Scylla of equally strong but dismissive and visceral counterreactions to what many take to be the latest scourge of capitalism, in its highest and most virulent form. These reflections will be guided by the empirically informed but deeply sensitive work of Saskia Sassen, who has pioneered what we can call global sociology, or sociology of globalization. She has been contributing over the last two decades to what I take to be one of the most sophisticated, multilayered, detailed, and comprehensive analysis of the new world economy and how this new economy leaves the traces of its form of accumulation in the physiognomy of the city. Her work on immigration, sovereignty, the ascendancy of a new postnational legal regime, the unbundling of national economies, and the reterritorializing of global economic and social processes in the city have painted with broad but masterful strokes a rich canvass of the new geography of the political economy in the age of digitization and finance capital.[3]

One of the most important aspects of Sassen's work (and this is why it is an indispensable guide in our times), is the way it focuses on the city as a litmus test for one of the central motifs of her work, namely, the *denationalizing of the national and the nationalizing of the global*. In Sassen's work, globalization is not just about the mobility of capital; it is also about the mobility of peoples. It is about the contestation of national policies by transnational and global processes, and the emergence and formulation of new claims by social agents within local geopolitical spaces. Indeed, the recent ascent of the discourse of human rights, which supersede and supervene citizenship rights, along with the centrality of a politics of identity that is undergirded by a politics of presence, are to be understood as contestational and oppositional strategies that face up to the unaccountability, fluidity, superlegality, and concentration of finance capital in global cities. From among the many provocative aspects of her proposals for deciphering and making legible the geopolitics of information megapolises, I would like to highlight two aspects. The first aspect is what I take to be a kind of methodological caution that seems to lead Sassen to articulate her proposal in the form of a conditional, in the form of an option. The other has to do with what I take to be a seeming symmetry between agents and actors within the new information megapolises.

After this critical but sympathetic discussion of these two aspects of Sassen's work, I turn to the articulation of what I will call a "phenomenology of globalization." If we take globalization to be about *Weltanschuungen*, gestalts, and ways of seeing and reading the world, and how these may or may not correspond with our "experience" of the world, then the logical tool of analysis would appear to be phenomenology. By phenomenology, it is to be understood here that method that sees concepts as embodied practices, and practices as interpretative or meaning-granting schemata, which in turn are seen as being part of a form of life, or sociohistorical environment. There is no concept without a practice, and no practice without a world. In this second part, then, I seek to understand how globalization is an attempt to come to terms, in a concept and through a figure of thought, with how our world is lived differently in the age of simultaneity and the collapse of space-time, to use of Harvey's terms, and how new conceptual matrices are required to make sense of the emergent forms of life (i.e., exiles, displaced people, migrants, cyber nomads, jetzet nomad intelligentsia, not on the same plane of power and survival).[4] The chapter closes with a discussion of how "religion" is rediscovered in this new context and how resources may be located within it that can contribute to meeting the challenges of a globalized world. Such a turn might be unexpected although not unwarranted. In the age of cultural homogenization, of the collapse of cultural borders, in which MacDonald's and Hollywood have created a global lingua franca, differences must be highlighted and discovered, if not created. Religion has become important, again, because it seems to profile itself as the one element of cultures that has remained, and this is contestable, partially immune to the homogenizing thrust of globalization. Religion has become a reservoir of resistance and difference. Fundamentalism, as many have noted, is unthinkable without globalization.[5] Yet, religious renewals and the formation of new religions are also unthinkable without processes of globalization. Conversely, globalization itself is both augured and accelerated by processes of religious innovation, proselytism, and evangelization.[6] The conceptual moral here would be to disabuse ourselves of the Enlightenment prejudice, perpetuated and exploited by the discourses on modernity, that religion had not been important, had in fact ceased to perform a social function, and that suddenly it had become once again necessary. As José Casanova's work has illustrated beautifully, such myths defaced social reality and diminished theoretical reflexivity.[7]

The Territorialization of Globalization

> Large cities in the *highly* developed world are the places where globalization processes assume concrete, localized forms. These localized forms are, in good part, what globalization is about. We can then think of cities also as the place where the contradictions of the internationalization of capital either come to rest or conflict. If we consider, further, that large cities also concentrate a growing share of disadvantaged populations—immigrants in both Europe and the United States, African Americans and Latinos in the Unites States—then we can see that cities have become a strategic terrain for a whole series of conflicts and contradictions.[8]

Some of Sassen's work could be read as advocating a kind of "methodological humility." By this I mean that some of Sassen's texts seem to project the idea that if we want to understand the new geography of inequality, of the overvalorization of capital and the devalorization of human potential, as dual aspects of globalization that coagulate in specific contestations within localized spaces, then we better look at global cities. There is a conditionality here that seems to offer an option, as though we could understand the contemporary situation independent of the new megaurbanization and demographic explosion that humanity is undergoing. I grant Sassen the benefit of the doubt, and I assume that this *if-then* type of argumentation is really a rhetorical ploy. Nonetheless, I will suggest that there is no way in which we can understand what is happening to the world, to our societies, to our environments, to the seas, to the air around the entire planet, and so on, if we do not look at three related factors: the unprecedented concentration of humans in cities, the growth of the human population, and the increase in certain forms of consumption. Let me cite a few statistics. At the turn of the twentieth century, 150 million people lived in cities—that is about one-tenth of the world population were city dwellers. In contrast, by 2006 3.2 billion people are estimated to live in cities, which is a twenty-fold increase.[9] What this means is that for the first time in the history of our species we have begun to be predominantly city dwellers. But this is not the whole story. While the nineteenth and twentieth centuries were the centuries of the great industrial metropolis of the so-called advanced world, the so-called modern world, the cities of the twenty-first century will be the cities of the developing world, the so-called third world, the purportedly not-yet-modern world. Note, for instance, that some of the largest cities today are in the southern section of the geopolitical map: Mexico City, 18.1 million; Bombay, 18.0; Sao Paulo, 17.7; Shanghai, 14.2; Seoul, 12.9.[10]

In short, the largest urbanizing areas of the planet are those areas that are most vulnerable and perhaps least ready to assume the challenges of massive concentrations of people in their already overstretched urban centers. Let me be more specific. While more and more people migrate to cities in the so-called industrializing nations, the disparities between the developed and the developing world continue to grow. Let me cite the *Human Development Report of 1998*. Twenty percent of the world's people in the highest-income countries account for 86 percent of total private consumption, while the poorest 20 percent account for a minimal 1.3 percent. Note also that the richest fifth (living in the information cities that Sassen studies):

- Consume 58% of total energy, while the poorest fifth consume less than 4%;
- Have 74% of all telephone lines, while the poorest fifth have 1.5%;
- Consume 84% of all paper, while the poorest fifth consume 1.5%;
- Own 87% of the world's vehicle fleet, while the poorest fifth own less than 1%.[11]

To these ratios and statistics, we would have to add the telling statistics of the actual number of people who have computers, access to an internet connection, wireless connections, and electricity. Couple these abysmally asymmetrical levels of consumption and ownership with the fact that the 20 percent of world population in the wealthiest countries (United States, Canada, Germany, Japan, France, and England) account for 53 percent of carbon dioxide emissions, while the poorest fifth accounts for only 3.0 percent

This all paints an apocalyptic picture, a doomsday scenario not unlike that so prophetically captured by Ridley Scott in his film *Blade Runner*, which projects an anarchical urban bazaar, teeming with masses from all corners of the world, speaking some post-Babelian pidgin, ever in the shadow of dark clouds that conceal a fading sun, always bathed in radioactive rain.

I will now turn to the second aspect of my thematization of some aspects of Sassen's work. Her analysis, at least as it is reproduced here, seems to leave open the way for an interpretation that would see global financial interests, global capital, as possessing the same type of leverage as human global actors have. If we see the city as a strategic site for the deployment of denationalizing and reterritorializing processes and contestations, does this mean that all agents are on the same level? Is this new topology of power characterized by a leveled plain? And here, I would have to say no. In other words, it is not the case that the globalizing that is operated and executed by global financial networks is of the same character and extent as that enacted by immigrants and women of color, to mention the actors Sassen mentions.

I will go a step forward and focus on the United States. Home to at least four of the most important megapolises in the circuits of technology, information, finance capital, as well as immigration and urban oppositional politics from below (New York, Chicago, Los Angeles, and Miami), the United States has had a long history of bias against cities. These biases are built into the tax structures at the federal and local levels. They are built into the very policies of the Welfare State, along with the allocation of national wealth through development grants, tax incentives, and breaks, grants and loans, and so forth. A whole series of factors has built a complex web of legal and tax codes, infrastructure construction, development incentives, and so on, that adversely affects the core areas of cities and simultaneously rewards urban sprawl, privatization, highway construction, and urban capital flight. In brief, in the United States, at least very clearly and concertedly since the end of World War II, housing, taxation, education, highway constructions policies, and so on, have conspired to produce the hollowing of cities and the expansion of a socially wasteful and ecologically devastating urban sprawl. The major infomegapolises of the new brave world of surreal wealth are oases of grotesque luxury in the midst of vast deserts of poverty, crumbling infrastructure, rusting bridges, broken public phones, poor and unsuitable public schools ... and the litany can go on and on. This logic of urban development in the United States has been a luxury that can only be bought at the expense of the asymmetries that I pointed out earlier. And here I would like to refer people to the work of Daniel D. Luria and Joel Rogers on a new urban politics for the twenty-first century.[12]

The point, however, that I am trying to elaborate is this: It is simply not the case that different actors enter the territory of the global city on the same level. In fact, it is a territory that is already organized in such a way as to preclude certain agents from confronting, from elaborating their rights to the city with the same level of force and efficacy that transnationals enact and enforce their claims on urban space. My question, then would be: How do we develop an analysis that takes into account the unleveled terrain that constitutes the new topology of power in which certain actors are more clearly at a disadvantage than others? What new forms of legitimacy and politics can we appeal to, or begin to configure, when urban dwellers find themselves historically condemned to always stand in a substantively adverse situation of economic, political, and legal power vis-a-vis the substantively effective legal, financial, and political forces of globalizing finance capital? In what way, in short, can we begin to elaborate a politics of the *right to the city*, to use that felicitous phrase of Henri Lefebvre, which unquestionably will become the number one form of politics in this age of megacities and hyperurbanization, from the standpoint of those who have been historically excluded from exercising their rights to their cities?[13]

The Phenomenology of a Global Phenomena

> The expression "phenomenology" can be formulated in Greek as *legein ta phainomena*. But *legein* means *apophainesthai*. Hence phenomenology means: *apophphainesthai ta phainomena*—to let what shows itself be seen from itself, just as it shows itself from itself. That is the formal meaning of the type of research that calls itself "phenomenology." But this expresses nothing other than the maxim formulated above: "To the things themselves!"[14]

I turn now to the presentation of what I call a "phenomenology of globalization." By a phenomenology of globalization I mean the analysis of those experiences that human beings, in varying degrees, are undergoing due to new socioeconomic-cultural and political processes, which in turn condition the horizon of all possible expectations against which new experiences are possible at all. Human experience happens against a spatiotemporal background: the lifeworld. At the same time, human experience projects itself forward into a horizon of expectations that is conditioned by the structures of the lifeworld. Human experience, therefore, is always framed or structured by spatial and temporal coordinates. Ideas of the world, or worldviews, are coagulations of those spatiotemporal configurations.[15] Images of the world, or world images, are ways in which we understand our relationships to space and time. For this reason, the way we conceptualize the world, imagine the world, mirrors the way we conceptualize ourselves as humans. The point of these reflections is to begin to think of globalization as a way of viewing the world, as a image of the world.[16] And to this extent, then, globalization acquires a philosophical status that requires a phenomenological analysis.[17]

In the following I will describe what I take to be fundamental elements of a phenomenology of globalization. Neither because I take these to be most fundamental, nor because they constitute a comprehensive index. I will discuss only four points of departure for a phenomenology of globalization, which I hope will be unfolded from below; that is, from the perspective of those most adversely affected by the impacts and transformations unleashed by globalization. It is also clear that they betray a Western perspective, although one that is conscious of the privilege and narrowness that underwrites and supports it.

First. Any phenomenology of globalization will have to begin with the description, analysis and study of the exponential acceleration of the production and dissemination of information. Of course, information is not knowledge. Knowledge might be broadly defined as "a set of organized statements of facts or ideas, presenting a reasoned judgment or an experimental result, which is transmitted to others through some communication medium."[18] Information, on the other hand, presupposes knowledge and data. More precisely, information is the communication of knowledge and data in such a way that the latter has to be discriminated from the former. Data is made up of raw statements and experimental results without the reasoned judgment. No one will deny the leaps in knowledge acquisition and information transmission that have taken place over the years since the atom bomb was first invented and exploded over the desert at Los Alamos. It is this glaring transformation of our knowledge of the world, ourselves, and the cosmos in general that has incited some to call this the "information age."

If we follow Karl Jaspers, as well as Pierre Chaunu and Ferdinand Braudel, we might suggest that every major epochal transformation in human consciousness was catalyzed by transformations in the means of acquisition of knowledge and its communication through different media or tools of information. The axial period, of which Jaspers spoke in his work on *The Origin and Goal of History*, which took place between the sixth and second B.C., had to do with the invention of books, the development of major cities, and the expansion of networks of economic exchange in terms of trade routes.[19] At this time, however, paper and books were fragile, expensive, and to a large extent tools of luxury and privilege. Knowledge of the world was guided by mythological worldviews controlled by almost unassailable authorities. The sixteenth century, another axial age, was marked by the printing revolution inaugurated by Gutenberg, the establishment of new trade routes, and the secularization of knowledge production and distribution with the emergence of philosophers and intellectuals.

The twentieth century marked yet another shift in the way we produce and distribute knowledge and disseminate it as information. One of the greatest unsung and neglected triumphs of the twentieth century was the institutionalization of mass education. Many have been the horrors that have visited cultures through their encounter with the nation-state, but one of the clear benefits of this encounter was the development of mass literacy and the establishment of education institutions that are if not de facto at least nominally open to all citizens of the state. Talcott Parsons called this achievement of the nation-state the "educational revolution." Amartya Sen, for instance, has urged us to measure absolute poverty in terms of the years of schooling, along with access to potable water, quality of air, and access to minimally nutritious food.[20] But this is only the least noticeable, although perhaps the most important aspect of the information revolution of the twentieth century. The most noticeable is of course the computer and telecommunications revolution. Jeremy Rifkin has appropriately suggested that we talk in terms of the "biotech century" and that we understand that the genetic, computer, and telecommunications revolutions are different flanks of one same front: the information revolution.[21] DNA was discovered by Watson and Crick in 1953, in 1990 the United States launched the Genome project, by the turn of the third millennium, the entire human genome plus the genetic makeup of the most important foods are controlled by a few multinationals.[22] In the United States already more than 25 percent of the grains produced are genetically engineered. In recent years, one of the most important conflicts between the United States and Europe since the deployment of missiles throughout Western Europe during the sixties and eighties has been festering over the import of genetically altered produce and meats. You might want to call this "biotech imperialism," but you may also see it as carrying out to its logical conclusion of the "agricultural revolution."[23] Similarly, the computer was invented during the 1940s but only began to be mass produced in the 1970s. Today, any laptop has more computational power than all of the computers of the first generation put together. Microchips are superseded every few months, with each new cycle increasing exponentially the speed, memory, and concentration of microprocessors. In 1957, the Russians launched Sputnik, the first artificial satellite. The Americans followed in 1962 with the launching of Telstar 1, the first television satellite. Today there are between two hundred and three hundred satellites forming a canopy of electric nodes linking the world in a red of synchronous telecommunications. It is projected that by the first decade of the next millennium there will be more than 300 satellites.[24]

I conclude this overview by noting that one of the fundamental characteristics of the modern world is that the extraction of raw materials and their transformation into commodities has been demoted from its place of privilege in bourgeois capitalism by the production of scientific knowledge and its dissemination as information. This is what the information revolution amounts to—namely, the superseding of the industrial revolution by the transformation both in the means and object of production.[25] Today, what matters is not the raw material and the possession of the means of production; instead, what matters is the knowledge that allows to discover—even invent—raw materials, which are processed through ever-changing means of production. The clearest example of this is the biotech industry, where Monsanto is the perfect illustration of the supervening of raw materials and means of production by the production of knowledge that controls seeds and how they are processed.[26]

Second. The acceleration of the production and information dissemination has had a direct and evident impact on the way we think about history and tradition. The durability and unifying role of our worldviews, or images of the world, is a function of the relationship between our individual, bodily, experience of space and time and the way the world surrounding us undergoes change. The world around us, in turn, is made up of the social world and the natural world, each having has its own rhythms and time.[27] In light of this, we should speak of a biomorphic space-time, social space-time, and world space-time.[28] Biomorphic space-time is the way space and time are experienced by the individual. The clock that measures this space-time might be said to be the biological clock of each human being. Social space-time is what social groups, societies, and communities live and experience. This space-time is measured in generations, historical processes, events, the rise and fall of cities. The motor of this space-time is the level of sociotechnical development of a society: its infrastructures and superstructures. World space-time is the pace at which the natural world evolves and transforms, seasons come and go, rivers run and dry up, mountains erode, plains dry up and became deserts and forests are cut down and grow up, or turn into shrubbery and wasteland. The further back we look in the history of humanity, the more disjointed and separate were the rhythms at which these different clocks run and operate.

Today, there is a convergence of the speeds of these different space-times. If we compare the speed of world space-time and biomorphic spacetime, we find that they are running almost simultaneously. In other words, the more our own life spans are lengthened, and world space-time—the time or speed at which the world itself changes—shrinks, the more unstable and local are our worldviews or images of the world. Cosmological views, as well as abstract universality, were able to be sustained as long as the world did not seem to change, and humans had such short life spans that any substantive change in the world was not noticeable and experienceable by any two or three generations. Pierre Chaunu remarked that one of the fundamental elements in the possibility for the communication of knowledge was the lengthening of the life spans of humans during and after the sixteenth century. Today, we have the convergence of unprecedented human life spans (to the extent that some societies are registering the divergent vectors of the general aging of their populations and the lowering of infant mortality, where both are clearly a function of the improvement in general medicine and its having been made more broadly available) with unprecedented accelerated world changes. The latter is not simply a mere mirage occasioned by almost synchronous world communication. It is the case that we are changing the face of the planet in ways that not just generations but individuals are able to note and distinctly remember. In this way we can talk about the malleability of tradition and the arbitrariness of history. In other words, what Harvey and Giddens called, respectively, the compression and collapse of space-time, which manifests itself in the contemporary plurification of historical methodologies and renarrativation of histories, as well as the skepticism that any historical chronology is not a function of some ideological agenda. Historical revisions has become the daily bread of the historically cynical masses of peoples who cannot read in history the telos of either emancipation or rationality. In *the age of globalization, reason does not entail freedom, nor revolution freedom, nor reason revolution.* In this way, we can say with Heelas, Lash, and Morris that we live in posttraditional or detraditionalized world, in which these pairs that gave cohesion and direction to the project of modernity have been superseded, or rendered ideological and historicized.[29]

Third. Any phenomenology of globalization must also begin with what I take to be an equally momentous transformation of human societies, and this has to do with the megaurbanization of the world. We can say that for most of its history, most of humanity has been rural. Cities developed as appendages to large agricultural areas. Cities were functional principles of rural areas. Eventually this relationship reversed, but only after the city ceased to be a communication node for agricultural exchange. Cities started to acquire their independence when they could produce their own commodities, namely knowledge and political power. This only began to happen after the Renaissance when major cities are not just ports but also centers of learning, culture, and political power.[30] This trend however only takes off when industrialization allows cities to become their own productive centers, even if they still remain tied to rural centers. The reversal of the relationship between rural and urban areas, however, began to shift in the 1950s, during these years 30 percent of all humanity already lived in cities. The United Nations projects that by the year 2030, 60 percent of humanity will live in cities. Here we must pause, and reflect that this means that a substantive part of humanity will still remain rural, and that most of those farmer and peasants will be in so-called third world countries. Nonetheless, as Eric Hobsbawm remarked in his work *The Age of Extremes*, the "most dramatic and far-reaching social change of the second half of [the twentieth century] is the death of the peasantry."[31] The other side of this reversal of the relationship between city and country is that most megacities will be in what is called the third world. Early into the third millennium, the ten most populated metropolises of the world are neither in Europe nor in the United States. These trends can be attributed to a variety of factors. The most important factor in the elimination of the rural is the industrialization of agriculture, a process that reached its zenith with the so-called green revolution of the fifties and sixties. Under the industrialization of agriculture we must understand not just the introduction of better tools but the homogenization of agricultural production, by which I mean the introduction on a global scale of the *mono-cultivo*.[32] We must also include here the elimination of self-subsistent forms of farming through the elimination of self-renewing biodiverse ecosystems. One of the most effective ways, however, in which the city has imposed itself over the countryside is through the projection of images that de-stabilized the sense of tradition and cultural continuity so fundamental to the rhythms of the countryside. Through TV, radio, and now the internet, the city assaults the fabric of the countryside. Tradition is undermined by the promises and riches projected by the tube of plenty, the cornucopia of other possibilities: the TV, and its world of infotainment (see Bauman's wonderful discussion of how, under the globalization of entertainment, the Benthamian Panopticon turns into the MacWorld/Infotainment Synopticon).[33]

Indeed, one of the most characteristic aspects of globalization is what is called the decreasing importance of the local, the state, the national. We therefore need to speak with Jürgen Habermas and Paul Kennedy of a post-national constellation in which sovereign nation-states as territorially localized have become less important because of their decreasing ability to return control of their own spatiality.[34] Sovereignty is being decoupled from territoriality, in a way in which both political and economic self-determination diverge.[35] What is too frequently forgotten is that there is a simultaneous process of localization in which a certain specific place acquires a new significance and accrues both material and symbolic capital.[36] The city is the site in which the forces of the local and the global meet. This is the site where the forces of transnational, finance capital, and the local labor markets and national infrastructures enter into conflict and contestation over the city. As Saskia Sassen writes: "The city has indeed emerged as a site for new claims: by global capital which uses the city as an 'organizational commodity,' but also by disadvantaged sectors of the urban population, which in large cities are frequently as internationalized a presence as is capital. The denationalizing of urban space and the formation of new claims by transnational actors and involving contestation, raise the question—whose city is it?"[37] The city, in fact, has become the crossroad for a new denationalizing politics in which global actors, capitals, and moving peoples enter into conflict across a transnational urban system.

Habermas has noted with acuity that one of the characteristics of the eighteenth and nineteenth centuries was their pronounced fears of the "mass," "the crowd."[38] Such fears were summarized in the title of the prescient work by Ortega y Gasset: *The Revolt of the Masses*.[39] As was noted already, the eighteenth and the nineteenth centuries signaled the reversal of the relationship between countryside and city. This reversal meant the rapid urbanization and demographic explosion in cities, which accompany the rapid industrialization of certain metropolises of the West: London, Berlin, New York, Chicago, Newark, Mexico City, Porto Alegre; and the non-West: New Dehli, Tokyo, Beijing, Cairo, and so on. Urbanization and industrialization gave rise to the specter of the irascible, insatiable, uncontrollable mass that would raze everything in its path. Three classical responses emerged: Sorel, and the celebration of the creative power of anarchical and explosive unorganized mass mobilization; the Marxist-Leninist, and the attempt to domesticate and train the creative and transformative power of social unrest through the development of a party machinery that would guide the ire and discontent of gathered masses of unemployed and employed workers; and the conservative and reactionary response of an Edmund Burke, but which is also echoed in the works of philosophers like Heidegger, which disdained and vilified the common folk, the mass, in a simple term: *Das Man*. The crowd, the mass, is consumed and distracted by prattle, and curiosity, as it wallows in the miasma of inauthenticity and cowardice.[40]

Today such attitudes seem not just foreign but also unrealistic. Most of our experience is determined by a continuous mingling with crowds and large, undifferentiated masses of people. We get on the road and we are confronted with traffic jams; we get on the subway and people accost and touch us from all directions. We live in continuous friction with the stranger, the other. May we suggest that the "other" has become such an important point of departure for philosophical reflection precisely because we exist in such a continuous propinquity with it? Indeed, the *other* is no longer simply a phantasmagorical presence, projected and barely discernable beyond the boundaries of the ecumene, the polis, and the frontiers of the nation-state. At the same time, the discourse about the other, what is called the politics of alterity, marks a shift from the negative discourse of anxiety and fear epitomized in the term "anomie" so well diagnosed by Durkheim, Simmel, and Freud and so aptly described by Christopher Lasch,[41] to the positive discourse of solidarity, inclusion, acceptance, tolerance, citizenship, and justice, so well diagnosed and described by Zymut Bauman, Ulrich Beck, Anthony Giddens, and Jürgen Habermas.[42]

Are there any morals to be extracted from this profound transformation in the way humans—and humanity in general—understand themselves? For the longest period in the history of humankind, groups remained both sheltered from and inured to otherness by the solidity and stability of their traditions and their worlds. Cultures remained fairly segregated maps of the world in which the foreign, strange, and unknown was relegated beyond the boundaries of the controllable, and surveyable. To this extent, "otherness" was legislated over by religion, the state, nature, and even history; namely, those centers of gravity of culture and images of the world. In an age in which all traditions are under constant revision, and human temporality converges with the age of the world itself, then "otherness" appears before us as naked, unmediated otherness: We are all others before each other. In other words, neither our sense of identity nor the sense of difference of the other are given, apriori; they are always discovered, constituted, and dismantled in the very processes of encounter. The other was always constituted for us by extrinsic forces. Now, the other is constituted in the very process of our identity formation, but in a contingent fashion. We make others as we make ourselves. This reflections link up with some insights Enrique Dussel has had with respect to the relationship between the emergence of cities and the development of the first codes of ethics: the Hammurabi Code, and Book N of the Egyptian Book of the Dead.[43] Such codes arose precisely because individuals were thrown into the proximity of each other and were thus confronted with each other's vulnerability and injurability. The injuction to take care of the poor, the indigent, the orphan, the widow, the invalid could only arise out of the urban experience of the contiguity with the injurable flesh of the stranger. Today, the experience of the indigent other is of the immigrant, the exiled, the refugee, who build their enclaves in the shadows of the glamorous city of transnational capital.[44] For this reason, the other and the immigrant are interchangeable; but this also raises the issue of the new global city as a space for the representation and formation of postcolonial identities. Geo-cities are space for the reconfiguration of image, the imagination, and the imaginary, as Arjun Appadurai argued.[45] In this sense, the centrality of the urban experience for humanity means that otherness is not going to be a mere metaphysical or even phenomenological category and concern. *Under the reign of the city, otherness has become quotidian and practical.*

Fourth. Another fundamental point of departure for a phenomenology of globalization will have to be the analysis of the place of technology in our everyday lives. I understand *technology* in two senses. First, in its broadest sense as "the use of scientific knowledge to specify ways of doing things in a *reproducible* way."[46] Second, as a prosthesis of the human body. Technology, to paraphrase a wonderful aphorism of William Burroughs, is the mind wanting more body. I will discuss first the former sense of technology, as a scientific specification for the iterable way of doing things. In this sense, then, a hospital is a social technology, like agriculture and cattle raising are material technologies. By the same token, prisons, asylums, and ghettos are social technologies. There is, however, something unique about technology in the twentieth century, and that is that technology itself has become an object of technology; in other words, the use of science in order to produce ever more efficient ways of doing things in ever more reproducible ways itself has become a technological quest. This technology of technology is what one might call the institutionalization of invention. Alfred North Whitehead noted that "the greatest invention of the nineteenth century was the invention of the method of invention."[47] What Whitehead attributes to the nineteenth century reached its true apogee in the second half of the twentieth century with the institutionalization of the research university. While the program of the research university goes back to the German ideal of the university, it is in the United States that this idea gained its highest formalization and state support. Without question we have to attribute the greatest technological breakthroughs of the twentieth century to this unique convergence of the state, the military, and the research university: what Eisenhower called the "military-industrial complex," and what we now with hindsight should more appropriately term the military-university-industrial complex.[48]

The rise of the nation-state also signified the rise of state-sponsored education, and the state university. The university plays a dual role. On the one hand, it has the function of preparing citizens and workers for the material and cultural-political self-reproduction of society. On the other, it has the role of institutionalizing scientific investigation, the invention of invention. Through the university, the state invests in its future ability to transform its material technologies of self-reproduction. Winning the Nobel Prize is not just a matter of pride, it is above all a question of institutional power to support immense research budgets whose actual industrial and technical application might be far off into the future. This is one of the reasons why the United States has remained a world power, despite its apparent military stalemate; namely, because it still remains the center for the production of most technological innovation.

Related to the invention of invention, what I called the institutionalization of the technology of technology, as its other side, is the interpenetration of technology in every aspect of our lives. Even those who are not directly affected by technological revolutions in their daily life, are nonetheless indirectly affected insofar as their worlds, economies, and cultures are made vulnerable to takeovers and colonization by those who drive the technological revolutions of today. For the longest period in the history of humanity, technology remained distant from the lives and bodies of men and women, not because it did not impact them, but because it did so sporadically and in such tangential ways: fire, the wheel, the printing press, the metal plow, the steam engine, the automobile. Each technological innovation, however, has meant a further interpenetration between tool and human body. With this, I turn to the discussion of technology as prosthesis, the second sense of technology I want to consider in light of a phenomenology of globalization.

A technology is a way of doing things in ways that can be reproduced, again and again, and that therefore can be taught and passed on. Culture is in this sense the most complex and important technology of all. In this sense, a technology is a way for a society to extend itself across time, from generation to generation, century to century.[49] A technology generally instantiated itself in tools. Tools allow particular individuals to reach beyond the boundaries of their own bodies. A tool is an extension of a particular bodily organ that augments its original performance. Tool and body, however, have remained relatively distinct, even if one can claim that the hand is a product of our invention of tools.[50] Recognition of the distinctness between tool and body does not entail the negation of their dialectical interdependence and comodification. Their distinctness was sustained by what I have already referred to above as the temporality of humans and the time of the world. When the time of humans and the world converge, what mediates their encounter, tools, has already fused with the body, or has already made the world immediate. Our experience of the world is already so mediated by our technological tools that we cannot distinguish the world from the tool, and these from the body. We are our tools. We are our technological prosthesis because they are the world.[51] But this does not mean that technology is itself transparent. Rather, technology itself has become like our bodies in the sense that we do not know how our liver, heart, or brains work: we just assume that they will do what they were designed to do, and if they break down, then we go to a specialist.

Everywhere we are surrounded by technological devices that have insinuated themselves into our lives to the extent that we cannot do without them: the watch, the telephone, the car, the TV, but also, tooth paste, x-rays, vaccines, birth-control pills, condoms, sun screen, eyeglasses, shavers, purified and chlorinated water, and so on.

What I am talking about can be illustrated by comparing Mary Shelley's Frankenstein, in which a creation out of human parts becomes monstrous precisely because it entails the complete instrumentalization of our bodies, and thus a sacrilege of its alleged divine naturalness, and Donna Haraway's borgs, which demonstrate and theorize to what extent we are always already synthetic.[52] There is no nature outside the confines of the laboratory. *Resistance is futile* to the logic of technology because we are all already borg: we are products of our technologies, and nature exists only as an Arcadian fantasy. This reading should not be taken to be suggesting that nature does not exist in the sense that it is a fiction, the mirage of radical social constructivism. Rather, the point is to highlight the ways in which nature is to be thought of in terms of what today we call the recursive loops between technology and nature, in which nature is already an artifact and machines are natural.[53] Indeed, appropriating Marx's language from his 1844 manuscripts, we have to talk about the humanization of machines and the mechanization of humanity.

Is there a moral to be extracted by the interpenetration of humans and their technological prosthesis to the point that you cannot distinguish them any longer? I would say that a Heideggerian response to this question is anachronistic and indefensible. On the other hand, a dia-mat, in the sense of Engels's dialectical materialism, will not do either. Science is neither metaphysically bad nor a malleable ideological epiphenomenon. Against these two positions, I would advocate what has been called Kranzberg's Law, which reads: "Technology is neither good nor bad, nor is it neutral."[54]

I summarize my reflections by suggesting that once a phenomenology of globalization takes seriously the points of departure above discussed, we will discover that globalization might stand for another axial period. This new axial age will be characterized by at least these four themes: First, the perpetual revolutionizing of production technologies has turned into the technology of innovation, in such a way that the generation of capital is relocated to the production of new information technologies and not production and processing of raw materials. Second, because of the almost instantenous information transmission and reception across the world, and the convergence of natural, historical, and personal temporalities, we have the effect of the *detranscendentalization and temporalization of tradition*. These detranscendentalization and temporalization suggest that our images of the world will be at the reach of our own design. In this sense, we will be able to speak of the true secularization of the world and its complete humanization. Third, the hyper-urbanization of humanity has brought about the *routinization and demetaphysicalization of otherness* brought about by the hyper-urbanization of humanity. Otherness will become a product of society, and in this sense we will have to talk of regimes of alterization. The "other," then, will become a continuous presence that will require our constant concern and vigilance. Fourth, and finally, this new axial age will be characterized by the *dissolution of the boundary between the natural and synthetic, the body and tool, technology and nature.* We will have to speak, then, of the age in which humans have become their own creations, and in which the directions of the reproduction of both mind and body, culture and technology will become a concern of political practice of paramount importance.

The image of the world projected by globalization is one that collapses the differences between biomorphic space-time, social space-time, and world space-time: what we see is what we get. To put it in the language of an essay by Theodor Adorno, the history of nature is not different from the history of humanity.[55] Globalization also projects an image of the world in which otherness is not external and intractable but produced from within. Finally, globalization is an image of the world in which the natural and the social, the created and uncreated, have been brought together under the insight that we have been producing ourselves as we have been producing tools to alter the world. Now, however, the producing of our tools is not different from the production of ourselves and our world. In the image of the world projected by globalization, the world is humanity looking at itself through its eyes and not the eyes of a god, history, or nature.

City of Angels

> Who is the observer when it concerns the question about the function of religion: the system of religion itself, or science as an external observer?[56]

The kind of phenomenology of globalization that I sketched above allows us to ask about the kinds of challenges religion faces in an age of globalization. For religion appears as a resource of images, concepts, traditions, and practices that can allow individuals and communities to deal with a world that is changing around them by the hour.[57] In the new *Unübersichtlichkeit* [unsurveyability] of our global society, religion appears as compendium of intuitions that have not been extinguished by the so-called process of secularization.[58] Most importantly, however, religion cannot be dismissed or derided because it is the privileged, if not the primary, form in which the impoverished masses of the invisible cities of the world (those cities to which I pointed in the first part of this chapter) articulate their hopes as well as a critique of their world.

The first challenge to religion that our phenomenology of globalization allows us to articulate has to do with the "detranscendentalizing of otherness," or what I also call the "routinization of otherness." There is a correlation between the way humanity has conceptualized otherness, metaphysically and conceptually, on the one hand, and humanity's relationship to real and concrete otherness, as it has been experienced existentially and phenomenologically, on the other hand. This correlation has been mediated by humanity's decreasing ruralism. In other words, the less rural—and thus the more urban dwelling—humans have become, the less other is the otherness that we can think of or dream up. The suggestion is that the metaphysics of alterity that has guided so much of Western theology and religious thinking over the last two thousand years has been determined by a particular asymmetry between the country and the city. For the longest history of humanity most societies have been farming and rural-dwelling communities and associations. Contact between extremely different communities and societies was sporadic and rare, and when contact did occur, this was meditated by city dwellers and the long memory of popular mythologies. But as was noted above, in the dawning twenty-first century most humans are city dwellers. Furthermore, in the twenty-first century most of humanity is conglomerated in the megaurbes of the third world. Under this circumstance, the holy other, the absolutely other, will be deflated. Alterity and the extraordinary, what can also be called the *tremendum*, are demystified and demetaphysicalized.[59] Either everyone will be a stranger, or no one will be, because we will all be strangers in a city of strangers. In such a situation, otherness will have become a routine, an unextraordinary event. How then are we to think divine alterity, the otherness of the holy, in a situation in which ontologically and metaphysically all alterity has been deflated, demoted, rendered normal, leveled to the quotidian? Are we in a situation of having to "risk a new idea of holiness" as Barry Taylor, pastor at the Sanctuary Church in Santa Monica, put it. This would have to be a holiness that is not other worldly, but a holiness that is about the difference and uniqueness of others, those who are our everyday other, with whom we ride the subway, with whom we walk the streets of populated megaurbes of the new age, with whom we share in anonymity the crowded spaces of the new cities. The real and metaphorical wilderness of the world, of its jungles and forests, of its undiscovered continents and untamed seas, of its unmapped deserts and unnavigated rivers, were excuses as well as instigations to go searching for God beyond the familial, the urbane, the too close and already "domesticated." God was beyond the world, other than the world. Now, the question is How do we discover the other in the mundane difference of every fellow human being and the crowded city of strangers?

The second challenge has to do with the city as locus of the culture of consumption, as the site for an ethos of immediacy, hedonism, and hyperexcitation. Sassen speaks of the city as the crossroads of a confrontation between the flows of capital and the flows of peoples. One of the ways these flows clash in cities is through the confrontation between cultures, that is, between different modalities of life. The more people become urban dwellers, the more people are exposed to the cornucopia of cultural possibilities. It is not just that more people are in cities, it is also that more people are seeking to participate in the standards of life promised by urban dwelling. The challenges are unprecedented. We are presently choking in our own refuse, in our own garbage. The psychological toil must also be unprecedented. The level of unmet expectations, unfilled desires, the gap between universally promised but exorbitantly expensive commodities that shatter self-images and worth and that are available to a relatively small fraction of the world population, has grown exponentially. There is another underside to the city as the crossroads of the clash of modalities of life. The more cities grow, the more they exert their pull on the so-called hinterland, the rural areas. The more agriculture is mechanized and industrialized, the more we adopt biotechnology, the more superfluous "farmers" become. At the same time, the expansion of telecommunications, television, paid-for TV, and satellite connections have made it easier to link up and peer into the "tube of plenty," to use that wonderful phrase by Erik Barnouw.[60] The city literally and metaphorically consumes its hinterland, its outlying areas of supply: it consumes its resources and produce, but also its cultures and its peoples.

It is perhaps unnecessary to underscore again that most of the consumption of rural resources is taking place in the metropolises of the so-called first world. So, not only must we address the rampant and rapacious consumerism of cities in general, but also the particularly scandalous and grotesque asymmetry between the consumption of first-world cities and third-world cities. This issue becomes particularly pressing when in the so-called advanced nations of the world we have thinkers, intellectuals, and critics talking about a politics and culture of inclusion and tolerance.[61] This politics of inclusion is articulated with the best intentions in mind. The assumption guiding it is that people throughout the world would be better if they could participate more equitably in the same kinds of so called basic needs and luxuries that we Westerners enjoy. But there is something profoundly disingenuous and deleteriously naive about such a view. In some cases the poverty of those across the world to whom we would like to extend our standard of living is due precisely to our luxury. That which we want to share is the cause of the privation we want to alleviate. Thus, perhaps the agenda should not be one of inclusion but of dismantling the system that occasioned in the first place the exclusions we benefited and continue to benefit from.

In this situation, then, the challenge becomes how to think of an urban culture of frugality. The challenge is how to translate the religious message and teaching of poverty as a holy way, as a holy calling, into a secular value, a secular calling. Another way of putting it would be, How do we translate the visions of the desert fathers, Saint Francis of Assisi, or Mahatma Gandhi into an urban vision for a spiritually starving youth? Or, alternatively, if we think of what Arnold Toynbee and Eric Hobsbawm said about the twentieth century—namely that its greatest achievement was the expansion of the middle class—then the goal for the twenty-first century should be the expansion of a globalized "living level class." In other words, we have to develop a culture for which the greatest achievement is not that everyone else will live like us, but that we will live at the level that allows the most people to share in the most fundamental goods: potable water, clean air, infant nutrition to sustain healthy standards of unstunted growth, and the possibility of basic education. Here, I would have to say that I concur with Negri and Hardt on their canonization of Assisi as a saint in the hagiography of revolutionary militancy.[62]

The third challenge that our phenomenology of globalization allows us to elucidate has to do with one of its central locus of analysis, namely the city. If cities have become the sites where the unbundling of the state takes place, that is, if we take cities to be the sites for the denationalizing of the national, and if we at the same time take the city as the locus of an emergent juridification, or process of legalization of new forms of relationships, then are we not in need of having to rethink the relationship between the legal and political structures of the emergent supranational state and the parastatist or extrastatist "church." Another way of putting it would be to note that the church, at least in the West, antecedes the modern nation-state. In fact, the church was the state, and that partly because of this, the quest for modernity, the process of modernization, entailed a secularization of state and legal structures. In the process, the church's sphere of operation became restricted or constrained by the spaces drawn by the boundaries of nation-states. Churches and denominations became identified with national boundaries, which took place notwithstanding the underlying and fundamental universalist trust of Christianity. If we accept Sassen's analysis, which we must given the overwhelming evidence, then we are inescapably put in the situation of having to rethink the relationship between the church and the state. In fact, as the nation-states of the nineteenth and twentieth century are unbundled, and new forms of political and legal rights emerge in deterritorialized and denationalized forms of political self-determination, then the church itself will have to face its denationalization and deterritoritalization. At the same time, however, one of the fundamental conditions of the presence of the church in the twenty-first century will have to be that it must have learned the lessons of the last five hundred years of colonialism, imperialism, and postcolonialism. This means that the challenge is dual. On the one hand, the new church must find a place beyond the nation-states of political modernity; but on the other hand, it must do so with a postcolonialist and postimperialist attitude. In the age of global transformations, the new church cannot and will not be able to serve as an agent of globalization for the new imperial masters that began to profile themselves on the horizon—namely, a united front of European nations (an expanded NATO), a technological elite bent on redesigning nature, and a cosmopolitan nobility without controls, allegiances, or consciences.

Fourth, and finally, another extremely important challenge has to do with the insight that cities are the places where cultures come to cultivate each other. In other words, cities are the places where old cultures are cannibalized but also carnivalized, where old cultures that are dying come to be renewed, but also where new cultures are produced from the remains of old ones.[63] Cities are germinals of new cultures. Indeed, just as we are very likely to find microclimates in most global cities, we are likely to find cultural enclaves: little Italies, Chinatowns, Japantowns, little Bombays, and so on. These places are where the centripetal and centrifugal forces of homogenization and heterogenization interact to produce new cultural formations. Underlying this new cultural genesis is its evident and almost presentist character. The processes of cultural genesis take place right in front of our eyes. Cultures are not millennial sedimentations; and even that which is peddled as the oldest is a present-day version of the old. Most importantly, cultures have become something we produce, and choose; cultures are something that we either nurture and preserve or abandon and disavow. In all of these cases, we are not passive but active agents of transformation. In this situation, the challenge for the new church, for an urban ministry for the twenty-first century, is how to develop an ecclesiology of cultural diversity. How will the new church participate in this cultural genesis that is germinating in global cities while retaining a sense of identity? Or, conversely, how will it retain a sense of cultural identity without becoming either ethnocentric or jingoistic about its cultural bequest, without contributing to the ossification of its own culture? On what terms can the new church participate in the creation of new cultures and the preservation of successful ones?

Conclusion

Cities are the vortex of the convergence of the processes of globalization and localization. Cities are epitomes of glocalization, to use Robertson's language.[64] They are also sites of the sedimentation of history. In this chapter, I have sought to advance the research agenda that would take the "invisible cities" of the so-called third world as their primary object of analysis. At the same time, however, I have urged that we look at the cities in the developed, industrialized world through the eyes of their invisible inhabitants and citizens: immigrants, ethnic minorities, disenfranchised groups, workers, women, and the youth. There are invisible cities within the cities that are so visible in most urban theory and analysis, as well as invisible cities that remain unseen because they are not in the horizon of the academic agendas of researchers in the universities of the developed world.

In tandem, I have suspended judgment on whether to be for or against globalization, not because I do not think that we can make moral judgments in this case, but because I think we need to broaden our analyses of this new order of things. I developed some general points of departure for a phenomenological analysis of globalization. This particular approach, I think, exhibits how "globalization" can and ought to become a matter for serious philosophical reflection. I have identified the issues of alterity, temporality, tradition, the distinction between the natural and the synthetic, as *philosophemes* that are substantively impacted by the processes of globalization. Yet, the phenomenological approach I articulate is deliberate in assuming a particular perspective or angle of approach. I have sought to delineate a phenomenology of globalization *from below.* The world does not disclose itself in the same way to all subjects, much less globalization. Thus, the phenomenology here presented urges us to look at the world from below, from the perspective of those who seem to be more adversely than beneficially affected by the processes that make up globalization.

This is what the "below" in the subtitle of this chapter points to: the below of the poor and destitute, the below of those who are not seen and do not register in the radar of social theory. Furthermore, I have tried to further qualify that perspective from below by focusing my attention on the issue of religion. Religion can mean many things, but at the very least it means "the sigh of the oppressed," and the "encyclopedic compendium" of a heartless world, as Marx put it, if only because it is the form in which the destitute, the most vulnerable in our world, express their critiques, as well as hopes.[65] I have argued that we ought to look at cities as germinals of new cultures, and that if we want to trace the emergent cultures of those "below," then we better look at religious movements. In what ways is the religious language of the oppressed and disenfranchised of the invisible cities of globalization to be heard as a critique and resistance to globalization? This is clearly a research desiderata, rather than a description or even an assessment.

Part 2

LATINAMERICANISMS

3

From Modernity, through Postmodernity, to Globalization

Mapping Latin America

Introduction, or Without Apologies

From the outset we must dispense with what seem to be de rigueur declarations of either consternation or bafflement before the proliferation of positions and discourses on postmodernity. This proliferation, in fact, reaches exponential proportions when we include the challenges formulated from Latin America and the so-called postcolonial world. Consternation is unacceptable because it is the nature of *cultural analysis* to proliferate. Were there no massive accumulation of articles, books, or anthologies—even books devoted to bibliographies of this and other such topics—then we would surely have reason to be concerned. Such an absence would betray either a silence imposed by only the most severe forms of repression and extermination, or reveal an impossible univocity and homogeneity that belies the nature of culture. Cultural analysis must tend toward plurification because, as Werner Hamacher puts it:

> There is no single culture that constitutes an autarchic, self-established, and self-sufficient unity. Every culture cultivates itself with regard to other cultures and is cultivated by other cultures.... This means: there is no one culture. Culture is a *plurale tantum*: it exists only in the plural, and it exists only as given also by other cultures.[1]

We must take the cacophony of voices on modernity, the discordant, even mutually exclusive positions on postmodernity, and the no less disconcerting

---

This chapter appeared in a different form in Alfonso de Toro, ed. *Cartografías y estrategias de la 'posmodernidad' y la 'postcolonialidad' en Latinoamérica: 'Hibridez' y 'Globalización'* (Madrid and Frankfurt am Main: Iberoamerica–Vervuert, 2006), 61–91.

and challenging discourses on postcoloniality, to be signs of if not an entirely healthy, at least a partially operating worldwide public sphere—some might be less sanguine and call it a global marketplace of slogans passed for ideas. If anything, dismay should be amply expressed at the sorry state of the reception of other analyses and positions from across the world, concerning postmodernity and related concepts. Bafflement is unacceptable, also, because this would betray a naivete concerning the very nature of *critical discourse*: their intrinsic tendencies to plurify, diversify, fragment, redouble, contradict, and even in some cases self-contradict. Incomprehension would be the attitude of someone waking up and looking around, seeking only to see what he or she is already too used to seeing. Such an attitude is only possible to someone who is inured to the critique of social reality by others and is too sure of their own regal status in the world. Instead, when approaching the question of Latin America's relationship to posmodernity, a sense of recognition of an unsurveyable world should be accompanied by our dismay at the relative hegemony of certain positions. We ought to be open to be shocked and incited into dissent by the tower of Babel effect of the dissemination of discourses on postmodernity. Most importantly, debates concerning postmodernity and related monikers concern not just a name, a word, even a fashion. Rather, the debates are over the meanings, concepts, and ideas that explain and give coherence to our historical experience. Thus, not to have a plurality of discourses would signal that we would have lost our claim to name our times, our world. Plurality is a mark of dissent, if not a sign of sedition. It is in this spirit that the following chapter is articulated.

Some "operating instructions" are in order. The following is a prolegomena, and a guide; thus many of the insights remain schematic and stand only as signposts and warnings. In the first part, I undertake a clarification of some methodological issues that must be handled with care if we are to proceed with the ambitious undertaking that this chapter prepares. In the second I proceed to offer another version of the debate on modernity/postmodernity, although now with the benefit of the insights gained in the first section. This final section is not a supplement, but rather stands as testimony to the idea that if modernity/postmodernity are brought to bear—that is, they are rubbed against the harsh reality of Latin America—then neither will remain the same. The lowest common denominator in this concatenation of concepts and meanings—Latin America too is a meaning and concept—is that our understanding of modernity/postmodernity will be deepened just as we will have begun to think Latin America otherwise, or in another light. Some readers might bemoan the absence of close readings of particular positions. Such discussions have a place in specialized articles and monographs. I wanted to offer more a road map and even a compass, and less another attempt at a failed encyclopaedic compendium that tries to parrot what authors themselves have said in exemplary ways. Furthermore, in endnotes and explicit references in the text, I direct the reader to already extant detailed and insightful discussions of particular readings. The reader is presently directed to what are by now the canonical texts in this field, namely the works by Santiago Castro-Gómez, Herlinghaus and Walter, and Beverly, Oviedo, and Aronna.[2]

Borders, Maps, Chronologies, and Typologies

Some methodological questions must be broached before any detailed discussion can be initiated. In no particular order of importance, for in fact the following considerations are entwined in a web of interdependences and codeterminations, one would have to discuss the question of periodization with respect to postmodernity. In other words, before the question of postmodernity's relationship to Latin America can be undertaken, we would have to clarify the question of when, and perhaps most importantly, where did postmodernity begin. As the moniker itself so loudly announces, *post*modernity refers to a temporal, epochal marker.[3] Inevitably, we must ask, When did this post begin, and has it ended? There are some positions, however, that contest this meaning of postmodernity. For them, postmodernity refers to a cultural orientation, a *Weltanschauung*, a mental state, a conceptual episteme. In that sense it is less like an epochal marker and more like the designation of a mental orientation of a particular lifeworld.[4] Nonetheless, even when we speak of postmodernity in this latter sense, we must still answer when, or about when did society begin to think of itself as postmodern. As Dussel has noted with respect to Habermas's timeline for modernity, chronologies are not innocent, but rather are weighted with ideological baggage.[5] Postmodernity, in fundamental ways turns around the question of chronologies, temporal maps. Who traces the boundaries of these maps, gets to determine who is behind, ahead, outside, or beyond history?[6]

A particularly tangled methodological consideration that must be carefully articulated concerns the locus of postmodernization. Postmodernity, no less than modernity, is surrounded by the halo bestowed upon it by what Wolfgang Welsch has called the "Magie des falschen Namens."[7] The word is used as a noun, adjective, verb, as an adverb, to refer in different ways to processes, events, social facts, that span the entire spectrum of social spheres of interaction: economy, politics, art, religion, and society in general.[8] Thus, philosophers, artists, cultural critics, theologians, sociologists, political theorists, economists, and so on, write about their respective spheres of investigation as though it had sole responsibility for the entire societal phenomenon of postmodernity. In other words, a sociologist will talk about urbanization, mass culture, the rise of cybersociety, the decline of marriage, the effects of television on critical consciousness, the demise of heavy industry, and so forth, as catalysts of postmodernity/postmodernization.[9] Economists, for instance, might point to the rise of flexible production, the development of a postnational, global financial market, and the decline of the Fordist and Keynesian models of the economy, as fundamental factors in the rise of a postmodern milieu. A cultural critique, on the other hand, might refer to the demise of the "novel," and coherent narrative, and the development of nontraditional forms of narrative, or the cross fertilization of different forms of narrativity, in tandem with the dissemination of the authorial voice and the decentering of subjectivity.[10] The world, in short, in no longer representable, not just because of the insufficiency of the means (language, writing, reporting, etc.), but because what would stand in opposition to the world, as that which registers the world's intractability and resistance, itself has dissolved—namely, the subject. Postmodernity as apriori indeterminacy and aposteriori social fiat—by which I mean that there is no extraterrestrial or transcendental realm that can offer warrant for claims to justice or normativity—has even colonized the realm of law and jurisprudence, the last bastion of determinacy and rational transparency that would allegedly foil all covert coercion or power deployment.[11] Philosophers, similarly, talk about rationality, historical progress, the criteria of normative evaluation, the possibility of legitimation, and thrust in the power of rational determinability of interpellations and critical claims.[12] In short, the point is that postmodernity looks different in accordance to the social locus from which it is observed. A sociologist paints a different picture of postmodernity from the way a philosopher, an economist, or a political scientist would paint it. In many cases, there is a willful attempt to make the facts and processes of one realm fit the descriptions and norms of another. A philosopher, thus, might look at postmodernity through the lens of Enlightenment values, without regard for either the historicity of the French *philosophes* themselves or of our times. An art critic, in a similar fashion, might attempt to offer a cultural diagnosis on the basis of an analysis of certain aesthetic trends and genres. There are as many theories of postmodernity, or there should be, as there are spheres of human interaction. Each such sphere claims for itself a privileged place in the order of social interactions. Analogously, theories departing from a specific sphere—value realms, in the Weberian language—abrogate for themselves higher survey and explanatory power. While it is important not to surrender to such claims of primacy or priority, it is just as important not to lose sight of the plurality of social forms of the determination of the social. Just as there is no one culture, there is no one society. Society exists in the plural of social variations of the arrangement of social spheres of interaction. A relevant question, perhaps to parallel the question, When do you mark the inception of modernity/postmodernity? would be Where do you place the locus of modernity/postmodernity? Whether a thinker gives primacy to technology, the political, social, economic, or aesthetic realms discloses plenty about that particular thinker's ideological commitments, and blind spots, and concomitantly, shortcomings as well as advantages. Finally, what the contentions and disagreements between, let us say, philosophers and sociologists reveals concerning the indeterminacy of postmodernity, where it resides most smugly, is that perhaps we are learning through the via negativa that society is not determinable by or through solely one social sphere, and this is one way in which we can read Baudrillard's pronouncement of the death of the social.[13]

Taking up Hamacher's insights, cited above, just as cultures are cultivated by other cultures, rendering it impossible to speak of one culture, or a culture, societies are determined by other societies. There is no society but in societies. The determination of societies is both synchronic and diachronic, and also multilayered. Some societies determine others more, and at more fundamental levels, than others. Postmodernity, like modernity, has been predominantly used to refer to so-called advanced industrialized nations in the North Atlantic corridor. Yet, as the present chapter testifies, postmodernity is intricately enmeshed with the third world, or most derogatorily called "the Rest," that which is not the "West" (of course, this word must be put in quotation marks because its referent is not an entity but a whole historical ideology and an ideology of history). One may find sprinkled with varying degrees of haphazardry throughout the seminal texts on postmodernity references to immigrants, underclass, ethnicity, race, the colonial, and subaltern, hybridity, and *mestizaje*, as well as the contestation of the West by former colonies, and the entire process of decolonization and colonization of the metropolis by the colonial periphery.[14] One cannot, for instance, separate the rise of a postmodern sensibility from the rise of "race pride movements"—which in many ways mirrored in the "center" the insurrection of the periphery in the colonial outpost. In the United States, for instance, conservatives and neoconservatives perhaps not entirely wrongly lumped together the rise of identity politics, poststructuralism, deconstruction, and postmodernism as signs of the barbarian onslaught upon the venerable walls of the citadel of Western culture. The cultural war of the eighties, again in the United States, which had its analogues in Europe with the debates about the meaning of the holocaust, also pointed in the direction of the elective affinity between the internal criticism of the venerable truths of the Western canon and their external challenges, and deligitimation by those who suffered their untruth, severity, and intolerance.[15]

The point: it is fundamental that any approximation to the question concerning postmodernity include an examination of the relations between the signifier "The West" and its "Other"—put more correctly between the ideologeme "the West" and its putative "others." Indeed, notwithstanding the invidiousness of the parallelism "modernity is to monologisms as postmodernity is to alterity," a politics of difference and a differential politics has come to dominate the scene in ways that underscore the foregrounding of heterogeneity and diversity that points outward but also inward. Difference is not just outside, beyond, but also inside, amongst us. This means, succinctly, that a viable analysis of postmodernity must also contend with the issues of postcolonialism and globalization. For as John Beverly and

José Oviedo point out "postmodernism might be better understood as precisely the effect in that center of postcoloniality."[16] To which I would add, and globalization is the response to postcoloniality, as it is felt by the center in its metropolises, in such a way that the contestation and insurgency named by postcolonianism is attempted to be deflected and co-opted. None of this entails a Manichean view of geopolitics; it merely reflects a struggle over meanings and concepts that make contemporary social reality legible, or surveyable. Thus, and not to overextend this crucial discussion, the core notion to be foregrounded is that, and in tandem with our reference to chronologies and temporal maps, any discussion concerning postmodernity must also point in the direction of both historical and contemporary geopolitics.[17] Postmodernity, when appropriately matched up, arranges in a constellation of related concepts and must yield insights into the geopolitics of contemporary societies. The issue is not just who is, was, or will be postmodern, but also who, and under what conditions, gets to modernize/ postmodernize whom.

We have thus far remained at a fairly abstract level. Yet, the point of these reflections is to sift postmodernity through the sieve of Latin America. In fact, a more apt metaphor would be to suggest that we intend to metabolize postmodernity with Latin America in such a way that neither remains unchanged at the end of the process. We are therefore required at the methodological level at which we still remain, but at a lower level of abstraction, that we elucidate at least these two central issues. On the one hand, and just as it is true for any theory of postmodernity in general, we must begin with the explication of the criteria by means of which we can offer a typology of discourses about postmodernity in Latin America. On the other hand, there is the issue of the character and nature of the producers of these discourses within Latin America. A significant aspect of postmodernity as a concept, as a way to describe social reality, is that it is a description produced by intellectuals and/or academicians, for intellectuals and/or academicians.[18] From this perspective, postmodernity turns into a register of the transformations undergone by the offices of the "cultural critic," "academic," and "public intellectual."

With respect to the first issue, it is by now possible to develop a typology that would categorize positions in accordance with a matrix that would contain the following coefficients, or grids: a main subheading would be comprised by those positions that see postmodernity as something extrinsic to and colonizing of Latin America. In essence, under this heading we would find agglutinated those positions that see postmodernity as another metropolitan discourse or fashion that more or less seeks to have an ideological effect—namely, to obfuscate social reality and to neutralize all criticism of the center (Vázquez, Roig, Larsen, Hinkelammert, Dussel). Under an adjacent heading we would find all those positions that would accept and theorize postmodernity not just as an intrasocial and endemic aspect of

Latin American reality (Brunner, Monsiváis, Lechner, Canclini), but go so far as to claim that Latin America is prepostmodern; that is, in a fundamental sense, inasmuch as we take postmodernity to be a *Weltanschauung*, postmodernity has been the natural outlook of Latin America (Ortiz, Retamar, Yúdice, Colás). Where as the prior two subheadings gravitate around the axis of Latin America, the next two gravitate around postmodernity. Thus, one heading would gather all those positions that are propostmodernity (again Lechner, Brunner, Monsiváis, Yúdice, Beverly, Laclau), while its adjacent heading would gather all those that are antipostmodernity (Guadarrama, Roig, Dussel, Paz, Larsen). Evidently, not everyone who is antipostmodern is so for the same reasons, just as not everyone who is propostmodern is so for the same reasons.[19] Thus, some who are antipostmodern are also antimodern, antimodernity (Dussel), while there are some who are antipostmodern who are unequivocally promodernity (like Roig, Vázquez, Guadarrama). Analogously, there are some propostmoderns who are antimodernity (Lechner, Brunner, Monsiváis, Canclini), while there are some propostmodernity who are also promodernity (Zea, and Paz in a particular reading). The intention here is neither to be exhaustive nor baroque, but rather to point in the direction of a plurality of positions. The point: there is no one position that can be said to be the Latin American position on postmodernity. Echoing an earlier formulation, there are as many Latin American positions on postmodernity as there are Latin Americas, and by this later I do not mean Latin American countries, but interpretations of Latin America (Paz's, Dussel's, O'Gorman's, Arciniegas's, Retamar's, Martí's, Vasconcelos's, etc.).

Turning to the issue of the transformation of the offices of the "cultural critic," "public intellectual," or "academic," in Latin America, we would have to suggest that a proper analysis of the metapolitical encounter between postmodernity and Latin America should include a chapter on the archaeology or genealogy of the social space for social self-reflection within and about Latin America. Just like the explosion of postmodern theorizing in the industrialized and modern nations of the North Atlantic corridor occurred in tandem with the transformation of the university, the rise of popular mass culture, the development of new social movements, and the transformation of public cultures through either colonization by commodified culture or relocation through popular displacement, in Latin America similar but also significantly different factors determined the rise and response to postmodern theorizing. In Latin America, for instance, we have to pay close attention to the transformation of the public university, which grew in unprecedented forms during the fifties and sixties, under the tutelage of the modernization thrusts led by paternal states. But at the same time that the university grew, the role of the critic was not co-opted, or assimilated to the university; instead, and in opposition, it was marginalized. In Latin America, the university was used as a sign of the modernity of the state; thus, it was heavily monitored by the state and became a privileged locus of contestation and insurrection. Two related processes were the failure of traditional communist and socialist parties, what Castañeda called "disarmed utopias," and the assimilation and co-option of their utopian energies by grassroots movements like the Christian Base Communities that then spawned the liberation theology movements of the seventies and eighties. These two processes are in fact almost opposite faces of the same coin, namely the coin of social activism under what some might called premodern conditions, and others would called alternate routes through modernity, where postmodernity is the name for Latin American's path to modernity as Brunner put it so poignantly. At the same time, it would be a massive oversight to overlook the fact that Latin America underwent a rapid, accelerated, inordinate growth in the first half of the last century: urbanization, industrialization, literacy, mass media, and so on. Indeed, one may say that postmodernity is the name of an accelerated and hypertrophied modernity in Latin America. Monsiváis, Lechner, Brunner, and Canclini have documented the ways in which new social movements have entered the scene at the very moment that mass media is commodifying everything, and that spaces for critical reflection are displaced from both the socialist and communists parties and the university, to think tanks and nontraditional spaces of contestation, like the pulpit, the seminary, and the bible-study group.

Whose (Post)modernity, Which Latin America?

"A place on a map is a place in history," says Adrienne Rich.[20] If that is so, where does Latin America fit in the map of history? The following questions are but a mere sample of the problems that arose as a result of the mapping of Latin America vis-à-vis the rest of the world.

Does Latin America refer to a part of the "American" continent? And if so, why has the United States claimed exclusivity to the term "America," preempting everyone else's claim to the name? Does Latin America refer to those countries below the Rio Grande but excluding Brazil? Is Latin America a subcontinent determined by linguistic identity, the lands where Spanish and Portuguese are predominantly spoken? Where does the Caribbean fit into this linguistic map? Why is Latin America the "third world" while parts of the south of Brazil are more developed than parts of the south of the United States? In what way are modernized cities like Mexico City, Rio de Janeiro, Caracas, and Buenos Aires different from Los Angeles, Miami, and New York? Is Latin America the land of vibrant Catholicism, to the exclusion of all syncretism? And if so, what do we do with all the Afro-American religions not just in Brazil, but also in the Caribbean and the south of the United States? And what of the "mestizo" face of Jesus in Central America and the Andes, and liberation theology, seen by many as a second reformation? Is Mexico part of Latin America? And if so, why is it that in the United

States *Chicanos* are not *Hispanics*, while Argentineans are *Hispanic* but not *Latinos*? and what is the difference between Haitians, Puerto Ricans, and Dominicans? Or, along the same lines, what are the differences among "New World Africans" in Brazil, the Caribbean, and the United States? How is the map of Latin America to be drawn—demographically, politically, economically, culturally, linguistically, or on the basis of race and religion? Furthermore, when did Latin America become Latin America?[21] Like Heidegger's *Dasein*, Latin America is defined above all by the fact that its being is always in question. This questioning, however, always betrays the trace of imperial designs.[22]

The impossibility of absolute representations is foregrounded by the fact that totalizing discourses are threatened from the outset by incoherence. Such is the challenge we must face in dealing with (post)modernity (from now on I will use this typographical monstrosity in order to underscore the point, addressed later on, that there is a fundamental parasitism between these two cognates.) I begin with the following claim: Latin America is not supplemental or external to (post)modernity. Instead, it is integral to it. Neither can be thought without the other. In other words, there is a correspondence between (post)modernity and Latin America inasmuch as they are projects and conditions, as well as worldviews and mental states. My central thesis is that (post)modernity is no less important to Latin America than it is to Europe and the United States. And, conversely, that Latin America is no less important to (post)modernity than either the United States or the crisis of the European project. I will have accomplished my goals if I have offered not only a window into how the debate on (post)modernity has been dealt with within Latin America, but also a window that looks back into the dyad itself: (Post)modernity. If Latin America will be seen as a product of (post)modernity, whether in terms of its failure or triumph, its point of origin, or its dénouement, then I hope that the reader will also think of (post)modernity as a significant Latin American cultural and social by-product. In other words, it is not that (post)modernity has arrived too late to Latin America; it is that we have failed to note how Latin America has always been there as both subject and object of this global process. Above all, I will have done my job if readers think of (post)modernity as a dynamic process whereby a society can name itself, a process that is always global and local, contingent and ineluctable.

When and Where Was (Post)modernity?

I must also begin with the truism—often forgotten—that one's understanding of (post)modernity is dependent on one's construing of modernity. (Post)modernity is a provisional category that awaits the elucidation of its root. Who coins the meaning of one is thus also able to coin the referent and promise of the other. It is therefore imperative that we make explicit what we understand by modernity.

Part and parcel of the struggle over the meaning of modernity is the dating of its birth: When did modernity begin? Who is able to give a date to its inauguration has also already prejudged a substantive part of the discussion concerning the meaning of modernity. The selection of a particular set of events or historical processes as being emblematic of the birth of modernity discloses the refraction caused by a particular theoretical perspective. The selection of a particular set of historical events or social processes discloses not only the theoretical angle from which a particular analysis of modernity is enunciated but also the geographical locality from which it is pronounced. Dates are always a matter of geography, and geography is mapped by history. Evidently, when one gives primacy to the Reformation over the Renaissance, one is also giving primacy to Northern Europe over Southern Europe, just as when one speaks of capitalism without mentioning imperialism one actually gives primacy to the metropolis while occluding the colonial outpost. Therefore, it behoves me, here in particular, to establish my own chronology, not only because I want to disclose my theoretical orientation but also because part of the significance I attach to the (post)modernity dyad is determined by this chronology.

As part of my move to challenge and disclose modernity's hegemonic chronology, I would like to underscore the spatiotemporal coordinates of the following historical events and processes: Above all, the "discovery of the New World" in 1492; the Renaissance; the Reformation; the French and American revolutions; the scientific revolutions; the revolutions in energy production and harnessing; and the economic or bourgeois revolutions. Although the events just mentioned are intricately related, we would like to agglutinate them under four significant subheadings: the revolution in subjectivities; political revolutions; scientific and energy revolutions; and the economic revolutions.[23] Any one of the above listed historical events may have participated in more than one of these four processes of social transformation and upheaval.

The revolution in subjectivities took place as a combination not only of the Reformation, which represented the liberation of individual conscience, and the Renaissance, which established the dignity of humans as reasoning and undetermined (*exocentric* in the language of philosophical anthropology) creatures who are "like" God in their capacity to create, but also through the despiritualization of reason and the detranscendentalizing of nature. While the Renaissance implemented the objectification of nature, by inscribing it mathematically, the Reformation made of religion an individual and private experience.[24]

If one considers Bartolomé de las Casas's defense of the "indians" and his debate with Sepúlveda, the issue of individual conscience and religious pluralism is put into greater relief. To this extent, the valorization of "individuality" and "subjectivity" usually associated with the Reformation is essential to Fray Bartolomé de las Casas's defense of the indians. It is this type of debate that stands behind the reflections of Vitoria, Suárez, and a host of other Spanish political theoreticians who basically laid the foundations for the theories of international rights and religious tolerance that became seminal for European nation-states. Nonetheless, the discovery of individual "conscience" that parallels the objectification and quantification of nature alone would not have transformed European societies.[25] Transformations in the political and economic realms were called for and presupposed. Indeed, rational and spiritual individuality only obtained currency in the context of the assertion of economic independence and political autonomy. The latter, in turn, would not have been possible if the production of social wealth had not expanded exponentially due to the quantification of nature, the harnessing of energy sources for the transformation of raw materials into social goods, and, in tandem, the regimentation of humans into wealth-producing entities.[26]

Yet, economic and political transformations of nature and humans would not have been possible without the colonization of the so-called New World that allowed for economic integration and political unification as the simultaneous but converse result of economic polarization and political exclusion. 1492, therefore, is a *condition of possibility* of modernity, and I cannot stress enough this perspective.

The moral I want to establish is that, from its inception, modernity has been plagued by the problem of the other. The other, in turn, has been a coparticipant of modernity, even if in most cases that participation has been represented asymmetrically and solely from the standpoint of the West's effects and initiative. This, however, is not a question of the presence of the other, but of their representation, which is one of the reasons I take this debate to be so important. At the same time, by pointing to 1492 as the date that inaugurates modernity, I want to contest the prevalent mapping of modernity that locates it in the center or in the north of Europe (England, Germany, and France), while also making suspect the Protestant flavor that has been given to it by the theoreticians who see modernization as secularization. The development of Catholicism as a reactive ideology that contained its particular responses to the modernization of social relations, I want to suggest, is a form of modernity. Not all paths to modernity lead through the doors of the church at the castle of Wittenberg. At the same time, it is not to be forgotten than 1492 marks the expulsion of the Jews and Muslims from the Iberian peninsula. The struggle against heathen and infidel, the reconquest of the Mediterranean Sea, the drive to homogenize language is all made manifest in the struggle against the Jews and the Muslims. It is for this reason that modernity as the thrust toward homogeneity and totalization was already presaged in the inquisition, the birth of modern bureaucracy. Note that 1492 is the axis around which purity of blood, belief, and language gravitate. If I foreground 1492, it is in order to keep within our horizon of comprehension the codetermining role that the "Orient" has had not only vis-à-vis "Europe," but the "West" in general.[27] For modernity has been constituted in a tug of war with the "Orient," Here 1492 stands for the inception of a new global world system, in which "Europe" is able to bypass the Mediterranean Sea and reach the East by way of the West.[28]

Modernity, seen from the perspective of the production, appropriation, and distribution of social wealth has been capitalism: who speaks of modernity must also speak of capitalism. Capitalism in turn is an economic system that is based on integration through the exclusionary polarization of productive localities. Capitalism establishes topographies of subordination (public/private, domestic/factory, city/country, nation/empire, metropolis/colony, etc.). These oppositions exclusively channel the flow of accumulated wealth toward the metropolis, the urban center from which colonial and neocolonial power is exercised and deployed. This dynamic of exclusion through subordination is also true of the different political systems that have accompanied the expansion of capitalism, be it liberalism, socialism, and/or fascism, all of which are in more than one way predicated on the sovereignty of the state and the unity of the nation-state. The history of the political systems constitutive of modernity has been accompanied by the history of imperialism, colonization, and thus of globalization. More explicitly, the constitution of differential geographies (or geographies of difference) is fundamental to political and economic integration through exclusionary polarization. We may therefore define differential geographies as the political economy of gentrification, now, however, thought of with reference to all the different levels of human interaction. In fact, these geographies of difference—gentrified localities—map social space at all levels: at the level of subjectivities, at the level of social/communal interaction, at the level of national and international exchange, and at the level of planetary gerrymandering. As examples of these differential geographies, constitutive of capitalism and modernity, let us take the "New World" in relationship with Europe, the "Western" frontier as a trope of salvation and regeneration in the United States, and the relationship between the *mono-cultivos* countries of Central and South America and the United States.[29] In short, modernity not only has a *when* but also a *where* within geopolitical space. Any discourse about (post)modernity, thus, must theorize not only about the convergence of these two coordinates, but also about the occlusion of one by the other. By highlighting the subordination of the spatial by the temporal we seek to unveil the eurocentrism of most theories about modernity that are emerging from the intellectual capitals of the West.[30]

Postmodernity as a Temporal Panopticon

It is clear that modernity is a complex historical phenomenon that has involved the seismic transformation of all levels of human interaction.[31] To account for this transformation, it is necessary to underscore the global nature of modernity. This is what we intend by focusing on 1492. From its birth modernity has been a global phenomenon, one that has entailed the transformation of every corner of the world according to the political economy of its spatiotemporal gentrification. Because modernity maps social spaces according to certain differential geographies, it calls for a *chronotopology*, the science of macromapping time and space.[32] Here I want to underscore that, from the perspective of a chronotopology, modernity appears always as local and global, plural and heterogeneous. Modernity is *glocal*, an epochal configuration in which the local is produced by the global and the global is determined by certain localities (center/periphery), and in which traditions are retroactively created and innovation becomes routine.[33] Modernity occurs within the coordinates of the local/global, the new/ancient, or innovation/tradition. Modernity secretes both space and time configurations that obey a logic of exclusion and inclusion. This logic can be best named *spatiotemporal gentrification*. Because modernity postulates universal claims that determine and regiment notions of space and time for the rest of the world, and because these claims are self-legitimating, one could argue that *modernity wants to be a panopticon whose tower (space) is the omniscient eye of time*.[34]

Modernity works in fact as a mechanism for the sundering of timing (temporalizing) and being timed (being temporalized). It is for this reason that while every one must write his or her history in terms of his or her interaction with the West, the West in turn can write the history of the world as the history of itself. Linked to modernity's panoptical structure, we discover that modernity is also the epochal situation in which society comes to the fore as a conceptual structure for the organization and constitution of agents. Society is born with modernity, for modernity constitutes individuals as subjects; that is, selves are individuated through subjection, their becoming subjects, while their economic and political associations, which aid in their subjection, are incorporated into the totalities of the state and nation. To be a subject is to be a political, economic, and social individual, possessing certain rights, duties, and economic claims. Modernity, conversely, is the constitution of society according to the regimentation of the temporal-spatial coordinates that enable or disable subjects to act: private and public domains, nation, law, and so on.

Given this geographical fixing of modernity, what can be and must be said about (post)modernity? (Post)*modernity* is above all disenchantment with disenchantment, to use Norbert Lechner's wonderful phrasing.[35] Postmodernity is: the crisis and abandonment of the pursuit of the unity of reason, selves, societies, and history. Hence its celebration of the heterogeneous, the hybrid, the Other as total difference. To this extent, the postmodern is also the announcement of the dedifferentiation of social structures, the explosion of the carnivalesque, the asynchronous, the dysfunctional, and the transversal.

Postmodernity, with respect to epistemic means and machines, is the denunciation of the impossibility of the purity and transparency of representation and perception, where language is not just a tool for the faithful representation of the world, but the very condition of possibility of its experience, its naming. Language is not aleatory to experience; it is its sine qua non. Structure, form, and schema were contaminated by the arbitrariness, refractoriness, duplicity, and fogginess of language, as Derrida has established so well. And mind, at best, is the name of our second-order reflection on language, and at worst, a linguistic ghost, a solecism. We are not idle bystanders to reality. We are constituted with it as we constitute it. The real is always the shadow of our gaze: that which we do not see when we are looking at it (as Luhmann aptly put it).[36] Reality is a detritus of human subjectivity, but no less important for that reason; hence postmodernity's announcement of the death of science and the intrinsic impurity of all knowledge. What we have instead are particular, contingent, epistemic configurations that obey social imperatives and that reflect images of themselves. Postmodernity is thus the pronouncement of the death of the innocence of science—this has become no more than our own particular magic: the fetishism of the totem instrumental reason. Postmodernity, thus, is the simultaneous denaturalization and resocialization of reality and perception. Everything is always, has always been, a second nature.[37]

Postmodernity, it is claimed, is concomitantly the end of history. As such, postmodernity abandons the pursuit of the great teleologies that fueled the modernization of Europe and the colonization of the world. History, the history of development, enlightenment, technological innovation, and social transformation died, postulates postmodernity, with Auschwitz, Hiroshima, and the gulags of the Soviet Union. Postmodernity is the collapse of the grand *récits*, the metanarratives that gave coherence and legitimacy to the homogenizing drive of modernity. Telos turned into eschaton, eschaton into holocaust, and holocaust into the end of history. Postmodernity is mainly the disenchantment of Western society with its own enchantment, its narcissism, and its plenipontency.

When did postmodernity begin? In contrast to a chronology of modernity, a periodization of postmodernity lacks the benefit of temporal distance. Also, the difficulty of addressing the "when" of postmodernity is linked with the fact that historical events as temporal markers reflect and sediment a particular ideology. However, regardless of what spatiotemporal coordinates we provided as the markers of inception of the postmodern, these remain determined by the modern, by modernity as an epochal situation. We could begin by offering the end of World War II as the beginning of the postmodern. Many of the thinkers who were later to become the theoreticians of the postmodern were born and grew up in the shadow not just of the Holocaust, but also of Hiroshima and Nagasaki. Yet, the end of the European age also inaugurated the beginning of the postcolonial. The struggles for decolonization and national liberation marked indelibly the ascendancy of a postmodern sensibility. In addition, and not necessarily as an extension of postcolonial struggles, the political and social mobilizations for minority rights also provided the context for the emergence of a postmodern suspicion of the modern. In contrast to the homogeneous and state-oriented political movements of modernity, the new social movements brought about a heterogenization of the political. And, without forgetting that 1968 was a world phenomena and not just a "French" experience, we have to consider the intellectual innovations that crystallized during the sixties: poststructuralism, deconstruction, post-Marxism, liberation theologies, and feminisms. This explosion of minority discourses vitiated the notion of a homogeneous, autochthonous, and continuous Western intellectual tradition, as well as the fetish of a wholly Other.

Along with these Western temporal markers, I also would have to consider the Cuban Revolution (1959), the rise and fall of the Berlin Wall (1949–1989), the Vietnam War, the 1973 petroleum embargo by OPEC, but also the democratic election of Allende and the Nicaraguan Revolution, as well as the struggles for national liberation in Africa. Not unlike modernity, postmodernity has been determined by *glocal* events, colonial and postcolonial dynamics.

It is against the background circumscribed by these twentieth-century events that one can trace the processes that characterize postmodernity. In terms of the subjectivites, postmodernity does not mean the end of the individual, as it is mistakenly assumed. Instead, it signifies the politicization of agency in terms of the denaturalization of humanity. Central here is the discovery that individuality is both the medium and telos of the subjection of agents. Agency is not to be taken for granted. The processes of its constitution are the questions of politics and the political par excellance. Postmodern posthumanism is not antihumanism but, rather, the call for new forms of agency, the rehumanization of social relations that have been left outside the realm of social determination. Simultaneously, the notion that the unity and stability of selfhood could be traced back to some warrant, such as the psychological, the epistemic, the volitional, the economic, or the social, is jettisoned. Thus, the repoliticization of social agency converges with the denaturalization of selfhood. Agency is social through and through.[38]

The converse of individuation as subjection is socialization as totalization. This was a central logic of modernity. In other words, the more agents became individuals, atomized as economic and political entities, the greater the need to contain them within the totality of the political. The state became the site for the dispensation of autonomy and individuation. This in turn entailed its growth and strengthening. The converse of political individuation and aesthetic subjectification is massification and totalitarianism.

Thus, under postmodernity, the repoliticization of agency entails the remapping of the boundaries between the social and the political. At work here is a logic of dedifferentiation, of hybridization and detotalization. Power is everywhere, especially where the state is not. The flows of power are to be mapped in a nonstatist strategy. Micropolitics replaces macropolitics, the microagent supplants the meta and macrosubject (the proletariat, class, race). This entails the plurification of micronarratives and the (re)turn to collective memory, to a memory that is nonstatist and nonuniversal as a point of condensation for political identity (the idea of postethnic identity). Under postmodernity identity politics is pursued as a critique of identity brokers and authenticators. To this extent, identity politics are oxymoronic and a performative self-contradiction, albeit to be pursued strategically for the purposes of the remapping of the social and the political.

In a fashion analogous to modernity, postmodernity also presupposed a revolution in energy production and energy harnessing. Part of this revolution was catalyzed by the petroleum crisis of the early seventies, but also by the use of nuclear energy (and the confrontation with its hazards), the automatization of production lines (the beginning of the end of Fordism), the introduction of the computer, and the mass production of microchips (the informatization of culture as a whole and the possible colonization of the lifeworld by the hyperreal of cyberspace).[39] These technological changes brought about a revolution in the modes of production that had two clearly related consequences: one, the virtualization of the economy, and the other, the reconfiguration in social relations. In the center, the transformation from industrial to finance capitalism, along with the parallel transformation in the periphery from semiindustrialized to industrialized capitalism (mass culture finally arrived to the third world), reversed the fundamental logic of modernity: industrialization and differentiation in the metropolis, marginalization and homogenization in the periphery. It is clear, however, that this apparent reversal of the logic of the production and appropriation of wealth had as a result the collapse of the progressive conquest of nature and the exponential growth of science. Technological prowess turned into dystopian forecasting. Science's mesmerizing development turned into stasis. Between the paralysis brought on by technophobia and the dizzying speed in the overturning of scientific paradigms, science and technology discovered their specificity, limits, and ideological character. The end of the metanarratives of emancipation and development was accompanied by the collapse of the metanarrative of the growth of knowledge and the intrinsic benignity of technology. This collapse was not only announced already by the success of the concentration camps and the slaughter machine of World War II, but also in the considerations of Canguilhem and Kuhn that bespeak the crisis of the belief in the teleological and cumulative development of science.

Whereas the technological sublime of modernity presupposed the strict separation of society and nature so that nature could be entirely subordinated to society, in postmodernity nature is denaturalized in such a way that the boundaries between nature and society are erased. Nature is already society and society is what is not nature, that is, itself in the negative. This is clearly the paradigm under which the ecological movements operate, even if some deep ecologists have turned to nature by remythologizing it, renaturalizing it by othering it. Indeed, just as postmodernity announced the end of the natural human being, pronounced as the death of "man" or death of the subject, postmodernity announced the end of nature as nature: nature is the darkness of the negation of our social responsibility; it is a phantasmagoric alibi for manufactured irresponsibility.[40] In Ulrich Beck's terms, the rhetoric of naturalness becomes the rhetoric of risk, which is more appropriate to the acknowledgment that nature is always a shadow of the social. Looked at from the standpoint of technology, the sociopolitical-economic transformation of scientific models and fantasies about the substratum secreted as nature is unmasked precisely as that: just another social imaginary, just another social strategy for regimentation and control. The myths of technology's teleology and its purported neutrality are dismantled. The denaturing of nature is the twin of technology's resocialization. The real of science is the hyperreal of technology and technology is not for the control of nature; rather technology produces it as its excrement and fantasy. Nature is what technology refuses to touch after it has already produced it. It is the preserve of a society that has discovered its permeation of everything.

From the perspective of the production and accumulation of wealth, we also have a redefinition of the economic under the postmodern. Whereas under modernity economic processes were regulated through the nation-state, under the postmodern the territorial nation state has been rendered almost if not entirely obsolete. This has taken place as the metropolis-to-colony relationship has imploded so that now the third world has come to the first world. Cities in turn have become nodes in global migrations in which the relations between international cities are closer than between cities and the respective nations in which they reside. This shift has been registered in what has been called the deindustrialization of capitalism. Heavy industry has been replaced by the service sector, just as high-tech jobs have gone beyond the reach of the undereducated. In other words, as the creation and processing of information comes to the fore, labor is pushed down in the economic ladder. Knowledge elites have become the nouveau riches of a postindustrial economy.[41]

The ascendancy of economies of information with its concomitant creation of the overworked and underpaid service sector laborer has resulted in the rolling back of labor's gains at the level of the welfare state. The less capital is accountable to the territorial nation-state, the less labor is able to enter into negotiation with transnational capital. This new economic configuration of social relations has been given the name "disorganized capitalism," but this is overstating the case, not only because capitalism has an intrinsic anarchical dimension but also because regulation and monitoring still take place through international market agreements and national strategies of redevelopment (NAFTA and the European Union.) Part and parcel of the displacement of industry by the production of information is the greater role played by "culture" in the economy. In fact, research and development have come to assume equal roles in the actual production of commodities. It is this phenomena which Baudrillard has given expression in his postmodern economies of the sign, in which simulacra is commodification to the second power.[42] This is the triumph of the culture industry, and with it triumphs not just massification, but also the aestheticization of culture. Goods are bought and sold less for their use value and more for their exchange value, a value that exists more and more in its accrued symbolic status. Implicit here is the process of the aestheticization of the economy and the virtualization of money. The fact is that the so-called deindustrialization of first-world nations has not proceeded at the same pace in all industrialized nations, to say the least about the industrialization of developing nations. It is also not clear that Fordism is at an end, even as flexible production expands into larger and larger sectors of production. If anything, we have a Fordism that has become global where nations, or global regions, play out the role of subordinate production centers specialized in the assembly of one or two products. Just as the gap between the rich and poor has grown exponentially and preposterously, the life standards and consumption levels between the geographical "third world" and "first world" has widened scandolously and equally absurdly.

Nonetheless, we must speak of postmodernities just as we must speak of modernities. The paths to modernization followed by the United States, Japan, and Germany, as John Urry and Scott Lash have shown masterfully, followed different logics, in which one was not more "modern" than the others.[43] Similarly, the paths to the postmodernization of world economies have been plural; again, witness the differences between Germany and Japan, on the one hand, and the United States and England, on the other. This same heterogeneity of paths to and through modernity/postmodernity is evident in Latin America. It would be entirely inappropriate to try to assimilate to one pattern the experiences of modernization that Mexico, Argentina, Brazil, and Venezuela have undergone.

The onus, in fact and to close these reflections, is not on showing whether Latin America is postmodern, but on how a certain path to and through postmodernity is Latin American; more precisely, how certain postmodernity is very Latin American. Culturally, economically, and politically many Latin American countries have struggled with the issues of the heterogeneity of the "cultural" realm, the hybridization of "high" culture by so-called low culture, the permeation of the political by the economic and the overdetermination of both by "cultural" icons and ideologies that have been products as much of colonial traditions as of neocolonialism, nationalism, and the striving after democratic self-determination. It is true that many Latin American countries have and continue to deal with the promise and crisis of modernity, but this is no less true of the United States than of Germany and England. In tandem, if postmodernity is the awareness of this tension, then Latin America is no less exempt from experiencing its vertiginous awareness than, let us say, Italy and France." It is true: revolutions have failed, many violently suppressed and defeated, Marxism seems dead, labor is decimated, nationalism has become a perverse and defunct ideology, many Latin American countries sink further into poverty as their corrupt governments continue to squeeze the poor poorer by duly obliging the economic policies dictated by the World Bank, the IMF, and the multinationals, and prospects for transformation seem distant and demanding of great utopian imagination. These same complaints can be heard in London, Chicago, Mexico, Bogotá, or Lima. What is clear is the imperative need to understand the specificity of the Latin American confrontation with the obsolescence of certain ideals and utopias of modernity and the way this recognition has been registered in Latin America. Latin America must be allowed to offer its own diagnosis. Unless the postmodern permits the other to pronounce the nature of its own time, it will continue to perpetuate the colonial trust of modernity. Now, however, this perpetuation will exist in the mode of the negative, as a negation of any alternatives except that of the exhaustion of the West's own failed dreams. If freedom is insight into necessity, as Marx noted, then the others' emancipation is predicated in their naming of their present and their being able to paint their own future.

4

Remapping Latin American Studies

Postcolonialism, Subaltern Studies, Postoccidentalism, and Globalization Theory

Introduction

When we think about Latin America from the perspective of the United States we cannot help but to think of a series of pivotal dates: 1848 and the Mexican American War; 1898 and the Spanish American War; 1910 and the Mexican Revolution; 1945 and the end of World War II; 1959, the Cuban Revolution; 1973, Pinochet and the assassination of Allende; 1979, the Nicaraguan Revolution, and 1990 the end of the Sandinista Government; 1994, NAFTA going into effect and the Zapatista uprising in the South of Mexico in the Lacandonian jungle. These are very recent historical events, but they have in very decisive ways shaped the way the United States and Latin America have related. I want to suggest that these events have determined four axes around which four types of Latinamericanisms have emerged. Furthermore, I want to suggest that these events in Latin American history are related to general ruptures in the fabric of knowledge as it has been woven over the past two hundred years or so. I will first discuss the four types of Latinamericanisms that have emerged since the late nineteenth century. (In chapter 5, I will return to these four types, but I will approach them from slightly different angles. Since these differences are central to my claims, it is imperative that I rehearse them at least twice, with different words and more extensively.) Next, I will turn to the crises of the knowledge, and how we might address them. The point is to discern on what grounds we can begin to develop a new form of Latinamericanism.

Latinamericanisms

The first type of Latinamericanism to emerge did so in part as a response to the events of both 1848 and 1898. This Latinamericanism juxtaposed the United States to Latin America in terms of their distinctive and opposite cultural and spiritual outlooks. One is crass, materialistic, utilitarian, soulless, and without cultural roots, while the other is the true inheritor of the European spirit of culture, civilization, and idealistic principles grounded in love and tradition. These distinctions are made in the work of someone like Rodó, but we also find them in the work of José Martí. This opposition was influential for generations of thinkers in Latin America, even when these did not share the original set of terms or animus. In the work of some Mexican thinkers like José Vasconcelos and even Leopoldo Zea, we find these kinds of differentiations. Another source of this type of Latinamericanism was the Latin American affirmation of its identity vis-à-vis Europe for similar reasons that Latin America sought to differentiate itself from the United States; namely, imperialism, war, and their putative patrician cultures of disdain for the colonized and the racially mixed. Yet, not all intellectuals rejected unequivocally Latin America's relationship to Europe. For some, in fact, the problem was that Latin America was not enough like Europe. This is a view that we find expressed in the work of Domingo Sarmiento who basically established a whole school of thought based on the opposition "civilization and barbarism."[1] This first type of Latinamericanism then was one that descended from the era of the colonial and imperialistic expansion of the United States and Latin America's affirmation of its distinctive cultural traditions. This Latinamericanism was based on a geopolitics of culture, and one may therefore correctly characterize it as a *Kulturkampf* Latinamericanism, one which juxtaposed the spirit of an imperialistic modernity to the promise of a humanistic and pluralistic form of modernization that, in the words of Pedro Henriquez Ureña, was embodied in the idea of America as the fatherland of justice.

The second type of Latinamericanism is the one that emerged after the cold war in the United States, as part of the area studies programs developed in North America. This area studies Latinamericanism had as its goal to gather and disseminate knowledge about "third world" countries. This Latinamericanism treated Latin America like any other foreign land, although there was from the inception an ambiguity about treating Latin America like Asia and Africa were treated. There were some fascinating debates, the Eugene Bolton debates for instance, that argued that Latin America should be studied in the same way that the United States and Canada should be studied. Nonetheless, cold war knowledge interests dictated the research model. This type of Latinamericanism, then, was a way to think about or represent Latin America from the standpoint of the North American academy. But to be fair, one should note that what we are here calling "area studies Latinamericanism" could be said to have two foci: one which is a Latinamericanism of Latin America as the land of underdevelopment, bringing in tow all of what this entails—that is, lack of proper stages of modernization, weak public spheres, lack of technological innovations, and so on. The other foci would be a Latinamericanism of third worldism, or a form of first-world romanticization and exocitization of the Latin American.

But this form of viewing Latin America is the negative picture of the Latinamericanism of Latin America as underdevelopment. It is this second form of Latin Americanism that romanticizes Latin America that explains the fetishization of the Latin American novel. And it is these two types of Latinamericanisms reacting to each other that gives rise to the collapse of the epistemological and aesthetic with respect to Latin America that Román de la Campa points out in his book *Latinamericanism*.[2]

In the wake of the moral bankruptcy of the West because of World War II, the Gulags and concentration camps, after a decade of postcolonial revolutionizing, and the introduction of a new fracture in the mythological identity of the West because of the sundering of Russia from the rest of Europe, a new epistemological horizon began to open up in which Latin America could think itself without its alter ego, Europe. The crises and delinking from Europe took shape and acquired expression in the 1959 Cuban revolution, the 1968 Medellín meeting of the Latin American Bishop's Conference, which established the theological foundation for the ecclesial Christian base communities and interpreted Vatican II in such away that liberation theology was legitimated, and the emergence of liberation sociology and underdevelopment theory. These intellectual, cultural, and social movements and creative fervor laid the foundations for, what I will call, critical Latinamericanism. This form of Latinamericanism articulates Latin American in opposition to the US, in which anti-Imperialism is matched by a critique of epistemological practices. Critical Latinamericanism can be discerned in the works of Orlando Fals Borda, Darcy Riberio, Leopoldo Zea, Augusto Salazar Bondy, Gustavo Gutierrez, and Enrique Dussel. This form of thinking Latin America is thought from Latin America and it is about thinking Latin American from its own historical reality and in accordance with its own epistemological needs.

Finally, there is a fourth type of Latinamericanism that has began to develop over three decades and that is linked to the aftermath of the Latino diaspora in the United States, and the emergence of a critical consciousness in the Latino populations in the United States as they came to be expressed in the Chicano and Puerto Rican movements of the sixties. This is a transnational, diasporic, and postcultural type of Latinamericanism that brings together the critical Latinamericanism produced in Latin America since the sixties and the homegrown epistemological and social critique that identity movements develop simultaneously but separately. Thus, this Latino Latinamericanism has two foci and loci of enunciation and enactment and operates at various levels of criticism: It is critical of the West but also of the way Occidentalism was deployed in order to normalize and regiment the very internal sociality of the West in the Americas. The thinkers that give expression to this type of thought are trans-American intellectuals like Juan Flores, Retamar, Román de la Campa, Subcomandante Marcos, Lewis Gordon, José Saldivar, Walter Mignolo, and Santiago Castro-Gómez.

On the Relationship between Geopolitics and Knowledge Production

I would like now to take a brief detour through two important theorizations of the crisis of theory. In a 1981 essay entitled "The Three Worlds, of the Division of Social Scientific Labor, circa 1950–1975," Carl E. Pletsch looked at the emergence of the threefold division of the world into "first, second and third world." He looked at the ideological context of the emergence of these now-suspect distinctions; but most importantly, he looked into their conceptual matrix in order to discern some fundamental epistemological categories that belong to the most elemental aspects of Western thought, or what today we call "logocentrism." The distinctions among first, second, and third world allowed Western social scientists to develop a disciplinary division of labor that nonetheless permitted them to assume a privileged place in the order of things. Talk of three worlds was based on a pair of abstract and always reinscribable binary oppositions that in turn were underwritten by ontology of history, or teleology of history. The two pairs of binary opposites were, on the one hand, the binary of modern and traditional; that is the world was divided into those societies that were either modern or those that were traditional—unmodern, or premodern, or on the way to becoming modern. The second pair, moved ahead in the implicit temporal continuum, referred to the opposition between "communist" (or socialist) and "free" (or democratic). While "communist" stood for authoritarian, "free" stood for liberal, constitutional, and rule of law. Thus, while the former was seen as a distortion, the latter was seen as the natural and logical outcome of societies that have overcome and superseded an earlier stage of unenlightened and even enlightened despotism. In this way, then, the social semantics of the three worlds cashes out into a cultural semantics that assigns the following invidious distinctions to each world: "The third world is the world of tradition, culture, religion, irrationality, underdevelopment, overpopulation, political chaos, and so on. The second world is modern, technologically sophisticated, rational to a degree, but authoritarian (or totalitarian) and repressive, and ultimately inefficient and impoverished by contamination with ideological preconceptions and burdened with an ideologically socialist elite. The first world is purely modern, a haven of science and utilitarian decision making, technological, efficient, democratic, free—in short, a natural society unfettered by religion or ideology."[3] The cultural semantics here—namely the way in which the words carried a whole conceptual badge that allows us to see certain things while putting others under erasure—operates due to a prior commitment to modernization theory, but this in turn is but an expression of a more deeply seated belief in a telos of history, or what I called earlier an "ontology of history." In this way the cultural semantics of first, second, and third worlds allowed social scientists to make the following distinctions: between degrees of economic and technological "development," on the one hand, and between kinds of "mentalities," on the other hand. Evidently, these distinctions are deployed from the standpoint of the blind spot of those who think they are granted by the logic of history to look upon those that are heading to where they now stand. On the basis of this cultural semantics, then a division of labor emerged that assigned to the third world and second world the ideographic sciences, while to the first world were assigned the nomothetic sciences. While the third world was studied by anthropology and ethnography, the second was studied as case studies in earlier stages of the emergent spheres of economic, social, and political theory that nomothetic sciences studies in the first world.

Immanuel Wallerstein has been urging a revision of the social sciences for the last two decades. He has been advocating a world-system analysis that goes beyond nation-states and even types of economic systems. In a 1995 essay entitled "What Are We Bounding, and Whom, When We Bound Social Research?" Wallerstein offers the most succinct expression to his critique of the social sciences as they have developed over the past 150 years.[4] Some aspects of his argument appearing in this chapter are elaborated at greater length in the small and significant volume *Open the Social Sciences*, which is the report of the Gulbenkian Commission on the status of the social sciences.[5] Wallerstein's argument is that the fundamental categories of contemporary social analysis were forged between 1850 and 1914 and were crystallized and firmed in the period from 1914 to 1945. While Wallerstein does not explicitly say this, it can be seen that this chronological distinction refers to a transfer of the center of social scientific production from Europe to the United States. This chronology also traces the zenith of the age of European imperialism, and the ascendancy of American imperialism. The categories of all the social sciences, in Wallerstein's view, fell along three great "cleavages": first, between the past and the present, between the West and the rest; and the divisions among state, market, and civil society. The first cleavage was particularly important because it had to do with the very nature of the social sciences; and this debate continued as the methods debate, the explanation and understanding debates, and the positivism debates of the sixties. A nice complementary division of labor was worked out in the end. History, generally identified with the ideographic sciences, was relegated to the study of the past, while the nomothetic sciences were assigned the study of the present. The study of the past, however, became a significant endeavor as it contributed to the socialization and pacification of the potentially revolutionary proletariat. Social scientists, in turn, focused on the task of providing legitimate science for the guidance of the liberal state. The complementary division of labor however did not hold or operate with respect to what was the non-West. For the study of the non-Western, which was putatively far away spatially and temporally, two different types of disciplines were assigned: on the one hand anthropology, to study the past of non-Western societies, and on the other hand orientalist studies, a motley crew of disciplines, to study the present of non-Western societies. The former focused on non-Western societies as though they were in the mythological past, while the latter focused on the present societies, as though they had never emerged from a later but still past stage of historical development: here the focus was on languages and texts that seemed to be unrelated to contemporary social realities of non-Western societies. The overall thrust of these disciplines was to dehistoricize and freeze non-Western societies. The third cleavage had to do with the state, the economy, and civil society. With respect to each sphere, particular social sciences emerged that abrogated for themselves normative status: economics, political theory, and sociology. Evidently, these social sciences preoccupied themselves primarily with the West, or modern, technologically advanced, and democratic nations of the North. The economies, political bodies, and societies of non-Western societies, however, could only be studied as either preliminary stages or pathological versions of the Western norm. The avowed intension of Wallerstein was to show how the core categories that established the "epistemological matrix" of the social sciences over the past 150 years had to do with a specific path of social development in the West, which was hypostatized into transhistorical verities. Since we are in the position of seeing their contingency, we are consequently able to displace them from the privileged place that they were given. It needs to be noted that neither in the essay nor in the book-length version of this line of argumentation do Wallerstein and his colleagues offer positive suggestions. The suggestions that they offer are of a cosmetic character, that is, a mere rearrangement of the theoretical furniture without being consequent with their own argumentation that requires an overhaul of the very categories that make up the epistemological matrix of the social sciences.[6]

The Space of Theory

I have briefly looked at two very insightful and critical approaches to the crises of the social sciences. Yet, I find them inadequate not just because they are bereft of any constructive suggestions, but also because they fail to give an account of their own theoretical position that does not presuppose what they are ultimately criticizing—namely the epistemological primacy of ontology of history, or what we generally call a triumphalist teleology of the West. Both Pletsch and Wallerstein presuppose the historical soil of theory when they criticize the conceptual matrix of twentieth century social science; that is, they are able to criticize what stands before their eyes because they stand at the most forward moment in that continuum. But, in what way can I engage in a criticism of a conceptual apparatus without at some level presupposing the very elements that constitute the normativity of that very apparatus. I want to suggest that in order to be aware of our own blind spot, or, in other words, in order to be able to justify our criticism without occluding the place from which we enunciate that criticisms, we have to engage in a doubling operation. We observe ourselves in the act of observing. If we cannot see the place from which we observe, we can at least observe what it is that we observe and how it is that we observe it. The language is that of systems analysis, or complex systems, but the intent is different, as we will see. The goal is to make sense of the plethora of theories that are available now in the marketplace of ideas. I am interested in making sense of this theoretical cacophony, not because I think that theoretical diversity is a sign of the decay or obsolescence of theory. The opposite is more true: the plurality of theoretical wares in the marketplace of ideas reflects the very level of commodification of theory that is necessary for the health of the exchange of ideas as the exchange of a cultural semantics that imposes a certain type of social semantics. I am interested in how theories operate in the circulation of cultural wealth, and how they grease the wheels of a global market in which what is traded is as much a product whose use value is as important as its exchange value, where cultural and theoretical capital stand on the same level as commercial and technological capital. But at the same time, I am interested in how, in this uncircumventable situation of extreme commodification and reification of the theoretical, of its coagulation into theory, we might nonetheless discover a place of criticism. I will begin by laying out a criteria for the development of typology of theories. Thus, in contrast to Pletsch and Wallerstein who wanted to get to the conceptual matrix of social theory writ large, I am interested in the ways in which in a saturated theoretical market we might begin to differentiate between theories and their effects.

First criterion: We have to determine what is the epistemograph or ontograph that is inscribed by a theory or group of theories? This is the language of Spivak,[7] but it is a terminology that one can claim descends also from Henri Lefebvre and David Harvey. By ontograph or epistemograph, I mean the following: Every theory, whether consciously or unconsciously, is determined by a spatial imaginary. This spatial imaginary operates at both macro and microlevels. The classic example is Hegel with his idea that Europe is the privileged center for the substantialization of reason. Another example would be how in Kant, as Spivak and LeDouff have shown, the categories of cognition are inscribed within a particular geography of the imagination. In Dussel's language, every philosophy participates in a geopolitical locus, not only in the sense that philosophy is determined by its place of enunciation, but also in the sense that philosophy also projects a certain image of the planet, the ecumene, and the polis as the space of what is the civilized, or the place of civilization, which may or may not be besieged by the barbarians. Philosophy enacts an act of spatialization at the very same time that it is spatialized by its locus of enunciation. Every philosophy, again, inscribes an ontos or epistemograph.

Second criterion: We have to make explicit the locus of the instantiation of the social. Every theory offers one or a group of structures and social processes that are the privileged locus for the substantialization of the reason or logos. In other words, reason materializes in certain social structures in a form, and some might claim, a normative way. It is for this reason, for instance, that Hegel could undertake a phenomenology of the spirit as an analysis of sociality, or society. Clearly, this relation between reason and social structure is what allows someone like Habermas, for example, to speak of modernity as the process of the rationalization of the systems level and the lifeworld. A theory of rationality in turn becomes a theory of social differentiation, which in turn becomes a theory about the modernity (read rationality) of certain forms of society that results in a differential hierarchy in which some societies are primitive, others premodern, and still others are modern. Conversely, in this view there are social spheres that have not been rationalized, or have been insufficiently rationalized. For this criterion the central question is What is the institutional focus of a theory or group of theories?

Third criterion: This one refers to what is taken to be the normative criteria of criteria or evaluation that allows us to adjudicate on whether a society has achieved what is putatively taken to be the actualization of reason in the social world. In other words: What is normative for each theory or group of theories? Let me illustrate: In some theories of modernity the criteria of whether societies are modern is dependent on whether a society has obtained a high level of bureaucratization, formalization, institutionalization of abstract universality, self-reflexivity, or even contextual uncoupling (as one can say that both Giddens and Habermas argue). Another example: What is the operating evaluative norm when one says that societies are globalized or have been globalized, or that they should be globalized—that a society has accepted the austere policies of the World Bank, that national economies have been liberalized and are open to the onslaught of transnationals?

Fourth criterion: What are the political consequences of an epistemological project? Or to put it differently, In what ways does a certain ontograph or epistemograph turn into an actual political project? Put differently, every theory has a political impact, or rather, it contributes toward sanctioning or legitimating and turning normal certain forms of social violence. Or, conversely, a theory or group of theories contributes to the demystification of the supposed naturalness of certain social processes and, in this way, can call into question the impact of certain forms of social violence that are tolerated and neglected because they had been naturalized. The question that is important with respect to this criterion is: What political projects are sanctioned when certain processes, loci of materialization of reason, epistemograph, or ontographs are theoretically defended and articulated?

Fifth criterion, and finally: This whole form of articulating criteria could be stylized and formalized by asking, Who is the subject who thinks what object? And more acutely still, Where is this subject and how does it project and localize its object of knowledge? A different way of saying the same would be: Who speaks for whom and who speaks over or about whom? This is a way of asking questions about the production of theory and the position of theoretical agents, agents that produce theory. It is a form of looking at the production of theory that makes explicit how there are subjects who are authorized to make theoretical pronouncements while there are other "subjects" that are merely spectators and who are relegated to being mere objects of knowledge. Some subjects are credible epistemic and theoretical witnesses, while others are from the outset suspect and illegitimate subjects of credible theoretical reflection. This all concerns the practices of partitioning, parceling, or one may say in Mexico, of *fraccionamientos*, and what we in the United States might call theoretical gerrymandering or gentrification. Who speaks, or who is authorized to speak about and for others, occupies a privileged epistemological place. This place, in turn, is made available by the theories and epistemological practices that are used by theorists. There is what Walter Mignolo calls a locus of enunciation and a practice of *enactment*. Theorizing, or philosophizing, is a habitus that is always accompanied or framed by a configuration of both social and imaginary space (all space is imaginary and social, and the social is always conditioned by a certain imaginary). To think our locus of epistemological privilege, or to think the place of our epistemological scorn and segregation, this is what Raymond Pannikar has called a "plurotopic hermeneutics."

One final note of clarification. The goal of this type of analysis that I am profiling with the help of Spivak, Pannikar, Dussel, and Mignolo, and which I am formalizing in terms of a set of criteria of discernment, is to supersede, to go beyond the cybernetic and systems-theoretical proposal of thinkers, such as Niklas Luhmann, who juxtapose the mere observer to the solely observed, on one side, and the observer who is observed, on the other. In other words, Luhmann juxtaposes what merely observes objects to the observing observer, or subjects, that looks at other subjects. The second type of observation is what Luhmann calls "second-order observation." Analogously, it is necessary to go beyond the distinction that Habermas makes, supporting himself on Luhmann but translating him into the language of hermeneutics and the philosophy of language, between the first- and third-person perspectives. The first, the position of the first person, is the position of the participant in a community of communication that is at the same time a community of interpretation, and who for this reason is thoroughly soaked by a hermeneutical immersion. The second position is that of the one who observes, but in an objectivating manner. This position is allegedly of someone who can objectify because she is not a participant of the lifeworld she observes. In fact, the grammar of the observer and the observed, the participant and the nonparticipant, is much more complicated that these two types of distinctions allow. We are always already, *immer schon*, as Heidegger would say, and simultaneously both observer and observed. We are observed observators, and observers who observe themselves. The gaze is not monological but always mediated by a third. In the language of semiology we could say that observation is always a triadic relation: there is always a gazing of an observer who is in turn observed in its very act of gazing. Who is observed can always return the gaze: the observed can gaze back, can look back. Using Mignolo's language, I would put it now in the following way: We always speak about something, or someone, from a given perspective, and when we do so, we are enacting, performing, deploying certain forms of knowledge-power. Now, what this type of analysis allows us to make explicit are the power dimensions, or the dimensions of coercion and epistemological violence that every knowledge pronouncement entails. At the same time, this type of analysis also allow us to unmask the form in which allegedly universal propositions and formulations, pronouncements that are putatively not contaminated and damaged by the subjective or local, are in fact make possible by an epistemological machine that has specific goals and functions. Behind every theory there is what, echoing Foucault, we could call an apparatus of knowledge-power, and that he called specifically a *dispositif*: an apparatus of coercion and control.

With these criteria on hand, now we can turn to a comparative analysis of the theories on display and up for sale in the global marketplace of ideas. Theories of modernity, looked at from afar and as a type of theories, are forms of theorizing that think from the *ontograph* of Europe. These are theories that are primordially about how Europe is the *locus classicus* for the actualization of reason. Europe is their subject of preoccupation, and furthermore, the world must mimic Europe. In this way the object of study is not the world but an entirely ideological construct. The institutional locus of analysis for theories of modernity is society understood as the unfolding of a social and state logic, on one side, and scientific logic, on the other. Thus, the institutional locus is the sociopolitical bureaucracies, such as the rule of law state, or the economy supposedly rationalized through abstract economic exchange mediated by money. That on one hand, but on the other we have the idea that technology is institutionalized as a socio-state project. This is science at the service of the state and society. The normative criteria of evaluation are formalization, the imposition of self-reflexivity (through science), and most importantly, whether political, economic, and scientific institutions are sufficiently formalized in order to be spatially translated. This is what Giddens calls the "uncoupling of institutions." This means that these institutions can be translated to different contexts. It bears remarking here how strange it is that one of the criteria of evaluation is that the most modern structures and institutions are those that are most simply and rapidly exportable and translatable. The political consequences already begin to be observable. The goal of these theories is of legitimating certain historical violence. Once processes of conquest, of the institutionalization of certain forms of science, are naturalized, then culpability, responsibility, and the possibility to call to account cultures for genocide are neutralized and disallowed. These theories, viewed from an epistemological angle, impose an epistemological blindness and an ethical silence. Finally, these theories are about a subject purified of all alterity, a subject that speaks for and about others. This subject is in a place that is different from that of its object of knowledge. In this type of theory we have the classic case of what Spivak diagnosed as speaking for the subaltern and, in this way, silencing him or her.

Postmodern theories do not digress or divert too much from this epistemograph. The ontograph continues to be Europe, the locus of reason or rationalization continues to be the Euromodern institutions, but now as those that have exhausted or have arrived at their logical extremes. The normative focus is the critique to the ontoteleology of the homogenizing and suicidal logos of modernity. As a critique of the rational project of modernity and its violent univocity, postmodern theories become the celebration of and reverence for alterity, which includes what is most singular, all of that which belies the triumph of Weber's iron cage of modernity. However, this other that is supposedly placed on a pedestal is merely the other face of the self-sameness of modernity's "I conquer" that Dussel has studied and unmasked so eloquently. Politically, the consequences are that all projects of emancipation are pronounced exhausted at best or totalitarian at worst. Every project of social transformation that would be designed and projected from out of the matrix of modernity is deemed failed and genocidal. Here we have the same phenomenon of the impossibility for the other to speak for himself or herself. The future is closed. Since the West has arrived at its own exhaustion, then it is impossible to conceive of the future in any different form. In this way, and once again, criticism is neutralized and silenced. Responsibility for the other is recognized, but this is unfulfillable because the great narratives of modernity that supported the possibility of being responsible for the other have been extinguished. Clearly we have here a subject that abrogates for itself the authority of speaking for others, and furthermore, it says that not even they are able to speak since the languages of liberation and responsibility have become anachronisms. The locus of enunciation is then the very same institutions, academic as well as of quotidian life, of the modern countries, which also announce that no other path is acceptable. For subjects located in this *locus enunciationis* the end of modernity has become the end of history *tout court*.

Until now I have been discussing chronologically a series of theories and have been offering a diagnosis or an analysis that looks at how these theories have power-knowledge effects. Following this chronological line, the next series of theories would be globalization theories. But at the same time a whole host of theories that compete with globalization has emerged. Such competition can be expressed in the following way: Where are localized the discourses about globalization with respect to the discourses of modernity and postmodernity, on the one hand, and discourses of postcolonialism and postoccidentalism, on the other? A note of clarification about the nomenclature is in order. I want to suggest that the distinction between one group of theories or discourses is not made just chronologically, but is fundamentally related to the place from which and about which they theorize. Insofar as the discourses of globalization seem to have become the discourses of a *pax Americana*, that is, insofar as they are discourses about the celebration of the triumph of so-called democracy and the defeat of the soviet project and, therefore, of the triumph of neoliberalism; and insofar as the discourses of globalization are understood primarily from the standpoint of an economic, technological, and even political perspective (that is, insofar as globalization is understood as the planetarization of an economic, technological, and political system), then we have to see these discourses that are primarily about who the West globalizes, as discourses about how the West also modernizes the world. Again, if we accept the discourses of White House and Pentagon apologists, *à la* Huntington and Fukayama, then the discourses on globalization are the renewal of the triumphalist discourses of modernity. Globalization thus becomes a modernized modernity, an actualized and updated modernity, and a "second modernity" to use Ulrich Beck's term. Globalization is the new name for modernity, but now seen from the United States, which has become the inheritor of the Western project. If Europe modernized, now the United States globalizes. The goal, the means, and the justification are the same. For this reason a radiography of globalization will make evident how this is a theorization that continues to trace and map the same epistemograph or ontograph that modernity traced. Europe, along with the United States, is the vortex of globalization. Evidently, positions like those of Canclini and Robertson have shown how globalization is as much the projection of the local as it is also the acculturation of the global, and for this reason it is more appropriate to talk of *glocalization*. Canclini, furthermore, has shown how the supposedly premodern or so-called traditional is an investure, or a form of fitting and appropriating transnational, modernizing, and globalizing projects. Using the language of Hobsbawm, the premodern and the traditional are inventions of the modern—the modern cannot be defined without inventing that which is its opposite.[8] And as Canclini shows, it is for this reason that hybridity is an already globalized strategy to enter modernity, or a modern strategy to access globality. Yet, both Canclini and Roberston illustrate exactly what it is that I am circling around—namely, the need to shift the epistemological locus of enunciation. For to accept Canclini's and Robertson's corrections requires that we see globalization as a global process in which there is not one agent, one society that globalizes, or one catalyst that inaugurates or accelerates an allegedly inevitable process, but a plurality of agents, both cultural and social, that transform in unexpected ways the directions and telos of globalization.

The difference between globalization and modernity is that the first seems to have abandoned all strong universalistic claims and pretensions, as was fundamental to modernity. While modernity operated on the logic of an ontoteleology, globalization transfers its alibi to a naturalized history of social development. History is the realm of contingency and chaos, but it also abides by the rules of selection and elimination that control the organic world. What survives is selected out. If it has survived, it is because it has been selected by nature. In fact, globalization presents itself as a second nature, as something that is inevitable. Globalization will happen, regardless of whether we want it or not. The formulation is that we are already globalized; or, rather, whoever does not want to be globalized will be, despite their own desires. Globalization, then, is a new philosophy of history that does not tell us that the telos that guides everything is in the future but, instead, tells us that the future is already here. There is no future, because we are already in the future. Here it would be fitting to appropriate Habermas's expression and we can say that globalization constitutes a closure of the horizon of the future. There are no other futures, since we already live there. And this is precisely what Microsoft suggests when it asks in its commercials: Where do you want to go today? Everything is at our disposal and at our reach. Postmodern cynicism is synthesized with the plenipotentiary and absolutist logic of modernity, and thus we have the discourses of globalization. Turning to our criteria, we could say, then, that the institutional locus is Euro–North American politics, economics, and technology. It is obvious that neither Indian, African, Nicaraguan, nor even French technology can globalize. Politically, the effect once again is of the neutralization of all critique. Who would want to stand in the way of the inevitable and logical path of social development? Of course, there are resistances, but these are caricaturized as Luddites and countermoderns, a type of antimodern romanticism. There is one difference with respect to both modernity and postmodernity: The discourses of globalization pretend to situate themselves beyond the borders of Europe and the United States. Here one could say that they share certain preoccupations and methodologies with the postcolonial and postoccidentalist theories. Globalization theories pretend to think the world from the perspective of the other. However, all that they can see or think is themselves. Put differently, they go to the other in order to see only themselves. In this form the locus of enunciation is the world, as a horizon of knowledge and concern, but what it enacts is a negation of this very locus of enunciation—for the world is not the world of cultural, social, and technological heterogeneity, but of a mere tabula rasa for the actualization of one global design.

Postcolonial theories began as a methodological critique of Marxism, and they were first elaborated in regions and countries that have been European colonies. Seen through this optic, postcolonial theories participate in a general discontent and disenchantment with Western culture that discredited itself so thoroughly and irreversibly with the massacres of the two world wars, the genocides of the concentration camps, and the communist gulags.

Postcolonial theories attempt to rescue certain Marxist-inspired methods of analysis for postcolonial societies. For this reason the Indian subaltern group was launched initially as an internal critique to Marxism, which because of its focus on European industrial capitalism cannot understand or appreciate the logic and originality of revolutionary movements that have nothing to do with the revolutionary logic of late capitalism as was diagnosed by Marx, Engels, and Lenin. Eventually, this methodological critique became an epistemological revolution, even a paradigm revolution. The goal is no longer one of transforming historical materialism and the cultural studies inaugurated by Raymond Williams and E. P. Thompson in order to acculturate and adapt them to the historical reality of the Indian world. On the contrary, now the goal is of abandoning these methods, for their epistemological as well as ontohistorical presuppositions are what hinder the possibility of understanding Indian reality in its own terms. Postcolonial theories are an epistemological and ontohistorical revolution that put in question all the science that is made, written, and exported by the Euro–North American pedagogical and ideological machine. For this reason, then, postcolonial theories change the epistemograph and the ontograph. The world requires many chronotopographs—different historical and geographical maps (Spivak and Chakrabarty). In addition, there are different ways of being historical and contemporary with the modern project—there are different ways of being modern. Here we can refer to a distinction that Dussel makes between modernity understood as a project that is supposedly accomplished only by Europe, and modernity as a global or planetary project.[9] The normative criterion is enunciated in the negative: Theories that negate reject and occlude the contribution, real or potential, of all cultures to an emergent planetary human culture, are unacceptable. Modernity is the product of the globality or *mundialidad* of humanity, and it would be hubristic to negate most or any contributions to such a project. The political consequences of this form of theories are evident. They are a critique of all forms of Eurocentrism, Americanism, and Ethnocentrism. The subject is at the same time the object of study, and its locus of enunciation is the locus of enactment and actualization. Here the other speaks about itself from its own place: from its quotidianity. The question, Can the subaltern speak? is provisionally answered with No, so long as the same ontoepistemological-historical categories of the Euro–North American project of modernity and globalization continue to be used (Derrida has written "theo-onto-epistemology," and I accept this neologism if we also accept how theoontology masks and harbors an entire philosophy of history).[10]

I am using the word "postoccidentalism" to refer to those theories that emerged in Latin America during the sixties.[11] This is a paradigm of Latin American thinking that gathers and synthesizes many theoretical currents: theories of dependence, the sociology of liberation, the philosophy of liberation, Freire's pedagogy of the oppressed, including the works on history by

Darcy Ribeiro, Samuel Ramos, Edmundo O'Gorman, and Octavio Paz. Methodologically, postoccidentalism emerges from a confrontation not only with historical materialism, but also from a synergistic synthesis and transformation of the existential ontology of Heidegger, the historicism of Gaos and Ortega y Gasset, and a symbolics, or cultural semantics and hermeneutics in the tradition of Ricoeur. I mention all of these precedents because I want to underscore how there is also an epistemological revolution in Latin American thought that is similar but anterior to that which took place within Indian thought, as well as in Marxist thought in England in the late sixties and early seventies. To look at Latin American thought from the perspective of postcolonial theory allows us to appreciate the innovation and originality of Latin American thought. One, and only one, of the many critical foci of what here I will call postoccidentalism is a critique to eurocentrism and European ethnocentrism, a critique that is carried from within. The central tenet of postoccidentalism is that Europe constitutes itself through a political economy of alterization of its others (a process that was so masterfully discussed by Edward Said). The logic of alterization creates others, but in order to define that which must remain unsoiled, pristine, which is the same, the identical. The grammar of abjection that determines the entire text of modernity in its relation to its others is not criticized from outside, but from within. What is a threat, what is vile and a possible contaminant, is within. Thus, the postoccidentalist critique begins by discovering the abject alterity within, inside. The figure is not the despised and feared Moor or the despotic Byzantium. The figure is now of Caliban cursing Prospero. The civilizing project, justified and imposed by a sanctified teleology but disguised behind the mantle of a historical reason, shipwrecks on the shoals of indigenous and mestizo culture, the Amerindian and the American slave. From its inception, the occidentalist project begins its failure, but it is nonetheless continued and perpetuated, as management of those others that it produces but that must be at the same time quarantined. Formulaically put: Already the Amerindians, the slaves of the New World, the mestizos and mulattos that are born with the modern project, knew in their flesh and sequestered and quarantined sociality what the postcolonial thinkers began to discover after the sixties and seventies in light of a process of decolonization begun in the aftermath of World War II.

It is evident, then, there has been a change in the locus of enunciation. Now, it is no longer admissible to permit a subject to speak for others, to epistemologize about them, without allowing them in turn to speak or to make knowledge claims. Nor is it acceptable to suppose that there is another who is silent and merely known. Postoccidentalist thought is that in which the other answers and responds back in his and her polluted and vulgar tongues. This speaking subaltern confronts the master with his voice and answers back: I do not recognize myself in your caricatures of me. The goal here is to acknowledge that we are always objects of a fantasy of control, and that this control materializes if we accept to live under the fictions of the master and his discourse. In short, postoccidentalism is what Luhmann would call a second-order observation, an observation of observations. In this way, postoccidentalism contributes to a critique of the modernist disciplines that occlude their political dimensions behind the curtains of scientization. Thus, postoccidentalism, in a manner analogous to postcolonial theories, is a critique of the political economy of knowledge.

There are fundamental differences between postoccidentalism and postorientalism, however. Postoccidentalism is a tradition that is sociotheoretical critique as much as it is philosophical critique, which has behind it five hundred years of experience and accumulated work. Yet, at a deeper level, we would have to note that postcolonialism elaborates a critique of European colonialism in the epoch of its last stage. It is a critique that for that reason is focused on the more recent and visible consequences of the colonial-modern project (as Mignolo thinks we should write it) in its second stage (where the first stage was when the colonial-modern project is inaugurated with the discovery of the New World, and the Spanish hegemony that is established in synchrony with the expulsion of the Jews and the Moors from the Iberian peninsula). In contrast, the postoccidentalist critique is articulated synchronically and diachronically. Postoccidentalism is a look that gazes back from the inauguration of the Western or Occidental project, which is prior to the orientalist project and that, inevitably, due to geopolitical and historical-cultural reasons, analyze from within a third and most recent stage of the colonial-modern project. This latest stage has to be understood as the continuation of the civilizing project by the United States, under the flag of the war against all wars that is benignly called the crusade for human rights and its condition of possibility, globalization. This convergence among the transfer of flags, exacerbation of the violence of the civilizing project masked by the fiscal and banking policies imposed by the G-7 (now G-8, since Russia came on board), backed up by the NATO armies, and the crisis itself of this rationalized irrationality that is given voice in the thinkers of the center (echoing the expressions of economic philosopher Franz Hinkelammert), requires that we opt for a long-term view that postcolonialism, which is so young, can neither admit nor provide.[12]

At a more elemental level, when we try to decipher the categories that allow postcolonial criticism, we are faced with an ambiguity or indeterminacy that seems to plague and render suspect the proposals of postcolonial criticism. Postcolonial theory advocates in favor of the subaltern, but who is the subaltern? How is the social, political, economic locus of the subaltern determined? How can one determine conceptually the theoretical locus of the subaltern? The subaltern sometimes appears to be part of the social system, at other times it seems to be beyond the system. As Spivak herself writes: "Subalternity is the name that I grant to the space that is outside any serious contact with the logic of capitalism and socialism."[13] In other words, the category of the subaltern is outside any historical determination. But this indeterminacy becomes an empty space and an inaccessible and intransigent opacity, at the very moment that it turns into the cancellation of the ethical response. To clarify: Faced with the challenge of the subaltern, who dominates? The hegemonic "I" of the ruling system has only two options: either respect absolutely and without reservations the alterity of the other, and in this way leave the status quo totally intact; or, on the other side, the hegemonic "I" must open up, respond to the other without trying to assimilate him.[14] This type of paradox is confronted directly in the philosophical corpus that animates the postoccidentalist critique. And to put it more concretely, the challenge of the encounter with the other, and of having to formulate an answer that is neither adulatory nor sacralizing, neither assimilating nor devastating, is the central theme of the work of the ethics of liberation that is at the center of so much postoccidentalist work. A philosophy of alterity is fundamental to the critiques of Occidentalism and Orientalism. The philosophical poverty of postcolonialism is justifiable; it is an epistemological critique that begins out of a methodological crisis. The critique of the political economy of knowledge that is developed by the postoccidentalist critique proceeds further since it begins from the crisis of reason itself. In this way, postoccidentalism is a critique of Western rationality, in favor of a reason that is universalistic but from and out of the different, alterity. It is a critique of reason from its hybridity and insufficiency.

5

The Emperor's Map

Latin American Critiques of Globalism

> Much of what ideologies say is true, and would be ineffectual if it were not, but ideologies also contain a good many propositions which are flagrantly false, and do so less because of some inherent quality than because of the distortions into which they are commonly forced n their attempts to ratify and legitimate unjust, oppressive political systems
>
> ... the concept of ideology aims to disclose something of the relation between an utterance and its material conditions of possibility, when those conditions of possibility are viewed in the light of certain power-struggles central to the reproduction (or also, for some theories, contestation) of a whole form of social life.
>
> —Terry Eagleton, *Ideology: An Introduction*

There are many globalizations, and all of them are not always in accord at any given time. Sometimes, some globalizations work against others. Generally, some globalizations are not simultaneous with others. Globalization is not global at once and all over. This internal heterogeneity breeds conflict, but also other perspectives on globalization. A way to deal with this internal heterogeneity of globalization has been to introduce lexical markers: globalization, globalism, planetarization, mundalization, and the like.[1] The globalization of globalization is a result of a conflict over who gets to define which globalization is assumed to be both inevitable and desirable. Some of the issues about which globalization gets to be globalized have been addressed in terms of globalization's relationship to modernity, posmodernity, postcolonialism, and most recently postoccidentalism.[2] What is

A shorter and different version of this chapter appeared in Manfred B Steger, ed., *Rethinking Globalism* (Lanham, MD: Rowman and Littlefield, 2004), 231–242.

common to all of these geopolitical macrotemporal markers (modernity, postmodernity, postcolonialism, etc.) is that like Foucault's panopticon, they seek to survey, monitor, and ultimately regiment the world in accordance with a *chronotope* that is itself immune to questioning and unassailable by historization.[3] Lest we continue to perpetuate the imperial designs and fantasies that underwrite these chronotopologies, it is necessary that we make explicit how this new chronotopological, or what I already called geopolitical metatemporal marker, relates to a "civilizational" mission that has come to define the West and its others. Such unveiling of the relationship between globalization and the millennial civilizational mission of the West may proceed by way of addressing some of the following questions: So long as there are many globalizations and not all of them are global simultaneously, we would have to ask: what globalization is imagined? Who imagines it? In what image, metaphor, or trope, is this imagined globalization imagined? And where, in geopolitical space-time, is located this imagining agent imaging his or her imagined globalization?

It would be uncontroversial to claim that Edward Said's classic work *Orientalism* was an incursion into these questions.[4] By documenting how the so-called West had imagined the "Orient," Said was able to disclose how the Western civilizational project also entailed a simultaneous logic of abjection and self-aggrandizement, of contempt for the other and self-immunization. One criticism that was leveled against Said was that he had enacted for the West, what he criticized the West for doing to its others, its Orientals. I want to bracket whether in fact Said can be criticized on this register. I am however interested in the suspicion voiced in this criticism. The suspicion points to something that I would like to make the focus of this chapter; namely, that within the logic of globalization, to which belongs the simultaneous westernization and orientalization of the world, to use Octavio Ianni's expression,[5] the West has had to imagine itself as it never was. A provocative way to put my thesis would be to plagiarize the title of one of Bruno Latour's most celebrated works and say that within the logic of globalization, within the contestation and drawing of battle lines, in which the goal is to globalize a certain globalization, the West has never been Western, although the West has been undergoing westernization. In other words, the struggle about globalization is a struggle about what the West will be, about what type of westernization we should submit not just the "others" of the West, but also the West itself. In order to approach my subject, however, I will focus most specifically on the way in which the United States has become the main agent and vendor of a certain type of globalization, which it peddles in and imposes over the world, while arguing that this is both the health and future of the West and the best the West has to bequeath itself and humanity. But more concretely still, I will focus on the relationship between the United States and Latin America in order to approach the way in which the United States has positioned itself as, and at the vanguard of the movement to save the West. (Note for instance the way Samuel P. Huntington's text *The Clash of Civilizations and the Remaking of the World Order*,[6] has become the point of reference de rigueur for White House and *pax Americana* intellectuals.) In order to discuss this relationship between the United States and Latin America, I will profile four types of Latinamericanisms, which in turn have become a register of that familial but fractious relationship. I will close with an overview of what I take to be the virtues of the Latinamericanist approach to globalization and globalisms.

Latinamericanisms

Latinamericanism is a name for forms of knowledge, ideological attitudes, and spectral mirrors. Latinamericanism as a form of knowledge has assumed different forms, as we will see; hence the plural in the title of this section. Analogously, Latinamericanism is plural because it has been about how Latin America has been portrayed by at least four major agents of imagination: Latin America itself, the United States, Europe, and most recently, Latinos. There are many Latin Americas, and not solely because of the waxing and waning of its boundaries and shifting place in the Western imaginary, as Arturo Ardao has documented so excellently,[7] but also because it has been imagined differently by different social actors. Finally, Latinamericanism has to do with the specters that haunt the rise of the West to global dominance, and because in it (the imagined Latin America) we also find reflected the dreams of an alternate "America" and possibly a different West. In the following, I will differentiate among four types of Latinamericanism that registers not just a particular chronology, but also the shifting of the location, or geopolitical place, of the imaging agent.

The *first* type of Latinamericanism emerged in part as a response to 1848 and 1898, the twin moments of American Empire.[8] This type of Latinamericanism juxtaposed the United States to Latin America in terms of invidiously distinctive and opposite cultural and spiritual outlooks. The ideology is that one is uncouth, materialistic, utilitarian, soulless, and without cultural roots, while the other is the proper inheritor of the European spirit of culture, civilization, and idealistic principles grounded in love and tradition. While this distinction has been best articulated by José Enrique Rodó,[9] we may also find it in the work of José Martí.[10] This opposition became a fundamental creedal pronouncement for generations of thinkers in Latin America, even if they did not share the same lexicon or emotional animus. Sometimes overtly, but most often covertly as a hermeneutical point of departure, we find the same prejudice in the work of seminal Mexican thinkers like José Vasconcelos, Leopoldo Zea, and even Octavio Paz. Another important point of departure for this type of Latinamericanism is the double bind in which a nascent Latin American identity found itself. This "criollo identity," this truly "American" identity was to be neither Anglo-Saxon, nor Spanish, and certainly not simply European. Thus, just as it sought to distance itself from Anglo-Saxon America, it also sought to distance itself from imperial and colonial Europe. Yet this distancing was not an outright rejection. America would become the land in which Europe's hope and promise would be fulfilled.[11] Some, in fact, went so far as to argue that the problem was that Latin America was not enough like Europe, or rather, that Latin America had yet to express the best of Europe, while dispensing with the work of patrician, royal, and feudal past and habit of old Europe. Such views are given voice in the works of of Domingo Sarmiento, who basically established a whole school of thought based on the opposition "civilization and barbarism."[12]

This first type of Latinamericanism then registered in thought the colonial and imperialistic expansion of the United States, and Latin America's resistance and rejection of this thrust into its own territories, culture, and traditions. This Latinamericanism was a cultural manifestation of a geopolitical confrontation of cultures. One should therefore properly define this first type of Latinamericanism as *Kulturkampf* Latinamericanism. This *Kulturkampf* confronted an imperialistic modernity with a protopostmodern promise of a humanistic and plurotopic (to use Mignolo's inflection of this term) modernity that in the words of Pedro Henriquez Ureña was embodied in the idea of America as the fatherland of justice (*La Patria de la Justicia*).[13] It is important that we linger briefly over the emergence of this *Kulturkampf* Latinamericanism for it emerges at the very moment that a semantic shift is taking place in Europe. Latin America, as the name for the nations and lands in South America formerly controlled by Spain, makes its appearance in the lexicon of geopolitics at the moment when Europe is ceasing to talk about Romania and Germania, the Gales and the Franks, and begins to talk about the Anglo-Saxons and the Latins, or the mixture of Gales and Franks that made up the western Holy Roman Empire. These shifts are registered over the span of about half a century, five decades in which England consolidates its power over the East, just as the United States begins to consolidate its power over the West. There is a division of labor, if one may speak in these terms: the United Kingdom conquers the East and Africa, while the United States launches itself over the American continent. As counterstrategy, France seeks to consolidate a cultural homogeneity between the Franks and Gauls in order to conform a unified front against the "Anglo-Saxons." These geopolitical struggles, waged in terms of the invention of cultural traditions that had irretrievably fragmented because of the Reformation and the discovery of the New World, left their trace in terms of names that conjure up fictions by fiat—notwithstanding Leopoldo von Ranke's attempt to see the histories of the Latin and Teutonic nations in terms of a series of common processes that included the migrations (*Volkwanderungen*), the Crusades, and the discovery of the New World.[14] The struggle for the heartland, the soul, the inheritance of the West, of Western culture, of Greco-Roman culture, was mirrored in this first type of Latinamericanism that struggled against the crass utilitarianism and hedonistic individualism of Anglo-Saxon culture, to use the despectives of the Arielists (Rodo's followers). These Arielists, however, were not thinking from and in Latin America, per se, but where thinking from the standpoint of a "Western" imaginary. When they thought about Latin America, they thought of it in terms of its prosthetic relationship to Europe. (And here the perfect example is Jose María Torres Caicedo, a Colombian who lived most of his professional life in France and who was one of the main promoters of the idea of "Latin America.")

The *second* type of Latinamericanism is the one that emerged after World War II with the onset of the cold war in the United States. More precisely, we should date the rise of this type of Latinamericanism with the National Defense Education Act of 1958, which determined that it was a priority of national security to invest in the educational programs that could contribute to the defense of the nation.[15] Guided by this national security and defense goals, area-studies programs were developed that sought to parcel the world in terms of areas of strategic interest. Clearly, Latin America was a major area of geopolitical strategic interest and, thus, arose what I will call area-studies Latinamericanism. This area-studies Latinamericanism had as its goal to gather and disseminate knowledge about "third world" countries. This Latinamericanism treated Latin America like any other foreign land, although there was from the inception an ambiguity about treating Latin America like Asia and Africa were treated. Nonetheless, cold war knowledge interests dictated the research model that sought to learn as much as possible about other cultures in terms of their vulnerability and potentiality for becoming germinals of sedition. The epistemological matrix that is going to undergird this research is determined by the ideas of a first, second, and third worlds, a sequence that is underwritten by the teleology of modernity.[16] Areas studies were a major tool for geopolitical gerrymandering, but also for epistemic surveillance. As it pertained to Latin America, area studies always imposed an analytical template that blinded its researchers to the very unique problems of Latin America—that is, hybridization, mestizaje, century-old inequities between the countryside and the city, as well as deeply entrenched traditions of *caciquismo* (or neopotism), on the one hand, and on the other, ideas about the common good that always conspired to promote social revolutions.

This type of Latin Americanism, then, was a way to think or represent Latin America from the standpoint of the North American academy, albeit explicitly at the service of the American cold-war project. But to be fair, one should note that what we are here calling "area-studies Latinamericanism" could be said to have two foci: one which is a Latinamericanism of Latin America as the land of underdevelopment, bringing in tow all of what this entails—that is, lack of proper stages of modernization, weak public spheres, lack of technological innovations, and so on. This would be the Latinamericanism of the technocrats and thinktank apparatchiks. The other foci would be a Latinamericanism of third worldism, or a form of first-world romanticization and exoticization of the Latin American. But this form of viewing Latin America is the negative picture of the Latinamericanism of Latin America as underdevelopment. It is this second form of Latinamericanism that romanticizes Latin America that explains the fetishization of the Latin American novel. This *third-worldist Latinamericanism* allows the agents in the United States to vicariously live a romantic, colonial, premodern past. This Latinamericanism is about ersatz tradition. Nonetheless, it is the interaction between these two types of Latinamericanisms that gave rise to the collapse of the epistemological and aesthetic, in which the place of the former is taken by the latter, with respect to the Latin America that Román de la Campa points out in his book *Latinamericanism* and that Jean Franco has also studied in her recent work *The Decline and Fall of the Lettered City*.[17]

The *third* type of Latinamericanism, which I call "critical Latinamericanism," can be unequivocally dated to the period after 1959, the Cuban Revolution, and 1969, the Medellín Bishop's meeting that essentially granted doctrinal justification to the Ecclesial Christian base communities and liberation theology. This third form of Latinamericanism sets Latin America in opposition to the United States, but now in terms of an antiimperialist and anticapitalist stand that is accompanied by a thorough critique of the epistemological regimes that had permitted the theorization of Latin America up to then. This is the Latinamericanism that we find in the works of Fals Borda, Darcy Ribeiro, Leopoldo Zea, Augusto Salazar Bondy, Gustavo Gutierrez, and Enrique Dussel. This is the idea of a Latin American developed in Latin America to explain the Latin American situation to Latin Americans and the United States. Undoubtedly, this Latinamericanism was explicitly developed to counter the obnoxious ideological effects of the Latinamericanism developed by the epistemological-military-industrial apparatus of the cold-war establishment of the United States during the fifties, sixties, and seventies. Indeed, as Subcomandante Marcos has articulated in some of his communiqués, while the United States was waging a cold war against the purported evil empire of the Soviet Union, a third world war was begin waged primarily in Latin America and Southeast Asia, the so-called third world. Thus, in marked difference to the area-studies Latinamericanism that emerged shortly after the two world wars, this *critical Latinamericanism* is one that was articulated by a historical agent situated in Latin America, thought as a *Latin* America, but also as an underdeveloped periphery. This type of Latinamericanism interjects already a new global dimension to the question of the relationship between the United States and the world system. To this Latinamericanism also belong the attempt to acculturate Marxism and all forms of critical theory. As the nations behind the so-called iron wall sought to develop socialisms with a human face, Latin Americans also sought to develop "Marxisms" with Indian faces. It would not be an exaggeration to say that this "historical materialism" with an indigenous and indigent face was articulated by liberation theology.[18]

Finally, there is a *fourth* type of Latinamericanism that has begun to be articulated over past several decades (depending on whether one takes the seventies or early eighties, either the rise of the Brown Beret and the Puerto Rican liberation movements, or the Nicaraguan Revolution and the Salvadorean and Guatemalan insurgencies). What is important is that this fourth type of Latinamericanism is directly and proportionally linked to the aftermath (and ongoing) Latino diaspora in, and to, the United States. Thus, this postorientalist and postoccidentalist, but also postimperialistic Latinamericanism is the expression of a nascent, although quite articulate, critical consciousness in the Latino populations in the United States. This is a transnational, diasporic, postcultural, and post-Latin America type of Latinamericanisms that brings together the critical Latinamericanism produced in Latin America since the sixties, and the homegrown (in the U.S.) epistemological and social critique that identity movements developed simultaneously but separately. Thus, this Latino Latinamericanism has two foci and loci of enunciation and enactment and operates at various levels of criticism: it is critical of the West, but also of the way Occidentalism was deployed in order to normalize and regiment the very internal sociality of the West in the Americas.[19] It is about the Latin America in the mind of the United States, and the Latin America in the mind of Latinos and Latin Americans in Latin America. It is a Latinamericanism that seeks to document and analyze the emergence of a *post–pax americana* American imaginary, an imaginary beyond the imperial dreams of a nineteenth- and twentieth-century United States and a "Latinized" Latin America.[20] Most importantly, this type of Latinamericanism seeks to unmake the emperor's map, regardless of whether it is the map of a new European Union asserting its claims over the "West," or the United States offering itself as the "future health of the West."[21] The thinkers that give expression to this type of thought are trans-American intellectuals like Juan Flores, Roberto Fernández Retamar, Román de la Campa, Subcomandante Marcos, Lewis Gordon, José Saldivar, Walter Mignolo, and Santiago Castro-Gómez. Yet, to underscore, what is important about this emergent Latinamericanism is how it is able to combine a dual critique: of Orientalism, insofar as Latin America itself has been orientalized, and of Occidentalism, insofar as Latin America has been the expiatory sacrifice to the homogenization of America as the West. To return to Ianni's stark formulation cited at the beginning, in the logic of globalization we encounter this simultaneous westernization and orientalization. Latin America is the trace of this dialectic, if I may be forgiven this rhetoric. It has been constituted as the Other of the United States and Europe, but it is also being the sameness, the "I," the oneself of an imagined identity that had to be dictated, projected, and enforced lest the hubristic project of taking over the moribund West collapse at the sight of the face of the other in our face.

The above analysis of four types of Latinamericanism would be incomplete if I did not discuss, if only briefly, what could be called a Latin American neoliberalism, or globalism with a human face.[22] Economists Hernando de Soto and Fernando Henrique Cardoso, and the past president of Peru, Alejandro Toledo, have put this type of globalism with a human face forward. Reversing decades of economic nationalism, and attempts to modernize stagnant economies through military coups, in the last two decades of the twentieth century, Brazil, Argentina, Peru, and Mexico experimented with neoliberal globalization—that is, opening their jealously guarded national markets to foreign (although mostly from the United States) investments. Cardoso and de Soto could be considered the theorists of this fin de siècle economic modernization. For both, the failure of economic growth in Latin America has been due to the lack of a thorough globalization of national capital and the strategic use of floating transnational capital to spur economic growth.[23] Yet, the devastation of the Argentine economy,[24] the growth of poverty in Mexico, the near collapse of the Brazilian economy and its bailing out by the IMF, as well as the recurring economic backsliding of most of the other Latin American countries, has seriously called into question the feasibility of a Latin American neoliberalism or globalism with a human face. On the contrary, the Harvard and Stanford School of Economics–type of classroom experimentation that has characterized Cardoso's and Carlos Menem's economic policies has spelled disaster for the Latin American people. Unsurprisingly, since neoliberal globalization entails privatization, which in Latin America is but another euphemism for the export of national capital, during the last decade the *Gini* coefficients (the ratio of income differential and ownership of national wealth between the richest and poorest within a country) in Latin America have grown to be some of the largest in the world.[25] By the same token, it should not come as a surprise that the recent electoral changes in Latin America could be taken as signs that neoliberal globalism in Latin America has come under serious attack. Luis Inácio Lula da Silva's electoral triumph in Brazil, during the 2002 election, are signs of growing skepticism and disenchantment with programs that have plunged Brazil into destabilizing debt.[26] Analogously, and notwithstanding his neoliberal rhetoric, Alejandro Toledo's electoral win against Alberto Fujimori could be attributed to a resurgence of grassroots populism. In fact, Hugo Chavez, Lula, and Toledo represent popular leaders who are calling for a new form of economic development that does not entail selling off the national patrimony. In the end, however, this type of globalism, which is not a critique but an attempt to acculturate it to Latin America, is perhaps less an episode in the narrative that I sought to develop here and more a chapter in the history of capitalism in its latest stage of neoliberal globalism.

The Economic Life of Culture(s) and Knowledge(s) in the Age of Globalizations

Under the term "Latinamericanism" are agglutinated various forms of knowledge or rather, techniques for the production of knowledges. In its most recent modalities, as a postnational, post-Latin America Latinamericanism and as a critical Latinamericanism, these techniques of the production of knowledge have been deliberately self-conscious about the relationship between what is known, how it is known, and who knows it—or at the very least who is authorized to know it. In this way, the most recent modalities of Latinamericanism have been avowedly about the critique of knowledge production or, more precisely, critiques of the political economy of the production of knowledges. For this reason, it would be entirely appropriate to catalogue these forms of Latinamericanism along with postcolonial and subaltern critiques of both Orientalism and Occidentalism. In tandem, and so long as we see the last two Latinamericanisms described as species of metacritiques, or metatheoretical self-reflections, then they are bound to share analogies with their siblings. Still, I will argue that the critical Latinamericanisms I have described have virtues that make them if not more useful, at least more appropriate for us, subjects located somewhere on the geopolitical and epistemological matrix of the West as it is imagined by the United States. For the sake of brevity I will highlight only five aspects that are, as I suggest in the title of this section of the chapter, about the "economic life" of both culture(s) and knowledge(s) in the age of globalizations. I will name the five virtues, and go on to describe only two of them, due to space constraints (for the moment, I will discuss only two virtues, and hold out the three others as Pro Forma or promissory notes): (1) transdisciplinarity; (2) globalization of antiglobalism and the antiglobalization of globalism; (3) critique of the commodification of culture and the culture of commodification (Canclini and Yúdice); (4) analysis of the manufacture of desire that projects and manipulates a global imaginary (de la Campa on *Buena Vista Socra Club*); and (5) as they offer genealogies of a transnational imaginary that oscillates between tradition and modernity producing as a trace an ersatz nostalgia that allows global nomads to live out vicariously a past that they never had, and that never was, but which allows them to affirm the validity of their present and the inevitability of their future, which is more of the same present (Santiago Castro-Gómez, Norbert Lechner).

The first virtue that Latinamericanism exhibits has to do with what is called "transdisciplinarity." As Roland Robertson has pointed out, globalization cuts across many disciplines, inter alia, sociology, political theory, economics, international relations, anthropology, and many more.[27] Furthermore, not only does globalization, as an object of study overlap and overflow some of these disciplinary boundaries, globalization vitiates the social realities around which these disciplines coalesced and crystallized. As the Gulbenkian report pointed out, the disciplines that have been housed in the different faculties and departments of the post–World War II university, with its roots in nineteenth-century romanticism, have entered into crises because their social signifiers and objects of study have been if not overtaken and corroded, at least rendered secondary and even superfluous.[28] If as John Urry put it, sociology has lost "society," and must rethink its object of study,[29] and the social and human sciences have lost their "world," the ground of their certitude, as Immanuel Wallerstein has been arguing, then new conceptual matrixes must be developed in order to deal with a new social cartography.[30] This is what transdisciplinarity names: the way in which globalization *transcends* the limits and applicability of nineteenth- and twentieth-century conceptual matrices, and the way in which those disciplines and conceptual matrixes might have become anachronistic and obsolete. Latinamericanism, both critical and postnational, has been laboring in this abject region of knowledge. The works of some of the figures I have mentioned cut across disciplines in ways never before thought possible: renaissance studies, semiotics, anthropology, american studies, literary studies, history of ideas, philosophy, political economy, and the like. For this reason, it is safest to say that Latinamericanism is less a circumscribed set of texts and objects of study and more a particular methodological orientation that always takes as both its point of departure and litmus test, Latin America. As a transdisciplinary approach par excellance, Latinamericanism is about how knowledge is produced out of, or at the vortex where the global meets the local and the local projects into the global. And more specifically, since this Latinamericanism has to do with the emergence of unique post–*pax Americana* imaginaries, is also about the way in which there are local agents within the United States who have become the exemplar of the global meeting the local qua flows of people, or ethnoscapes, as Appadurai put it so felicitously.

The second virtue of the critical Latinamericanisms that I have been profiling has to do with the dialectic between what we could call the globalization of antiglobalism and the antiglobalization of globalism. During the years of the cold war, Latin Americans, as well as Latinos, made use of the discourses of globalization as well as of its networks and infrastructures. Perfect examples are: the Nicaraguan failed attempts to use the world court against the United States (Nicaragua did get the world court to censor and demand that the United States pay reparations to Nicaragua, but the United States neither respected nor fulfilled the world court's injunction); the uses of what arguably was one of the first institutions of globalization, namely the Catholic Church, for socially emancipatory goals; and more recently the use of the internet and cybertechnologies to, on the one hand, destabilize local governments, and, on the other, to make transnational claims by local ethnic and racial minorities. These latter forms of the use of globalization's infrastructures have been excellently illustrated by the Zapatistas in the Lacandonian Jungle of southern Mexico.[31] But they have been followed by indigenous groups in Peru and Ecuador, who are making direct claims on their cultural inheritances by bypassing their regional and national governments. Other forms in which the Latinamericanisms under attention attend to this dialectic are illustrated by their focus on the uses of globalization to project a local imaginary that appeals to, seduces, and excites a global imaginary by promising tradition, the exotic, in short, the spice of culture. This has been done in terms of literature, music, and tourism. Yet, at the same time, Latinamericanists have been very careful to document and analyze the ways in which the crises of Latin America since the early nineties in particular, are illustrative of what I have here called the antiglobalization of globalism. NAFTA is perhaps the most illustrative example. This reference, however, allows us to make explicit how the antiglobalization of globalism is in fact another name for asymmetrical globalization, or what is now commonly called globalization from above, in which some globalize without allowing themselves to be globalized.

I will close by reaffirming the central theses of this chapter: The West has never been (solely and entirely) Western, albeit it is being westernized; and globalization has never been global, albeit it is being globalized. In this age of globalizations, the United States is pushing a particular agenda that entails that it assumed the mantle of the civilizational mission of the West, and in this way, globalization is another name for MacDonalization and MacDysnelization. Four different forms of Latinamericanism have emerged to counter these subterranean but determining relationships between empire, civilizational mission, globalization, and the alterization and homogenization of others and oneself. Two quotes from Eagleton serve as epigraphs for this chapter. One speaks for itself and, although it seems to be almost self-evident, what it expresses is too easily forgotten by many critics of globalization. The second epigraph requires a bit of commentary: Globalization is an ideology, indeed, although it is also, and without doubt, a reality. The prior sentence is probably an oxymoron for there is no reality that is not suffused by ideology and no ideology that is not real, or has reality effects. But as an ideology, what is its utterance, its performativity? And furthermore, what are the conditions of possibility of that very utterance, and what power struggles are being waged that both enable it and yet challenge it as it conditions the very reproduction of the society that makes the utterance of globalization, as a reality and as an ideal? What mode of life, what historicity is at stake and is being negotiated so that the pronouncement "globalization is the health and future of the world" can be made?

Part 3

CRITICAL THEORY

6

Beyond Universal History

Enrique Dussel's Critique of Globalization

Introduction

Geopolitics has always determined the cartography according to which history is written.[1] As Adrienne Rich put it: "A place on the map is a place in history."[2] Conversely, a time in history is also a place on a map. This is more than a question of perspective, for it insists that history happens more forcefully, authentically, as if for the first time, in certain places, with the concomitant that other places are relegated outside history, to the supplemental, to the epigonic. Universal history, as has been practiced in the "West," exemplifies this claim.[3] One may argue that the genre of universal history began with Saint Augustine's *City of God*. But here history is a thin veil for divine history. Nonetheless, it is Augustine's idea of world history as *Heilsgeschichte* (salvation history) that inspired a whole tradition of speculation about the logic and telos of history.[4] Since Guizot, Condorcet, Smith, Hegel, Marx, and Dilthey, history has been concerned with the elucidation and discernment of those processes and forces that explain humanity's history and future. And while Christendom stands behind many of these historian's speculations, most of them have secularized salvation history into Europe's civilizing mission. For many of these great philosophers of history, the issue of history was the question of "universal history," that is, of the unity of human historical experience. Their general contention was that this unity could be explained in terms of a series of processes or determining logics. These invariably turned out to be European, Western processes and logics: secularization, modernization, industrialization, juridification, *Entzauberung* (disenchantment), bureaucratization, and so on.[5] These, in turn, were allegedly absent, stagnant, lacking from non-Western societies—or at

This chapter first appeared in Linda Martín Alcoff and Eduardo Mendieta, eds., *Thinking from the Underside of History: Enrique Dussel's Philosophy of Liberation* (Lanham, MD: Rowman and Littlefield, 2000), 117–33.

the very least still to be brought to them via diffusion, contact, and exchange. Not unexpectedly, it was the West that would catalyze innovation in these non-Western societies. In this way, salvation history, became the West's civilizing mission, the "white man's burden." Universal history, however, emerged in the eighteenth and nineteenth centuries as the ideology of European world hegemony. This is the time when European colonialism and imperialism attained their farthest global reaches. Universal history, therefore, became the apologia for Western expansionism by writing the history of humanity in terms of any one, or several, of the following tropes: civilization and/or culture, freedom, the state, technology, civil society, urbanization, and so on—ideals and ciphers that stood for Europe and the West.[6] The type of universal history practiced in the West, in short, became a way of writing about the "West" and the "rest" in such a way that the latter were defined by a "cluster of absences" that turned out to be what the former possessed in abundance and exclusively.[7]

The project of universal history, however, entered into crisis in the early part of the twentieth century. Two world wars made it extremely difficult and suspect to project certain aspects of Western culture as possessing universal validity.[8] The moral and evaluative aspects of universal histories, taken from the Christian idea of a salvation history, became highly questionable and indefensible. Europe itself plunged into a deep moral identity crisis. Lord Acton was to be the last great universal historian, even as his work remained incomplete.[9] A new brand of history was to be inaugurated by Arnold Toynbee. His historical project began as a rejection of universal history as it had been understood by writers since Guizot, up through Lord Acton. Toynbee was to inaugurate what is today called "world history." A history of the world in terms of the history of civilizations that rise and fall with the ebb of time.[10] The West, in this new historical practice, became one of the many civilizations to have its time on the historical stage. The West was neither the most advanced nor the most moral, nor even the summation and synthesis of all prior cultures and civilization. Toynbee began to see history through a decentered and decentering historical perspective in which the West could no longer claim a place of privilege or prestige.[11] This orientation was to be furthered by William McNeill, the best-known American practitioner of world history. For McNeill, who is the author of the *Rise of the West: A History of the Human Community*,[12] however, Toynbee's approach remained too parochial and not global or planetary enough. More recently, McNeill has leveled the same criticism at his own work.[13]

Today, the proliferating discourses of globalization project themselves as a new version of universal history.[14] As with the universal histories of eighteenth- and nineteenth-century historians, the discourses of globalization put emphasis on certain civilizational forces that purportedly collapse all parochialism and cultural chauvinisms. With globalization theory we seem to be returning to the orientations of a Condorcet, Smith, Hume, Kant, Marx, or Weber, all of whom could only think of history in terms of the planetarization of certain concepts, processes, organizational principles, and the like. These, in turn, were taken to be unique, endemic, and autochthonous to Europe and the West. Globalization has become the West's new cartography according to which history's map is traced by the planetarization of the free market, laissez-faire liberalism, mass consumption, and mass culture.[15]

In the following I want to challenge the ways in which globalization is offered as a new apologia for, and of, the West. I will begin with the analysis of several recent theories of globalization. This analysis, although summary and sketchy, will suffice to illustrate the ideological character of some of these theories of globalization. I will then proceed to sketch the ways in which these theories have failed on several counts, namely with respect to the questions of ethics and history, and their respective but linked relationships to globalization. It is a central contention of the present text that globalization has raised the stakes on what kinds of analysis can and should be provided. Globalization demands of us not just greater attentiveness to detail but also greater circumspection concerning our conceptual apparatuses. I suggest we need to pay greater attention to the way globalization fits into history and how "Western" history looks when seen from a global perspective. Most importantly, however, globalization appears as an ethical challenge, and this is why I take up Dussel's challenge. Therefore, in the final section I will discuss the ways in which Dussel offers us a critical discourse about globalization that directly addresses the failures of its recent discourses.

Theorizing Globalization

Globalization might be understood in a variety of ways. It can be seen as a purely economic project, or the realization of one. This is for instance the view held by Barnett and Cavanaugh, who speak of globalization as the realization of global dreams by imperial corporations.[16] For them, globalization is the planetarization of a global bazaar, with its concomitant K-Mart realism aesthetic, the global casino economy, the global labor market, and the global shopping mall. Benjamin Barber shares some similarities with Barnett and Cavanaugh's approach. In Barber's case, however, globalization is merely the confrontation between McWorld and Jihad, which being ciphers of economic processes that register as cultural epiphenomena, results in the evisceration of politics by economics.[17] For Barber, the challenge of globalization is the threat to the possibility of civic participation. As he puts it succinctly, "Globalism is mandated by profit not citizenship."[18]

Globalization can also be seen as a cultural phenomenon or, rather, as the final fusing of economy and culture. Jameson has suggested that one of the distinctive qualities of postmodernity is that it registers this economization of the cultural and the culturization of economy. Or in other words, as culture becomes economy, the latter turns into the former. Globalization as Americanization is the epitome of this mutation of the one into the other.[19] In a recent article, Jameson has extended this analysis to globalization.[20] Arjun Appadurai, on the other hand, who also could be included under this rubric of interpreting globalization as a cultural process, is more interested in how sociopolitical processes unleashed by economic imperatives have turned into cultural projects that surpass and cunningly outwit these imperatives themselves. For Appadurai, globalization is a new space for a new social imaginary that works through the nation-state but also against it and beyond it. In the last instance, Appadurai is interested in the constitution of a new social imaginary that can no longer be matched or reduced to economic goals and processes alone.[21]

There are also political readings of globalization. This we find represented in the work of Jürgen Habermas and Malcom Waters,[22] although I will discuss only the former. For Habermas, globalization is the extension to the entire globe of the highest achievements of the Enlightenment and critical modernity. To this extent, globalization appears to be an extension of modernity, if not its final denouement. In two recent essays, Habermas has addressed directly the question of globalization.[23] He has suggested that globalization does indeed consist in a series of economic and political challenges, but that the appropriate answers to those challeneges requires instituting at a global level the rule of law and one of the greatest achievements of the twentieth century—namely, the welfare state. In fact, in the face of the many quandaries and problems that besiege the walls of European nation states, the appropriate answer is to reach out to the law.[24] Law becomes the civilizing element. Indeed, Habermas talks about the juridification of politics, at a global level, as the answer to the conflicts brought about by growing cultural ethnocentrism and the atavistic reactions by societies that are trying to survive the onslaught of Europanization and westernization. As Habermas puts it: "The only means of countering the factual oppression exercised by the dictatorships of developing nations is a juridification of politics [*Verrechtlichung der Politik*]. The integration problems that every highly complex society has to master can be solved by means of modern law, however, only if *legitimate* law helps to generate that abstract form of civic solidarity that stands and falls with the realization of basic rights."[25]

Then, there is a systems-theoretic perspective on globalization, which I think is represented best by Roland Robertson, Niklas Luhmann,[26] and Martin Albrow,[27] but for brevity's sake I will discuss only the first. Roland Robertson, the theorist who has most consistently contributed to our understanding of globalization, reads globalization as a profound challenge to the basic categories of sociology.[28] For Robertson, globalization results from the diachronic and synchronic interactions within a "global field" that is constituted by four axes, or components: (1) selves, (2) national societies, (3) a world system of societies, and (4) humankind. Synchronically, each one of these components has developed and transformed in relationship with one another. Diachronically, they stand in tension, and codetermination. More concretely, however, we ought to see the development of a global system, that is, a system that is increasingly interdependent and just as aware of this integration, in the following way:[29]

1. The individual self (1) is to be understood as a member of a community and/or nation-state that through its culture of citizenship endows that individual with inalienable rights, but these rights often stand in contrast to and tension with the inalienable rights and conceptions of self in other societies (3); even the individual is to be seen, in the last instance, as a particular instance of humanity as such (4).
2. A national community (2) stands in a particularly contentious relationship to its members (1), who are either seen as rights carriers or as members of a culture and language community. This national community, in turn, sees itself as a member of a community of national communities (3), one that makes claim to such status on the grounds that it provides to its members a status closest to those made by and for humanity on its behalf.
3. A global system of nations (3) is established through the coordination, attenuation, and acknowledgment of sovereignty on the part of individual communities. (Kant's project in *Perpetual Peace* is a perfect example.) This system elaborates, maintains, and legislates a certain set of expectations with respect to the ways in which human are treated as citizens within their respective body politics (1). Here the Nuremberg Trials are a perfect example, as well as the many challenges of nations before the world court. Finally, the ability of a global system of nations to legislate on human rights offers a test of feasibility for many humanitarian projects (3). Robertson calls this a reality check.
4. Humanity, in turn, is defined not just in terms of certain religiophilosophical perspectives but also in terms of concrete rights of persons qua human beings (1). These rights are sometimes granted by nation-states, but they are nevertheless possessed or claimable by all human beings (2). These rights in turn are enforced and are given weight by international arrangements and pressures (3).

These four components of the global field exert a relativizing force upon one another. Thus, selves are relativized with reference to the notion of humanity, and humanity in turn is made relative with respect to specific embodiments of selves. Individuals, as selves, stand in a problematic relationship to the nation-states that either nurtures and enables them or disables them. Similarly, nation-states are relativized when viewed from the perspective of humanity and other nation-states. Robertson has given nice expression to these forces of relativization with a schema in which arrows cross while extending from each corner of a square, whose right angles are made up of each component. Interestingly, Robertson notes, one of the most salient characteristics of this global field is that it both relativizes and further enhances the "identity" of each component. Robertson suggests that globalization is in fact the institutionalization of identity declarations, as much by individuals, nation-states, and world system of nations, as by humanity in general.

This dynamic of relativization and the institutionalization of identity declaration, is further stylized by Robertson in an insightful formulation. Globalization, for Robertson, consists in a twofold process "involving the interpenetration of the universalization of particularism and the particularization of universalism."[30] To this extent, globalization results as much in a quest for universalism as for particularism. Globalization, thus, involves the universalization of particularism, and not just the particularization of universalism.[31] In other words, under globalization, all societies must be both unique and individual, but they must be able to make universal claims about their uniqueness, particularity, and difference. Robertson is quick to note that the West is itself not exempt from this dissolving and integrating force of globalization. The West is just one of the many cultures in the world, one which, like all others, must present itself before the world court of universalism.

In contrast to Barnet, Cavanagh, and Barber, Robertson suggests that globalization is prior to modernity, and further, that the imperatives for globalization are, to a large extent, dictated by cultural or systemic-sociological imperatives and not by economic or political ones.[32] For Robertson, globalization is driven by the logic of social systems, as systems of agency, to which economics and politics are subsidiary. As he summarizes: "Globalization theory turns world-systems theory nearly on its head—by focusing, first, on *cultural* aspects of the world 'system' and, second, by systematic study of *internal* civilizational and societal attributes which shape orientations to the world as a whole and forms of participation of civilizations and societies in the global-human circumstance."[33]

Some of these different takes on globalization, however, have tried to elucidate the links that exist between globalization and history, history and ethics, and ethics and globalization, with varying degrees of success and self-consciousness.[34] If successful, they would have encountered that many of their assumptions, as well as ideals and models, would have been unmasked as eurocentric and ethnocentric. In contrast, Enrique Dussel's most recent work *Ethics of Liberation in the Age of Globalization and Exclusion*[35] is the most comprehensive, thorough, and systematic analysis of the relationship between ethics, globalization, and history. Before I discuss Dussel's magisterial contribution, I would like to briefly flush out the relevance of these conjunctives.

Globalization and History

Under this rubric I gather the question concerning the relationship between globalization and history. Is globalization a result or a catalyst of modernity? Can we subsume globalization into the dialectic of modernization, and to that extent is the latter a product of the spirit of the West alone? Could we in fact view globalization as reflexive modernity, as is suggested by Beck, Lash, and Giddens?[36] And concomitantly, can we then view globalization as a project, modernity's project, but now elevated to a planetary scale? On the other hand, if globalization entails the corrosion of all developmental projects and the agents that heralded them, such as the state and the economy, how then do we do history in a global age? It is not clear what relationship exists between a global age and a global history.[37]

History and Ethics

This dyad, although analyzed extensively, has not been framed appropriately with reference to global history. Ethical perspectives, on the one hand, are always the result of particular histories. An ethos is coagulated history, so to speak. Aristotelians and Hegelians share this view. History, on the other hand, also unleashes processes that challenge established ethicities (*Sittlichkeiten*), and insofar as histories are projects, certain ethical perspectives become the result of certain epochal shifts. We can see Protestantism, and its resultant ethos of privatization and individualism, in this light. This brings up the question, To what extent, for instance, can we speak of a new planetary ethical consciousness that surpasses the reaches of local and culturally based ethical perspectives? It must be acknowledged that this question has been at the center of Apel's[38] and Habermas's work.[39] Yet their views on a postconventional moral consciousness are too rooted in a particular view of socialization processes that seem to be endemic and unique to the West. If we take globalization to entail the relativization of other cultures as well as of the West itself, then we cannot work on the assumption that a global moral perspective can be forthcoming only from a globalization of Western formalism and neo-Kantianism. In short, we must ask what global history stands behind what new global ethos, and whether we can speak of a global ethos that challenges as well as actualizes what was inchoate in up to now relatively inward-looking ethicities.

Ethics and Globalization

Globalization, as Jameson has suggested, ought to be taken as a philosophical problem. Robertson, as was noted already, has suggested that globalization ought also to be taken as a major challenge to the basic categories of social analysis. Globalization should also be taken as an ethical problem. For globalization at the very least has meant the growing gap between rich and poor, developed and underdeveloped, linked up and unconnected to the flows of information, money, and power that as a storm elevates some to heights of obscene wealth while plunging others into abysmal levels of subhuman existence. Globalization, similarly, has also meant the relativization of cultures and their views about what human agents can and ought to do. If we begin with the simplistic realization that an ethical perspective consists of the coordination of the concepts of ethical agent, a criteria for the discernment of the validity of ethical judgments, and the guiding light provided by cultural goods that acts as moral compass, then we must ask what ethical systems are allowed by a global age in which agents, judgments and cultural goods have been destabilized, rendered fluid and suspect, and in which the reach of individuals and even communities is thwarted by global processes that even if locally unleashed have unforeseen planetary consequences. At the very minimum we must begin with the realization that globalization commands that we visualize new categories of ethical analysis.

The World Sytem of Inclusion Through Exclusion: Enrique Dussel's Critique of Globalization

It is my contention that Dussel's work addresses these challenges. His *Ethics of Liberation in an Age of Globalization and Exclusion* is a contribution of paramount importance because it explicitly and in an unprecedented fashion links up these dyads: globalization and history, history and ethics, and ethics and globalization. I will present his work as being guided by these dyads.

Globalization and History

Above all, Dussel seeks to dislodge the ethnocentric and eurocentric views that inform most of contemporary philosophy. He does this first by demonstrating that modernity must be read as the result not of an autochthonous dynamic of European culture, but rather, as the result of the management of a world system by the West. In order to demonstrate this thesis, Dussel periodizes world history into four stages of the "inter-regional system" (see schema 1).[40]

The thrust of Dussel's argument is that the West assumes a hegemonic position only vis-à-vis other cultures through becoming the center of a world system that is inaugurated with the discovery of the New World. In contrast to the standard chronologies and meta historical philosophical justifications for the success of the "miracle of the West," or the "rise of the West" (so much celebrated since Hegel, but which still informs Marx, Weber, Parsons, Habermas, and many recent world historians), Dussel argues that the "triumph" of the West can be understood appropriately only when we take

Schema 1: Schematic Representation of the Four Stages of the Interregional System Which Begins to Unfold as a World System after 1492

Stage	Diachronic Name of the Interregional System	Poles around a Center
I	Egyptian-Mesopotamian (since the fourth millennium BC): ∍ 0.1	Without center: Egypt & Mesopotamia
II	Indo-European (since 200 years BC): ∍ 0.1	Center: Persian Region, Hellenic World (seleucidic and ptolomaic) since the fourth century bc Eastern extreme: China Southeastern: Indian Kingdoms Western: Mediterranean New World
III	Asiatic-Afro-Mediterranean (since the fourth century AD): ∍ 0.4	Center of Commercial connections: Persian Region and the Turín and Tarim, later the Muslim World (since the seventh century AD) Productive center: China Southwestern: Bantú Africa Western: Byzantine- Russian World Extreme West: Western Europe
IV	World System (after 1492 AD): ∍ 0.5–0.6	Center: Western Europe (today U.S. and Japan, from 1945 to 1989 with Russia) Periphery: Latin America, Bantú Africa, Muslim World, India, Southwestern Asia, Eastern Europe. Semi autonomous: China and Russia (since 1989)

into consideration the management of the world system that allows the West to obtain a differential advantage over the East and over Africa. In Dussel's view, the willfully myopic conceptualization and chronology that informs most contemporary eurocentric philosophy has resulted in part from a series of conflations: *First*: from conflating the *formulation of the "new theorical paradigm"* (modernity) with its *historical origin*, as well as with the crisis and eventual demise of the *medieval* paradigm.[41] *Second*: from conflating European ontogenesis, so to speak, with world phylogenesis, in such a way that a *mirroring* (*espejismo*) effect takes place in which what were effects of a positioning within a world system are taken to be intrinsic advantages that belong to the very spirit of the West.[42] Most importantly, however, by reframing the question of modernity in terms of Europe's centrality within a world system, Dussel is able to talk about the "underside" of this purportedly "civilizing" project. Modernity emerges from Dussel's reframing of it as a project that entails a "sacrificial logic," one in which the perpetrator of the sacrifice is exculpated and left blameless for the demise and onslaught that it unleashes upon a world and its cultures, which are to be managed, civilized, bureaucratized, and secularized. Modernity, whether incomplete or already exhausted, cannot be understood comprehensively unless we give voice to the victims of this project.[43]

History and Ethics

In a fashion analogous to Hegel and Taylor, Dussel views ethical systems through the lens of history. Yet, he is also related to Habermas and Apel in that he views ethics not just as the actualization of a form of life, but also as the unfolding of formal aspects of moral thinking that, in coordination with ethical and cultural goods, lead ethicities to higher levels of abstraction, formalization, and universalization. His work, thus, is interested in demonstrating how the ethical material and moral formal levels of ethical consciousness are historically conditioned. Thus, he discerns in the first stage of the interregional system the dawning of an ethical consciousness that departs from the recognition of the material, corporeal individuality of the ethical agent. In the Egyptian Book of the Dead and in the Hammurabi Code, to mention just a few documents from the first interregional system we find enshrined, according to Dussel, the respect and reverence for the dignified unity of the ethical-corporeal subject. This subject is addressed in his/her individuality, in his/her suffering and vulnerable corporeality.

During the second stage of the interregional system, which is marked by the rise of the iron and bronze military empires, Dussel discerns the rise of metaphysical and anthropological dualism. For this dualism, matter, the body, living corporeality is a blemish, a fault, a prison, a hindrance. The poles of this ethical orientation are the rejection of corporeal life and the quest after the One. Thus, in Dussel's view, from Greece and Rome to the Persians and the kingdoms of India and Taoist China, a metaphysics of the absolute as One, and a dualist anthropology inaugurated an ascetic ethics. This ethics of the negation and overcoming of corporeal materiality meant the superseding of material plurality as a return—a *Heilweg*—to the originary unity of the fountainhead (Plotinus being the epitome of this voyage toward the divine).

In the third stage of the interregional system, the ethical perspective of the Egyptian-Mesopotamian stage of the interregional system reasserts itself. Partly through Christianity and Islam, an ethics of the suffering ethical-corporeal subject is proclaimed. Buddhism, Islam, and Christianity are reformation movements formulated in light of the empires that dominated antiquity.

With the fourth stage of the interregional system, we return to the ethicities of the second interregional system, during which the great empires of antiquity rose and brought about the unification of the Eurasian and African continental masses. The difference is that for the first time we have a world system in which the relatively autonomous regions of the world are subsumed into a system in which there is a center and a periphery. The center acts as manager and metropolis; the periphery as backwater and colonial outpost. In analogy to the second stage of the interregional system, anthropological dualism is reaffirmed, and the subject is conceptualized as a disembodied epistemic subjectivity. The ethical subject is reduced to an appendage of the epistemic subject.[44]

Ethics and Globalization

Perhaps like no other living philosopher, with the possible exception of Karl-Otto Apel, Enrique Dussel has been insisting since the early sixties on an ethical consideration and analysis of both modernity and globalization. For Dussel the processes of global integration, at first understood by him through the prism of underdevelopment theory, represents not just historical, or socioeconomic challenges, challenges which could be met by the conceptual tools that would refashion the edifice of social science. For him, modernity/globalization represents an ethical challenge of the first order. What secularization, urbanization, industrialization, and colonialism meant as ethical challenges for European philosophers during the past five hundred years of the world system, globalization means for Dussel. It is a point of departure for all ethical speculation. For Dussel, globalization profiles itself as an ethical problem in two senses, or under two registers. *First*, we cannot, and must not, circumvent, turn away from, minimize, or simply neglect the *brutal fact* that three-quarters of humanity lives in massive poverty. In absolute numbers, people today are poorer and more likely to become victims of famine, draught, and interregional or global conflicts.[45] In absolute numbers, developing nations are less likely to jumpstart their economies into the kind of development that would allow them to meet even the most minimal standards of dignified human living. Children and women, moreover, are the general victims of this spiraling into the abyss of subhuman levels of existence.[46] Ecologically, culturally, economically, and politically, the third world, fast becoming a fourth world (to use Samir Amin's term),[47] is succumbing to the logic of finance capitalism, a logic of chaos, disorder, and economic Russian roulette (although Cornel West's term "gangsterization" just as appropriately describes the present world economy.[48]) For Dussel, globalization spells the material, discursive, cultural, and philosophical exclusion of most of the world's peoples (most located south of the equator), just as a rhetoric of inclusion and interconnectivity announces their purported participation and coresponsibility for a globalized planet. Globalization, in short, means for Dussel what Hans-Peter Martin and Harald Schumman have called the "20:80 society," where only 20 percent of the world will suffice to produce all that is needed, and the remaining 80 percent will be entirely superfluous, supplemental, a burden, a perpetual lumpen proletariat. To this it should be added that of this 20 percent, only the top 5 percent will enjoy the riches produced by world society.[49]

The *second* sense in which globalization is an ethical challenge for Dussel concerns the development of appropriate ethical categories that will ground an ethics for the age of globalization and exclusion. At the core of Dussel's *Ética de la Liberación en la edad de globalización y de la exclusión* lies precisely the resolution to this challenge. In light of the threat to life (understood by Dussel in its plethora of manifestations, i.e., culture, thought, ecosystems) that globalization entails, all contemporary ethics must begin with an affirmation of life. Ethics, in Dussel's view, thus departs from recognition of the materiality of human agents, who are always first and foremost members of a community of life. Second, life in its human plurality, one which is recognized with greater appreciation due to a global awareness, requires an arbitration, negotiation, and discernment between different and competing moral goods projected by different and competing forms of life (the historical encounter between civilizations or cultures, each of which is generally informed by a mythicoethical core). Finally, the ethical, as what must be done in light of the preservation and nurturing of human life, must concern itself with what is feasible, what is materially and logically possible. These fundamental points of departure are summarized and expressed as principles for a foundational ethics: the material principle (practical truth) that enjoins to respect and preserve life; the discursive principle of formal validity (formal morality); and the principle of feasibility (strategic instrumental rationality). In this way, Dussel offers a middle path between Aristotelian-Hegelian historicist communitarianism and Kantian-Rawlsian idealist transcendentalist proceduralist universalism. These three principles concern foundational ethics. They in turn are, and must be, complemented by the principles that inform a critical ethics.

A critical ethics is an ethics that departs from not only the affirmation of life but life already under threat, life denied. Ethics thus must contain two necessary aspects: the negative (abstract and universal) and the positive (concrete and particular). It is the latter that critical ethics elaborates. Paralleling, but now articulating in a positive way, the principles of a critical ethics are enunciated thus: every system, practice, and norm that makes the life of any or all humans impossible must be criticized. Thus, every system that produces victims must be submitted to ethical censure. The *locus criticus* of ethics is thus the victim. This is the critical material principle. Inasmuch as all systems are blind to their victims (they are not recognized as victims, and much less as victims of their own logic), the imperative to include in all of their deliberations all possible affected individuals by the decisions they make, demands that all systems criticize their practices of inclusion and/or exclusion. When the victims of any system, practice, or norm recognize their victimization, the system is under compulsion to give privileged attention to their critique of the system, lest the principle of abstract validity be broached (that is, a system turns dogmatic and cynical). To this extent, the critical principle of abstract formalization and justification turns into the principle of the hermeneutical-ethical privilege of the victim. Finally, from every critique that arises from the recognition of the ways in which any given system makes life impossible, and from the imperative to submit every system's practices to validation and justification by all, must inescapably result the commandment to liberate the victims of the system from the conditions that oppress them, that make their life an impossibility. This last is the liberation principle that gives positive form to what was merely affirmed formally and negatively in the abstract and general principles of foundational ethics. In Dussel's view, then, the appropriate and necessary ethics for an age of globalization and exclusion must begin with the affirmation of life and must include a recognition of the plurality of ethical goods that must be submitted to a universalization test (whether these goods could be universalized by a community of discourse under conditions in which these discourses would not be vitiated by systematic exclusion), while at the same time recognizing what is both materially possible and feasible. But since every social system, practice, and norm is by definition imperfect, all ethical reflection must at the same time seek out the victims of the system, and the ways in which they enunciate a critique of the system, while also seeking to liberate these victims from their situation of negativity, privation, and lack.

7

Politics in an Age of Planetarization

Enrique Dussel's Critique of Political Reason

> "Solamente el que puede desear la libertad, la liberación del Otro que es el pobre, desde él y no desde la totalidad, es quien realmente puede instaurar una política de justicia."
>
> —Enrique Dussel, *Introducción a la filosofía de la liberación*

Introduction

The canon of political thought is not exempt from the identity crises that besiege all other similar practices of giving shape and continuity to a cultural identity. This means that like the religious, literary, legal, and philosophical canons that identify a culture, the political canon is at the mercy of the forces that shape history, while also contributing to the thrust of that history. This also means that canons serve as a register for the struggles that have catalyzed social transformations and, as such, they also serve as large compendia of social memory. It is for this reason that they are the focus of so much attention and the locus of much contestation.

Very much like during the times of the Magna Carta, the American Declaration of Independence, the French Revolution, the Russian Revolution, the Defeat of the Axis powers in 1945, and the fall of the Berlin Wall, in these years of the dawning of a new century, we also face a series of unprecedented political challenges that require innovative and forward-looking political thought, but also a rethinking of the key figures and concepts in our political canon. Globalization has become the shibboleth that points in the direction of these challenges. Unfortunately, at the same time, this term has become an excuse to glide over the immensity of the challenges and has, thus, in turn become a crystallization of ideology. It is

---

This chapter first appeared in David Ingram, ed., *The Political: Blackwell Readings in Continental Philosophy* (Cambridge: Blackwell, 2002), 280–97.

for this reason that many thinkers have reacted viscerally to the term dismissing it as useless, as a mere gimmick. These thinkers see this terms as the latest version of colonization, neocolonization, modernization, and the expansion of Western financial markets. Others have attempted to circumvent its co-opting by reinscribing it within a different etymology, like mundalization or planetarization.

There is a third group of thinkers that have neither dismissed it nor attempted to refunction the term in a different grammar. This group, instead, can be said to have been thinking about the processes, forces, institutions, concepts, and challenges associated with globalization for at least the last three decades. This group has been thinking about this phenomenon we call globalization, although naming it differently, and thinking it from and through different categories. In fact, this has been one of their main contributions, namely, to call for a rethinking of the fundamental concepts of political and social thought. This group, for instance, has been talking about the obsolescence of the classical nation-state; the planetary reach of the ecological crisis, which is just a general name for the demographic explosion of humanity and the concomitant problems this exponential growth means for the ecosystems on which all forms of life on our planet depend (erosion, deforestation, drying up of fresh-water sources, dioversity depletion, along with the introduction of genetically altered foods, more damaging herbicides, and the proliferation of luxury crops to feed the wealthy industrialized nations of the North); the need for a planetary ethic that supersedes the stalemate of Aristotelian communitarianisms and Kantian universalism; the need for supranational mechanisms to legislate, arbitrate, and enforce global laws and human rights. Although some of these thinkers do not share the same political allegiances and beliefs, they can all be considered as members of this third group because of the consistency and acuity with which they have thought the thoroughness and immensity of the challenges globalization entails for humanity. Among them we might list Karl-Otto Apel, Niklas Luhmann, Anthony Giddens, Immanuel Wallerstein, Benjamin Barber, Ulrich Beck, Daniel Bell, Zygmut Bauman, Jürgen Habermas, Vandana Shiva, and Enrique Dussel. It is against this background and in this company that Enrique Dussel's thought must be introduced and considered.

Enrique Dussel is unquestionably one of the most important Latin American philosophers of the last half a century. As one of the founders of the history of the Latin American church, a prolific historian of religious ideas, and a philosopher of religion, he is well known to theologians in general and Latin Americanists in particular. He is perhaps less well known by philosophers, although his extensive *oeuvre* is beginning to receive the attention it deserves. His contributions to political theory are certainly scarcely known by political theorists and philosophers. Such unfamiliarity is understandable, since most of Dussel's work on political philosophy and theory has not been translated, and, as with most systematic thinkers, his observations on the political are nested within an expansive philosophical system that encompases ethics, history, theoretical philosophy, and so on. I will begin, therefore, by giving a general overview of his thought and its evolution. In the last section, I will focus on the contribution to this volume and what it means for political thought in an age of planetarization.

Thinking from and about the "Third World"

Enrique Dussel was born in Argentina in 1934. After receiving his BA in philosophy, he traveled to Europe, where he proceeded to receive advanced degrees in philosophy, history, and theology. He studied in France and Germany, and lived in Israel for a year, earning his living as a day laborer. He has lived in Mexico since 1975, when he arrived there as an exile from Argentina. An intellectual itinerary that spans half a century, several continents, and many national crises (or as he puts it, the crises of the small—Argentina—and large—Latin America—fatherlands), as well as global crises cannot but have undergone several and severe transformations. Dussel's thought has transversed at least six stages, all of them determined by biographical factors: studies, travel abroad, return to the homeland, the discovery of Latin American political reality and the challenges to philosophy, exile, and so on.[1] For the purposes of our analysis and presentation, however, I would suggest that there are three significant intellectual stages or periods in Enrique Dussel's thought. Each stage was characterized by a quest or philosophical project. In this sense, Dussel's work has been marked with a conceptual and philosophical restlessness, albeit tempered by an ethical pertinacity.

The first stage is circumscribed by the trajectory from ontology to metaphysics. This stage covers the earliest years of Dussel's philosophical production, the decade of the sixties. Dussel was trained in Europe, mostly France and Germany. There he came under the influence of Ricoeur and Heidegger. Dussel's early work therefore was deeply influenced by hermeneutics and phenomenology. He related to them less as traditions and more as forms of philosophical analysis which he proceeded to deploy in discovering and forging a Latin American philosophical project.[2] From Heidegger, Dussel derived the idea that all worldviews are manifestations of existential attitudes. In other words, ideas are not absolute and abstract categories but, rather, they are coagulations of existential experience. Existence entails certain preunderstandings. We cannot comprehend the world without already having some preexperience of it. Conversely, certain forms of existence, or forms of social relations to put it in the language of sociology, entail certain conceptual schemas, or ways of making sense of the world. Our way of being with others and in relationship to the world result in particular ways of viewing those persons and things to which we are in relation.

Concepts and worldview are extensions of a web of existential relations. Another way of putting it would be to say that mind and world, ideas and things, consciousness and its other, are not ontologically different, but are part of a continuum.

From Ricoeur, Dussel learned that this continuum is always a circle of meaning: interpreted meaning and interpreting meaning. Everything is a crystallization of acts of interpretation. If we approach culture oriented by these intuitions, then culture is to be treated like a geological sediment, accumulations of layers of meaning. With these two methods in hand, Dussel set out to discover and recover the symbolics of Latin American culture that would yield to his investigations the layers of meaning accumulated by centuries of a unique Latin American existential experience. Ontology, however, is totalizing, as is already intimated by the correspondences established by Heidegger's ontology: mind and world, consciousness and its other, I and Thou. In this ontological circle, the other of both myself and my consciousness (or self-consciousness) can only be but a shadow of the already same. The other is prefigured in the same, the I, the self-enclosed hermeneutical world. There is no other, merely a refracted version of what an ontological horizon contains within itself.

In the late sixties and the seventies, challenged by the pedagogical inappropriateness of the methods he had learned in Europe, and urged on by the revolutionary fervor in Latin America and by the rise of populism in Argentina in particular, Dussel came to realize that existentially, hermeneutically, and culturally, Latin America occupied a place in world history that could not be assimilated into the European models of development, or even explanation. Biographically, the context was of political and cultural turmoil and ferment, as was the case for most world thinkers around the momentous years of the late sixties and early seventies. Philosophically, as Dussel undertook a massive philosophical work of ethics, *Towards an Ethics of Latin American Liberation*,[3] he discovered the work of the great Jewish thinker Emmanuel Levinas—in particular, *Totality and Infinity*.[4] This work produced in Dussel a "subversive disorientation" that challenge all of his preunderstandings, in particular his Heideggerianism.[5] The discovery of Levinas allowed Dussel to develop his own unique philosophical methodology, one he considered more appropriate to the task of the recovery of a Latin American symbolics and hermeneutics. This method he calls the "analectical method," sometimes he also calls it "anadialectical method."[6] Analectics, which comes from the Greek root *ano* (beyond), takes as its point of departure the unmitigated transcendence of the other. The other is never the mere shadow, faulty, incomplete image or realization of the same, the I, the one. The other is beyond the horizon of what is already experienced and comprehended. The method of the self-mirroring and self-projection of the same is dialectics, and it is this method that has ruled all of Western philosophy at least since the pre-Socratics (Parmenides and Heraclitus). But dialectics is war, the war of the same and the I to affirm itself in and through the other, and to wrest from the other what makes the other inassimilable alterity. The horizon of comprehension and existence of the I is a totality. Dialectics is the production of the totality. The other is an exteriority that is irreducible to the totality of the selfsame. As long as we subscribe to an ontological approach, the otherness of the other will remain inscrutable alterity. To open ourselves to the other requires that we destroy ontology and in its place institute a metaphysical approach, one that sets out from the fundamental principle that the truth of the world is never exhausted by the given. To put it formulaically, ontology is to dialectics as metaphysics is to analectics. The former is mobilized by exclusion and war, the later by expectant openness and solidarity.

In Dussel's works from the seventies, then, Western thought is seen as the succession of dialectically produced and maintained totalities, whose very constitution and preservation has been predicated on the exclusion of an abject alterity: a vilified, despised, exploited, annihilated other. Thus, the totality of the polis was predicated on the exclusion of women, slaves, and barbarians (those who did not speak Greek); the totality of Christendom was predicated on the exclusion of women, the infidel, the atheist, the heterodox; the totality of Modern Europe was predicated on the exclusion of the other of civilization and culture, namely the Amerindian, the African, and Asian cultures. Every hermeneutical and existential, or *ontologological* (epitomized in Hegel, the high priest of self-referential totalities) totality is totalitarian, belligerent, and martial. And as long as we approach them dialectically, we will remain within the domain of their domination. To break free from their coercion and subjugation, we must open ourselves to the other from the standpoint of the other. We must think, hear, see, feel, and taste the world from the standpoint of the other. This is the analectical moment. Thus, if dialectics is conditioned by magnanimity, analectics is conditioned by humility; if the one is conditioned by erotic love, the other by compassionate solidarity; if one is conditioned by quid pro quos, the other is conditioned by expectant solicitude; if one is about production and profit the other is about service and gift. We approach the other in a reverent attitude, disposed to service and to empathic solidarity. The alternative is war, dispossession, occlusion, exclusion, and genocide. A philosophy that tries to think this alternative, from the standpoint of the alterity of the other, is a philosophy of liberation and not just simply a radical hermeneutics or phenomenology. Philosophy at the service of liberation, and produced by the experience of liberation, of and about. It is this philosophy that Dussel has been working on since the late sixties and early seventies.[7]

Politics, looked at from a metaphysical point of view and dealt with from the analectical methods, yields the insight that there is a politics of the totality and a politics of the other. The former is the politics of the status quo, of the established and ruling totality. This is a politics of fetishization and divinification, of enthronement and intolerant homogenization. In fact, ontological politics turns into the science of the smooth functioning of the machine of power that assimilates otherness to the selfsame and excludes the indissoluble alterity of the other. Politics becomes the craft of the production and concentration of power with the telos of the control of the other within and outside the totality.

A political totality divides into the master and its oppressed, as oppressed within that particular system, and the other of the totality, as political alterity. Every totality has its internal and exterior others. The politics of the other, then, is an antipolitics, it is a politics of delegitimation, of subversion and contestation. It is a politics that challenges the established hierarchies and legal verities that justify and legitimized enforced exclusions. The politics of the other, the antipolitics of alterity, proclaims the injustice and illegitimacy of the present system, not in the name of chaos or lawlessness but in the name of a new legality, a new lawfulness, one which will be generalized, more universalized, where these two terms refer to the point of view of the abjected and excluded other. In Dussel's view, then, metaphysical politics, the politics of the other, the antipolitics of alterity, is energized and made dynamic by the struggles of the excluded, exploited, and disenfranchised. Its determining virtues are neither equality nor justice, but respect and solidarity. At the core of the politics of antipolitics is the fundamental insight that all power struggles are predicated on asymmetries, and what mobilizes us to shift the scales is not justice, which remains within the outlook of the totality that grants to similars the same, but respect and solidarity for him/her or it, whose interpellation remains incomprehensible lest we opt for utter gratuitous solidarity with they who clamor. The suffering of the other raises as a cry. This turns into an interpellation that challenges the verities and principles of the extant legal and political system. The more reticent a system is to the interpellation of its others, the more totalitarian, belligerent, and intolerant it turns. The intolerant homogenizing totalitarian totality is the ontological version of the annihilating terrorist state of the concentration camp, what Eugene Kogon called the *SS-Staat*.[8] This dual view of politics will remain a constant in Dussel's thought.

The second stage in Dussel's philosophical itinerary is circumscribed by the trajectory from metaphysics to Marxism.[9] This stage overlaps partially with Dussel's exile in Mexico, which begins in 1975. Philosophically, Dussel is confronted with the challenge of the increasing importance of a historically specific analysis of the systematic exclusion not just of a group within a nation (class and pueblo, for instance), but of even an entire continent within a world totality, more specifically Western culture.[10] Evidently, such a historically specific analysis took Dussel to a critique of capitalism, which at that time was seen as the only cause of the increasing impoverishment of the Latin American people. This critique could be executed only with the tools of Marxism. At the same time, however, this Marxism had to be wrested away from the entrenched and already solidified dogmatism of the Eastern Block nations.

Notwithstanding the shift from ontology to metaphysics we described above, Dussel had continued to read Marx as another functionary of the totality. As a child and follower of Hegel, Marx was a thinker of the totality and an executor of dialectics. During the middle seventies, Dussel began to revise his reading of Marx, but already skeptical of Western and in particular European philosophical readings, he realized that traditional approaches are insufficient for the task of the appropriation of Marx in a Latin American context. In fact, he realized that he must read Marx himself, and this meant reading the manuscripts that were being made available, too slowly for Dussel's interest and agenda, as the complete work of Marx and Engels were being published by the Marx-Lenin Institutes in Berlin and Moscow. Dussel immersed himself in a reading of the four redactions of *Capital*, as well as other manuscripts produced by Marx toward the end of his life. Out of this archival work, there emerged a three-volume commentary and analysis of the process and evolution of Marx's categories.[11]

Dussel's reading of Marx distinguishes itself by at least four unique aspects: *First*, Dussel's reading of Marx is based on an unparalleled and unprecedented knowledge of the trajectory of Marx's own intellectual development. Dussel not only read the recently published works, but also the preparatory notes, and different drafts Marx worked on as he began to elaborate his *Capital*, of which he saw through print only volume one.

Second, insofar as Dussel has studied, exegeted, and reconstructed for us an immense unknown corpus of theoretical productivity, he not only discovered a Marx that was relevant to the project of Latin American liberation, he also discovered a hitherto unknown Marx that made it indispensable to begin a critical assessment of Marx's reception in the twentieth century. To this extent, Dussel might have discovered a Marx for the twenty-first century.

Third, Dussel's careful reconstruction of the emergence of certain key categories in the *Grundrisse* and *Kapital* led Dussel to conclude that Marx in fact was not just a left Hegelian, but even a Schellingian. What this means is that in Dussel's reconstruction the fundamental method of Marx was not dialectics but what he called "analectics." Dussel thinks that the core philosophical and methodological insight in Marx's work is that the fountain of value—that which is appropriate as surplus value and which gives the commodity its ability to generate value that is accumulated in capital—is living labor (*lebendige Arbeit*). The capitalist system does not produce value. Value is extracted and appropriated from the living corporeality of the laborer. A commodity, then, is a coagulation, a crystallization, of living labor. In Dussel's view, such an analysis of the processes of commodity production and the accumulation of surplus value into capital correspond more to a late Schellingian metaphysical perspective than to a Hegelian dialectical perspective. For the late Schelling, specifically the one of the *Philosophie der*

Offerbarung [*Philosophy of Revelation*] of 1841/1842, the ground of the world is the mystery of God's wholly otherness. What is, is revelation of the mystery of God. In terms of philosophy, Being is posterior to the non-Being of the wholly other. Or, to put it in the terms of German idealism, the identity of the identical and the nonidentical is replaced in Schelling by the nonidentity of the identical and the nonidentical. There is always a surplus beyond the identical. The other is always the epiphany of an unsupersedeable alterity. In Dussel's view, this reverence and acknowledgment of the life of the other, as the living labor of the worker, is what makes Marx's method not Hegelian but Schellingian and, one may add, Levinasian. The Marx Dussel discovered is what we would call today, of course anachronistically but entirely suggestively and appropriately, a Levinasian Marx.

Fourth, and consequently, Dussel's Marx is not one who is correctly read through the Althusserian distinction between the young and the late Marx; where the former is a humanist and dialectical Marx, while the latter is a scientific and materialist Marx. Nor is Marx correctly understood when we try to dissociate him from Engels's dialectical materialism and appropriately associate him with historical materialism. Instead, and here Dussel enunciates a challenge for the twenty-first-century Marxists, Marx is to be read metaphysically, humanistically, and as a critic of Hegelian, Aristotelian, and Platonist totalities. Dussel thus calls us to dispense with the distorting reading of Marx executed by Western Marxism, as well as *diamat* (Soviet sanctioned and dogmatically thought in the socialist block dialectical materialism). In Dussel's view, the really humanist Marx is he whom we encounter in *Capital*, where we are confronted not with a science of economics but a critique of the political economy that produces the system for the expropriation of life of the laborer. *Capital* is less a scientific treatise and more an ethics. A nice parallel would be to say that *Capital* is not like Hegel's *Logic* but more like Levinas's *Totality and Infinity*, which at root is a fundamental ethics, a metaethics. The first philosophy, *prima philosophia*, of all philosophical speculation, in Levinas's view (and here Dussel concurs unequivocally), is ethics. In this sense, for Dussel, *Capital* is a *prima philosophia* that describes an ethics. In summary, Dussel discovers an ethical Marx that has been betrayed and eclipsed by decades of the ontologizing and Hegelinizing of his fundamental option for the creativity of the living corporeality of the worker.

The metaphysically criticized totalities of the first stage of Dussel's thought, turned into the Marxistically unmasked systems of exploitation. History is not just a succession of ontological totalities, it is also a succession of systems of the exploitation, expropriation, and extraction of value from the living labor of workers. This exploitation and expropriation has taken place at regional, national, and continental levels. It is in this way that totality and transcendentality (the alterity of the other) are translated in Dussel's Schellingian Marx into the categories of center and periphery. Of course, such a reinscription takes place against the background of the concepts developed by dependency and underdevelopment theory.[12] In the seventies and early eighties, the central question for Dussel became the *development of underdevelopment* on a global level. During this period, Dussel analysis of politics turns more economicist, in the sense that his books and essays are now suffused by careful studies of the flow of capital (i.e., accumulated value) from one continent to another (from Latin America to Europe, and from Latin America to the United States). From this perspective, then, the analysis of politics turns into the critique not just of political totalities but, most specifically, into the critique of the political economies of imperial systems of the transfer of life coagulated into commodities from a sphere or region of production to a region or sphere of consumption. Here, Dussel's critique of the imperial political economy of world systems converges with those critiques developed by Immanuel Wallerstein and Samir Amin.[13] During this second stage, Dussel adds to his analysis of antipolitical politics, the planetary and global perspective he assimilated from a Marxism read and discovered from a third-world perspective. In Dussel's view, whoever would like to speak of poverty and destitution, topics that are uncircumventable in the age of mass culture, world wars, and continental famines, must speak of global capitalism, imperialisms, and world accumulation of wealth for a minority and impoverishing expropriation of a majority. A nationalistic approach, an approach that only looks at regions within continents, and one that focuses only on the capitalist accumulation of certain "industrialized" Western nations contributes only to the distortion of the global nature of the capitalist system of production and accumulation of wealth. In short, during his second stage, the critique of Western philosophy as ontology has turned into a critique of the political and economic theories that misconstrued and contributed to the occlusion of the system of massive and global inequity.

The third stage of Dussel's philosophical development is traced by the trajectory from Marxism to discourse. Biographically, this stage overlaps, more or less, with the fall of the Berlin Wall, the voting out of office of the Sandinistas in 1990, and the splitting apart of the Soviet Union. This stage could be said to begin in 1989, when Enrique Dussel began a decade-long debate with Karl-Otto Apel, the founding father of discourse ethics.[14] Like the first stage was summarized in his five-volume *Latin American Philosophical Ethics*,[15] and the second in his three-volume reconstruction and commentary on Marx's redactions of *Capital*,[16] this third stage is summarized in the monumental *Ética de la Liberación en la edad de globalización y de la exclusión* [*Ethics of Liberation in the Age of Globalization and Exclusion*], from 1998.[17] In this work, Dussel sets out to reformulate the foundations of a planetary ethics of liberation of the oppressed and excluded, but now combining his particular brand of Levinasian and Ricoeurian phenomenology and hermeneutics with Apelian and Habermasian discourse ethics.[18] Much of the preliminary work for the *Ethics of*

Liberation, fortunately, has appeared in English under the title of *The Underside of Modernity: Apel, Ricoeur, Rorty, Taylor and the Philosophy of Liberation.*[19] In this collection of essays, as well as in the ethics of 1998, Dussel confronts the challenges of the linguistic turn and, in particular, the challenge of how to ground universalist ethics in the face of the dismantling and critique of monological and logocentric philosophy of consciousness. While Dussel proceeds to offer a third way between abstract and universalist (but now dialogically reconstituted) Kantianism and particularist and historicist Hegelianism, with already dialogically constituted agents, in debate with Rorty, Taylor, Ricoeur, and Vattimo, it is clear that the central dialogue partners are Apel and Habermas.[20]

At the center of the debates, summarily put, are three questions: *first*, whether the community of communication (*kommunikationsgemeinschaft*), which acts as the a priori condition of possibility of all discourse (or that acts as a counterfactual idealization that is both precondition and telos of all communication, in Habermas's less strict formulation) is either prior or posterior to a community of life (*comunidad de vida*). In Dussel's terms, before discourse there must be life (*bios*), in the sense that people must at the very least have secured the conditions for their survival and preservation. If these conditions are not met, then discourse, as conceived by both Apel and Habermas, becomes either an empty idealization, at best, or a way to conceal the factual lack of the conditions for true discourse (in which the only coercion is the noncoercion of the better argument and in which the primary goal is agreement and not deception or determination by fiat), at worst. *Second*, whether we can dichotomize in practice what both Apel and Habermas had distinguished as discourses of justification (or grounding) and discourses of application. Discourses of justification attend to the theoretical dimension of ethical questions; namely whether we can offer rational and universal warrants that are not vitiated by their historical and local contexts of discovery. Discourses of application attend to the circumstantial, historicized, contextual, and very singular application of principles. Dussel thinks that this disjunction contributes to the misrepresentation of the very practical character of ethical questions; that is, that ethical questions emerge from very specific context and that universal principles are generalizations of concrete problems. More concretely, Dussel thinks the generalized principles of an ethics already anticipate their contexts of application, and vice versa—specific context of moral consideration becomes visible as such precisely because of a certain ethical outlook. A *third* bone of contention is the degree to which any ethics should refer its affirmations to neurobiology, or, philosophically articulated, to the fact that ethical entities are biological organisms: with needs, desires, and a neurological system that filters the world and processes it into ideas and perceptions. As Kantians, neither Apel nor Habermas are prepared to accept the empirical evidence or insights offered by neurobiology in their moral philosophies, despite Habermas's call for a deflationary philosophy that works in close cooperation with the fallible sciences.[21] Dussel, instead, thinks that such extreme Kantianism leads to the erasure of the body or sentient corporeality. Most importantly, such intellectual rigorism and asceticism leads to the foreshortening of the ethical outlook. In other words, the exclusion of the body, as orienting being-in-the-world corporeality, leads to the misrepresentation of not just the source of ethics but also its goals.

A brief discussion of the *Ethics of Liberation* of 1998 will make it clear how Dussel has substantively replaced the philosophical infrastructure of his ethics, while retaining its fundamental concern and motivating telos: the oppression, exclusion, and genocide of the poor, destitute, suffering, vulnerable living corporeality of the victim. After a lengthy introduction, which is a monograph on its own, that traces the history of world ethical systems, the book is divided into two major sections. The first deals with what Dussel calls "foundational ethics." The second deals with critical ethics. Each part is divided into three chapters, each dealing with a major foundational aspect of ethics: the material moment, the formal moment, and the feasibility moment of ethics. The first chapter of the first part deals with the material or "content" moment of ethics. For Dussel, ethical questions have to do with our being in the world, not just in the Heideggerian sense of being interpreting entities whose world is always already interpreted, but also in the sense that we are in the world by virtue of our needs and desires. All ethics deals with specific choices and the principles that guided them, and these choices are "about" things and persons in the world. The second chapter of the first part deals with formal moralities, that is, with the question, or demand for, intersubjective validity. Validity remits us to the legitimation and application of the material principle. The next chapter deals with what Dussel calls "the good" (*das Gute*), or what he also calls "ethical feasibility." From these considerations, three principles emerge: the practical principle of the preservation of life, the formal principle of the discursive legitimation of norms and principles, and the goodness or feasibility principle.

The second part of the *Ética de la liberación* develops the critical principles of his ethics of liberation in a negative vein; that is, if the foundational ethics discussed in the first part concerns the positive formulation of the principles that guide ethical action, critical ethics concerns the formulation of the critical principles that guide all ethical critique. Thus, chapter 4, which is the first chapter of the second part, deals with the ethical critique of the ruling systems. This chapter concludes with the enunciation of the critical-material principle of ethics that commands that the affirmation of life calls for the critique of all systems in which the corporeality and dignity of the other is negated. All ethical critique emerges from the recognition of the suffering of the other. This suffering, however, is always material and bodily. The condition of possibility of all critique is the *recognition* of the dignity of the other subject, the cosubject, but from the perspective of their being seen and experienced above all as *human living beings*. The next chapter covers the antihegemonic validity of the community of victims. In this chapter Dussel deals with the problem that the ethical critique of the victims of any system always appears illegitimate from the standpoint of that system. To that extent, their critique turns into a delegitimizing critique of the legitimacy of the status quo. This chapter closes with the enunciation of the critical-discursive principle that commands that who *acts* ethically must participate in a community of victims, who having been excluded recognized themselves as such and, thus, issue a critique of the system. The closing chapter develops what Dussel has christened the "liberation principle." All ethics worth that name must culminate in the imperative to liberate all victims from the system that turns them into victims. Evidently, the question arises: How, under what conditions, and by what means is this liberation to be pursued and achieved? This chapter, in parallel with the preceding chapters, concludes with the elaboration of the "liberation principle," which commands that who *acts* critically-ethically *ought* to, or is compelled to pursue a feasible and performable *transformation* of the present system that is the cause of the suffering of the victims, while also being compelled to pursue the *construction* of a new order in which the life of the victim will be made possible.

From this overview it becomes clear that Dussel has not simply fused his early ethics with the discourse ethics of Apel and Habermas. Instead, what we find is a very detailed, elaborate, comprehensive, and innovative discussion of ethics that synthesizes while superseding both teleological and deontological ethics. Most importantly, it is quite clear that for Dussel, politics is not extrinsic or foreign to ethics. Instead, politics becomes the horizon for the realization of the ethical. Dussel in fact has already announced that the ethics of liberation has as its logical and conceptual complement a politics of liberation, which like the ethics must proceed by way of the positive enunciation of certain principles, but also by way of the critique of political reason.[22]

Critique of Political Reason

As we noted above, Enrique Dussel's philosophy is a philosophy of liberation that seeks to contribute to the actual liberation of victims and the oppressed by elucidating and unmasking the sources of that oppression. It is not because of hubris, or overvalorization of the philosophical disciplines, but precisely because every social science is informed by a series of acknowledged and unacknowledged preconceptions, which are at core philosophical ideas, that Dussel thinks that all projects of liberation must begin with a liberation of philosophy. In an unmistakable hermeneuticist attitude, social practices are seen as crystallization of conceptual schemes, and vice versa. Social life is suffused by ideas, concepts, and conceptual schemes, sometimes ossified into unchangeable verities and sacred truths. Liberation philosophy struggles against the tendency of both the social world and philosophy itself to conceal their interdependence.[23] In this way, a liberation of philosophy must begin with a critique of most of its mystifications and divinification. A philosophy of liberation is a critique of philosophical fetishizations. And one of the areas to which Dussel has paid closest attention is the fetishization of the inevitability and intractability of political systems of oppression.[24]

In the seventies, one of the major targets of Dussel's antifetishistic critique, at the political level, was the myth of modernity and modernization. Dussel demonstrated how the ideology of imposing on so-called third-world countries the expectation that they would overcome their poverty once they adopted the political and economic systems of the industrialized West, was in fact a way to mask the production of the underdevelopment of the underdeveloped. Dussel christened this ideology "the developmentalist fallacy,"[25] by which Dussel meant to point out that it is a fallacy to suppose that underdeveloped countries are poor merely because they have failed to attain the stages of development of advanced northern countries. Instead, their condition is dialectically related to the wealth and development of what is offered as the normative model. So it is the case, and Dussel points this out, that we must both critique the myth of historical progress (if by this we mean the purported ascent through stages of development already transversed by the Western world) and critique the myth of the autonomy of nations. We cannot understand the success of the West by looking at internal and allegedly autochthonous factors, a la Hegel, Weber, and Habermas.[26]

Another fundamental fallacy that Dussel has sought to unmask is what he calls in the contribution to the present volume ("the reductivist and formalist fallacy.") By naming this fallacy, Dussel seeks to make explicit how most of the dominant political theory of the past five hundred years has been ruled by two overriding mystifications: first, that the political can only concern that which is not individual, material, or related to the corporeal survival of human beings; and second, that politics can only concern the arbitration of abstractly construed formal principles. If one aspect of the fallacy seeks to exclude the economic dimensions of human life from political deliberation, the other seeks to exclude questions of material and substantive values from the formulations of political principles. In Dussel's view, these ruling fallacies have turned politics not into the art of living in community but the science of control that reduces political agents to automata, or mere numbers in a complex calculus of maximization or minimization of power accumulation. The scienticization of politics, executed in tandem with the scienticization of economics and sociology, has contributed to the denudation of all the social sciences of their practical and ethical aspects. All the social sciences, and in particular, political science have become disciplines of daily coercion, the regimentation of potentially subversive agents into docile and depoliticized consumers and agents of the state.[27] And this coercion and concomitant depoliticization becomes the more subtle and insidious the more the systems that enact it are baptized by the scientific social sciences as natural, logical, inevitable, or systematically autopoetic (a la Luhmann). It is for this reason that Dussel thinks that it is imperative that we abandon the already tiring and sterile debate between communitarians and liberals. In the same vein, Dussel also admonishes us to relativize, or provincialize, the Western focus on rights and the state. Not because these are not fundamental to any viable political theory, but because the way they are debated in most of the contemporary political philosophy literature broaches them from a series of unacceptable generalizations that are applicable to the West; and even within the West, they are to be seen as wild generalizations.

Following the structure of his *Ethics of Liberation*,[28] Dussel has divided his contribution to this volume in two sections: fundamental and critical politics. The former deals positively with the principles that should guide all political reflection. The latter deals with the principles that motivate all political critique. However, and in contrast to his ethics, instead of deriving a series of principles, he proceeds by way of theses. The text is made up of six theses and two corollaries. A note of clarification is in order. When Dussel refers to "fundamental politics," he has in mind both the Kantian sense of grounding and the Aristotelian-Heideggerian sense of foundational (as in foundation and fountain, from whence something flows and grows out of). This means that Dussel is interested in grounding something in the rationalist sense of elucidating the principles without which political reason would be unthinkable and impossible, and the hermeneutical and metaphysical sense of providing an insight into the whence, the where-from, of our interest in the political. Fundamental, therefore, should not be at all construed in the dogmatic or scholastic sense, in which we have a set of natural laws and principles that are unassailable and beyond criticism. It is imperative that this dual sense of Dussel's be kept in mind, lest we misinterpret him as another hubristic philosopher king (in the tradition of Plato, Aquinas, Hobbes, Heidegger, and recently Rawls.[29])

The first thesis of Dussel's critique of political reason is that all political rationality is both practical and material. This means that politics is first and foremost, a form of practical rationality, that is, a form of *prudentia* or *phronesis*, that has to do with the reproduction of the life of individuals in contexts of community and mutual cooperation. Politics is uncircumventable for humans, for they are creatures of community (in the fashionable language of contemporary philosophy, humans are a dialogic species). Furthermore, their dialogicity, or linguistically constituted intersubjectively, is practically oriented toward the production, reproduction, and development of human life. Political reason, *ratio politica*, is eminently practical, and precisely for that reason universal. But precisely because humans are dialogic creatures, their interactions must be discursively mediated. Hence the second thesis: political reason must proceed by way of discursive and legitimate procedures that neither mystify the rule of the majority nor sacrifice the autonomy of the political agent. Discursive legitimation and democratically achieved validity, in which each political subject is both materially and formally a participant, does not exclude dissent, but rather incorporates it procedurally. But what kinds of projects are acceptable and feasible depends on the careful consideration of options and a scrutiny of the means available for their realization. The third thesis, then, deals with the instrumental or strategic aspect of political rationality. It is this instrumental and even strategic rational aspect of political rationality that allows it to become a politics of the real and feasible, and not a politics of utopia, or atopia. In this way, a critique of political reason is also a critique of utopian reason, as Dussel already made explicit in his 1998 ethics (partly inspired by Franz Hinkelammert).[30] A political reason that is too far beyond the horizon of the possible, and too close this side of the incipient, becomes either a politics of the unreal or a politics of the modus vivendi. The synthesis of the above three theses gives us the first corollary. Only those norms, laws, and institutions that have been guided in their execution by a political reason that is material and practical (although also universal), has been dialogically and democratically legitimated and validated, and has looked at the real possibilities of the actualization of these norms, laws, and institutions, can make a claim to political justice. If one of these conditions is exempted or excluded, we have a faulty politics, a politics of power, and coercion, of the powerful and the autocrats, a politics of utopia that quickly turns into a totalitarian politics. How is political reason mindful of its own faults? How does it monitor its own penchant to consecrate the present as the most perfect system of political organization? For politics to live closest to its own ideals, it must turn into critical political reason. And it does so by turning critical from a particular perspective, guided by a particular series of concerns, advocating a specific agenda.

The second part of Dussel's critique of political reason develops the structure of a critical politics, what in the language of Dussel's earlier philosophical stage was called "antipolitics." The fourth thesis, or first of critical politics, hypothesizes that when political reason takes charge of the negative effects of any norm, law, or system, then political reason turns into critical political reason. For this reason critical politics now seeks not the legitimation of the existing system but its delegitimation, precisely because it is faulty and the cause of negative and adverse consequences. All systems have their victims, true. But this realization neither exempts any system nor makes victimization acceptable. Instead, it renders political rationality realistic, in the sense that its realism makes it suspicious of the perfection of any norm, law, or system that claims such honor for itself. Consequently, thesis five: all systems have their own victims, and these victims owe their existence to heterogenous factors. The interests of these diverse victims must be considered in the restructuring of the system. Critical political reason is discursively critical political reason; meaning, the claims of the excluded and victimized are brought to the fore and become the point of departure for future legislation or norm development. The guide is offered not by the most well off within a system but, rather, by the worst off within that very system.[31]

All critical political reason has only one telos: *liberación* (liberation). Critical political reason, which is at core a critique of established political systems, aims at a transformation of oppressive practices, be they institutional or existential (not that they can in practice be separated). But the transformation of the existing ruling and oppressive system, undertaken with the interest of the most disadvantaged of that system, must be guided by a politics of a realizable utopianism. Hence thesis six: mere critique is insufficient. This must be accompanied by the development of strategies and movements that aim at the heart of the oppressive present. In this way, critical political reason that is guided by the telos of liberation turns into a transformative politics, a politics of liberation. An antipolitics of the status quo turns into the politics of liberation of the future system. But only, in Dussel's formulation, a politics that has been guided by the insights offered by the above six theses, as a synthesis of the positive and negative moments of political rationality, can claim to be a just critical political reason of liberation. Political justice, in other words, is the obverse side of political liberation. Both are unified in a politics of transformation that is always provisional and fallible. For every system produces its victims. In Dussel's view, however, political reason, and consequently political philosophy, must look at the world of the political not through the lens of the system, but of the victim. The more victims a system produces, and the more blind and deaf that system is to their suffering and interpellation, the more unjust, and illegitimate that system turns. Politics is the practical craft, a *phronesis*, of living together. If there are victims, politics has turned into a technology of genocide. This is why true politics must be always accompanied by a critical political philosophy that from the outset looks at the world through the eyes of the suffering and vulnerable materiality of the most dispossessed and exploited of the world. For this reason, Dussel thinks that the only viable politics for an age of unprecedented interdependence but simultaneous massive exclusion from the sharing of the most elemental goods necessary for a humane life (water, food, education) is a transformative politics that aims at liberation from the side of the least of the world. In an age of globalization, our political solutions will not come from those who seek to include but those who have been excluded. The excluded understand best how our political systems have turned into machines of destitution and impoverishment. Despite all the changes and philosophical transformations, Dussel has remained obstinate in this principle: all truly liberating thinking must set out from the misery of the poor, the anguish of the destitute, the pain of the victim.

8

The Linguistification of the Sacred as a Catalyst of Modernity

Jürgen Habermas on Religion

The Question of Religion

The question of religion is once again at the forefront of critical thought precisely because in it are crystallized some of the most serious and pressing questions of contemporary social thought: the relationship between social structure and rationality; between reason as a universal standard and the inescapable fact that reason is embodied only historically and in contingent social practices; that reason as universality was, if not discovered, at least enunciated as a teleological standard by religions;[1] that in an age of secularization and scienticization, religion remains a major factor in the moral education and motivation of individuals uprooted from other traditions; and at the very least, in an age of accelerating homogenization and simultaneous manufacturing of difference, what sociologists of globalization have called *glocalization*, religions are articulated as the last refuge of unadulturated difference, the last reservoir of cultural autonomy.

Jürgen Habermas's work over the last four decades intersects at times directly and explicitly, at others tangentially and suggestively, with many of these questions. The impetus is to make explicit what to many has been implicit and unthematized. The goal, thus, is to foreground those resources in Habermas's immense intellectual contribution that may aid a critical confrontation with the new intellectual and social challenges that are entailed by new forms of obscurantism, fundamentalism, anarchical mysticism, religious irrationalism, and the like. Most importantly, this collection should make evident how those resources in Habermas's work were forged

---

A shorter version of this chapter first appeared as the editor's introduction to Jürgen Habermas, *Religion and Rationality: Essays on Reason, God, and Modernity*, ed. Eduardo Mendieta (Cambridge, UK: Polity, 2002), 1–36.

from the very sources and traditions that have shaped the identity and structure of Western societies. Habermas's "methodological atheism" is not a rejection but a response to and a dialectical sublation of the Jewish-Christian tradition that suffuses so pervasively the work of all of his precursors.

Another goal of this collection is to make explicit, if it ever was put in question, how Habermas's work inherited, appropriating and transforming, the critical tradition of Jewish utopian messianism of the early Frankfurt School. In the following, therefore, I turn to a brief and broad characterization of this Jewish messianic utopianism. I then proceed to reconstruct the main elements and strains of Habermas's treatment of religion. The central thesis of this later section is that Habermas's treatment is not correctly characterized by the image of a temporal rupture between an early positive and a later negative appraisal of the role of religion. Instead, textual evidence will be elicited that suggests an ever-present appreciation of religion that fluctuates with the angle of approach, or lens of analysis. In other words, it will be suggested that Habermas's statements, whether positive or negative, are determined by whether he is broaching the question from a philosophical and critical perspective or from a sociological, political, and legal perspective.

Religion as Critique

Albert Schweitzer began his classic work *The Quest of the Historical Jesus* with the statement, "When, at some future day, our period of civilization shall lie, closed and completed, before the eyes of later generations, German theology will stand out as a great, a unique phenomenon in the mental and spiritual life of our time."[2] He wrote this shortly after the turn of the century, in 1906. In parallel, today as we look back over the century of extremes, as Hobsbawm called the twentieth century, we may claim that Jewish thought will stand out as a unique social and intellectual phenomenon. In the secular, apocalyptic, utopian, and pessimistic messianism of the Jewish thinkers of the generation of 1914 were crystallized some of the most painful lessons of the age of mass extermination and mass culture. After Auschwitz, as Adorno put it, "[a] new categorical imperative has been imposed by Hitler upon unfree mankind: to arrange their thoughts and actions so that Auschwitz will not repeat itself, so that nothing similar will happen."[3]

Nonetheless, following Michael Löwy, we should seek to be less evocative and more precise.[4] It was the Central European Jews who were able to achieve one of the most creative and lasting synthesis and transformations, of both Judaism and Christianity, in the twentieth century. But we would have to go beyond Löwy and suggest that the height of this creative upsurge was best embodied in the work of the first generation of the Frankfurt School, in the work of Max Horkheimer, Theodor W. Adorno, Walter

Benjamin, Herbert Marcuse—and to extend legitimately Gershom Scholem's list, Erich Fromm and Leo Lowenthal.[5] Their work, it should be noted, was deeply influenced and guided by the work of Ernst Bloch, György Lukács, but also Franz Rosenzweig and Martin Buber.[6]

This creative furor during the first decades of the twentieth century—what has been called the Jewish generation of 1914—in Germany in particular and around Frankfurt as well as Berlin even more specifically, could be analyzed sociologically.[7] Jewish assimilation had reached its zenith in Germany at the very moment when industrialization, urbanization, and secularization had reach their most extreme levels of acceleration. The German-Jewish question had found its answer in the dissolution of the Jewish into the German without residue or trace. Simultaneously, a young generation of secular and assimilated Jewish intellectuals began to discover and make explicit this one-sided assimilation. They discovered themselves to be both pariahs and unwanted, marginalized and excluded, as Jews. Despite their confession of Germanness, they remained suspect: once a Jew, always a Jew. Assimilation is unmasked as a pyrrhic victory, as an asymmetrical and nonreciprocal immersion into a polis and culture that still resents their identity, as dispossession and abandonment of a tradition that at least offered a cultural and moral compass. At this very moment, the promise of modernity turns into a malaise: alienation, reification, rootlessness, superficiality, crassness, qualitative leveling for the sake of quantitative maximization (i.e., massification), and so on. It is thus that a romantic critique of capitalism, and modern society in general, begins to be enunciated. This anticapitalist romanticism, to use Lukács's apt expression, does not fit the traditional taxonomy of responses to modernization: left, centrist, or conservative. It is not easy to associate a particular political attitude to a particular philosophical and epistemological perspective. Elements of so-called conservative ontology and metaphysics are deployed with the intent of enunciating a radical and leftist critique of capitalism. Mostly committed to the values of the Enlightenment, which had catalyzed their incomplete assimilation, and set adrift from their traditions by centuries of secularization, deassimilation, and religious amnesia,[8] Jewish intellectuals were poised in a unique social position from which they could seek to salvage and refashion their religious traditions while at the same time trying to salvage the best of the Enlightenment from the corrosive effects of capitalism. It was out of this dialectical tension that a unique type of Jewish messianism was articulated by Central European Jews, and Frankfurt assimilated Jews in particular.[9]

Philosophically and conceptually, the Jewish Messianism of these central European and German Jews could be said to be made of four elements, always present with varying degrees of emphasis in different thinkers. Following Anson Rabinbach, we can differentiate them in the following way. First, this Jewish Messianism is profoundly characterized by a restorative element. This has to do with anamnesis as a fundamental aspect of rationality. In contrast to the idea of the restitution of an Arcadian past, or golden age, this messianism seeks to restore by way of an apocalyptic reenactment. Second, this messianism is utopian in that it projects a new age that is not brought about by the progressive accumulation of improvements, through a quantitative meliorism. This utopianism is unlike Enlightenment utopianism, which sees the future as the mere actualization of the present. Instead, the truly utopian is to be seen as an irruption into the historical continuum by a transhistorical agent. With Benjamin, we may say that progress is catastrophe and utopia is ahistorical. The third element, already alluded to, is the apocalyptic dimension of this messianism. The restoration of wholeness, *Tikkun*, and the irruption of utopia, two aspects of one and the same process, is only conceivable as a radical discontinuity with the present. The past, as the past of injustice, is not to be superficially reconciled in the present, and the future is not imaginable from the present, lest it become a mere mirror image of what that present can alone think and project. Radical reconciliation and utopia are possible only on the assumption of temporal discontinuity. Fourthly, and finally, the restorative, utopian, and apocalyptic elements converge in the ambivalent image of messianism. This messianism, most importantly, is not personalizable. It is not the waiting for or announcement of a messiah, but the call and discernment of the messianic forces and elements that, like fragments of utopia, rupture into the continuum of history. To this extent, this messianism is apriori undecidable, indeterminate. In other words, this messianism that rejects the present and the possibility of meliorative progress, stands poised ambiguously pessimistic and passive, but also wildly expectant and vigilant. Expectation, readiness, wakefulness, but also profound passivity, humility, and patience—these are the extremes between which the Jewish messianism of these turn-of-the-century Jewish pariahs wavered.[10]

A careful reading of the work produced by the members of the Institute for Social Research, as well the people attached to it, reveal a sustained and in-depth concern with questions of religion, theology, the sociology of religion, theological metaphysics, and the history of religious ideas.[11] Max Horkheimer himself contributed a series of essays in which the theme of religion is substantive if not central.[12] Yet it must also be acknowledged that a study of the particular critique of religion developed by the first generation of the Frankfurt School has remained unexecuted, because of the transdisciplinary or adisciplinary character of such a critique.[13] In other words, the work of the early Frankfurt School on religion has remained elusive because of the difficulty of placing it within the traditional disciplinary boundaries we associate with the study of religion. Their work did not fall within the category of the study of religions, sociology of religion, even philosophy of religion, much less could it have been assimilated to theology, notwithstanding repeated accusations that critical theory was really masked theology.[14] What makes the contributions of members of the early Frankfurt

School, like the early Fromm, Marcuse, even Lowenthal, Horkheimer, and Adorno, so unique is precisely the way they developed a sui generis approach to the question of religion. For them, the issue of religion had to be approached philosophically, historically, sociologically, psychologically, even from the standpoint of metaphysics and ontology. The point, in fact, was to rescue from theology and religion that which threatens to be extinguished and desecrated by their attempt to render positive that which can only be ciphered negatively.[15] As Horkheimer put it in a letter that became the foreword to Martin Jay's history of the Frankfurt School: "The appeal to an entirely other (*ein ganz Anderes*) than this world had primarily a social-philosophical impetus. It led finally to a more positive evaluation of certain metaphysical trends, because the empirical 'whole is the untrue' (Adorno). The hope that earthly horror does not possess the last word is, to be sure, a nonscientific wish."[16]

In order to further characterize the unique aspects of this critique of religion, and given our purposes in this chapter, it should suffice to focus on Max Horkheimer's and Theodor Adorno's relationship to the previously demarcated Jewish Messianism. Evidently, in their religious atheistic, to use an expression by Lukács,[17] or "nonsecular secularist," to use an expression by Scholem,[18] response to their Jewishness and the challenges of modernity, as well as to the crisis of Marxism in the early decades of the twentieth century, we find developed and summarized the critiques of religion that are exhibited in their two most extreme forms in the works of the key figures of Ernst Bloch and, of course, Walter Benjamin. The former stands for the utopian and forward looking while the latter stands for the redemptive and anamnestic. Although both remained institutionally peripheral to the Frankfurt School and the Institute for Social Research, they remained central to the intellectual constellation that configured that unique cultural phenomenon called Frankfurt School critical theory.[19]

It must be made clear from the outset that Max Horkheimer's work was marked by a continued and unwavering interest in religion.[20] From his earliest aphorisms to his last writings, interviews, and obituaries, there is an ever-present confrontation, treatment, and concern with the question of the role of religion in contemporary societies.[21] The best-known example of this preoccupation with the so-called demise of religion—that is, the secularization thesis—is to be found in Horkheimer's essay written for a *Festschrift* for Adorno, "Theism and Atheism." In this essay we find the statement that became the focus as well as the title of one of the essays by Habermas included in this book. The statement reads: "Without God one will try in vain to preserve absolute meaning. No matter how independent a given form of expression may be within its own sphere as in art or religion, and no matter how distinct and how necessary in itself, with the belief in God it will have to surrender all to being objectively something higher than a practical convenience.... The death of God is also the death of eternal truth."[22]

The other statement comes from an interview Horkheimer granted in 1967 on the occasion of Paul Tillich's death: "I believe that there is no philosophy to which I could assent which did not contain a theological moment, for it relates indeed to the recognition of how much the world in which we live is to be interpreted as relative."[23] Evidently, there are numerous analogous statements. A wonderful collection of aphorisms by Horkheimer on the need for the totally other, the entirely other, as a social, anthropological, and even metaphysical need could be easily edited.[24]

These and many, many more assertions, however, are marked by two central motifs. First, that religion retains an ineradicable philosophical and conceptual importance, without which criticism of actuality and society is unthinkable. And, second, that insofar as religion means belief in an absolutely transcendent god who hovers above history as ultimate judge, then the promise of justice and hope that is not exhausted by any social institution is kept alive. Indeed, as he suggests at the end of his essay "Theism and Atheism," our relationship to religion remains an index of resistance. In times of atheism and the glorification of terrestrial powers, theism becomes an act of defiance and nonconformism, of not going along with the powers that be. In times of theism, when again the powers that be are legitimated with reference to some projection of the divine, atheism becomes an act of resistance, precisely in the name of that which must always remain unrepresented. The Jewish forbiddance of the representation, even in writing, of the holy one is in Horkheimer's view not only a theologumenon, but even a fundamental concept of the dialectic. That we cannot say anything absolutely about god is assimilated into one of critical theory's foundational presuppositions: that the absolute is unrepresentable.[25] In Adorno's words, it is not that we have the identity of the identical and the nonidentical, but the nonidentity of the identical and the nonidentical. A thought that would claim to present the totality as representable in any form whatsoever would have already succumbed to the logic of identity thinking. But, as Horkheimer notes, the rejection of the possibility of the representation of the absolute is to be preserved for the sake of the individual, the singular, that which has suffered the ignominy of a history that has been lived hitherto as catastrophe. In Horkheimer's work, then, the yearning for a wholly other is a figure of thought that seeks to preserve the "longing that unites all men so that the horrible events, the injustice of history so far would not be permitted to the final, ultimate fate of the victims."[26]

In Adorno's case, his work is so permeated by the apocalyptic, utopian, Jewish messianism that some have thrown at it the accusation that it is no more than negative theology, a form of medieval mystical irrationalism.[27] Here what Benjamin says about his work's relationship to theology might also be said of Adorno's parallel relationship: "My thinking is related to theology as blotting pad is related to ink. It is saturated with it. Were one to go by the blotter, however, nothing of what is written would remain."[28]

Indeed, as Adorno himself wrote to Benjamin in 1935, "A restoration of theology, or better still, a radicalization dialectic introduced into the glowing heart of theology, would simultaneously require the utmost intensification of the social-dialectical, and indeed, economic motifs."[29] It is in the light of this double, dialectical strategy that we must read Adorno's critique of religion.

One may venture the assertion that Adorno's works are not just an attempt to do exactly what he calls us to do at the end of *Minima Moralia*; namely, to think from the standpoint of redemption, but further, to exalt the theological content of thought to its extreme. But to do so means to do it negatively: Preservation by negation, refusing to accept the assimilation of the singular into the concept, without relinquishing the means of the concept. The other, as the irreplaceable and unrepresentable singularity, can only be referred to indirectly and through the deciphering of the traces of violence inflicted on the other, the individual, by the concept itself. This is why negative dialectics is a synthesis of a phenomenology of existence that grants us the view from immanence with the dialectics of concepts that traces their genesis by way of determinate negation: how they emerged from a specific societal context. This means, specifically with reference to religion, that that which dwells in the religious can only be rescued and transmitted by way of the critique of the concepts and theologumenon in which it has been preserved. As he put it in his essay "Reason and Revelation": "If religion is accepted for the sake of something other than its own truth content, then it undermines itself."[30] In Adorno's view, we can no more unhinge critical thought from metaphysics, albeit transformed, than we can uncouple metaphysics from theology.[31]

Adorno, like Benjamin and Bloch, practiced the art of philosophizing by way of apothegms, verbal diamonds of refracted wisdom. Here, however, I will not succumb to the temptation to concatenate citation after citation. I will merely gloss over a few.[32] In *Negative Dialectics*, for instance, he writes: "Any one who would nail down transcendence can rightly be charged—as by Karl Kraus, for instance—with lack of imagination, anti-intellectualism, and thus a betrayal of transcendence. On the other hand, if the possibility, however feeble and distant, of redemption in existence is cut off altogether, the human spirit would become an illusion, and the finite, conditioned, merely existing subject would eventually be deified as carrier of the spirit."[33] Transcendence, as the wholly other, the numinous and divine, but also as the element of unconditionality in every human being, is neither to be shabbily represented nor to be skeptically disposed off. Metaphysics, and theology as its precursor, had the intention of capturing this reference to the other by way of the immanent in life and history, while being aware that such attempts were always in jeopardy. Thus, the critique of metaphysics is itself an instantiation of the metaphysical impulse to point to the transcendent. As Adorno continues in the same section from the *Negative Dialectics*: "The idea of truth is supreme among the metaphysical ideas, and this is where it takes us. It is why one who believes in God cannot believe in God, why the possibility represented by the divine name is maintained, rather, by him who does not believe. Once upon a time the image ban extended to pronouncing the name; now the ban itself has in that form come to evoke suspicions of superstition. The ban has been exacerbated: the mere thought of hope is a transgression against it, an act of working against it."[34] These echo the sentences that close his already cited essay "Reason and Revelation": "I see no other possibility than an extreme ascesis toward any type of revealed faith, an extreme loyalty to the prohibition of images, far beyond what this once originally meant."[35] We must reject hope for the sake of that which it pointed to, namely truth, but truth as the unconditional that renders everything intramundane something relative and contingent, as Horkheimer put it.

We have to wonder whether in fact Adorno meant to reject hoping, *toto caelo*. After all, he had written earlier in *Minima Moralia*: "In the end hope, wrested from reality by negating it, is the only form in which truth appears. Without hope, the idea of truth would be scarcely even thinkable, and it is the cardinal untruth, having recognized existence to be bad, to present it as truth simply because it has been recognized."[36] Hope is the guarantee of truth precisely because hope unmasks the givenness of reality. Hope, the yearning after the possibility of that which would totally transform the present, renders reality incomplete and inconclusive. Truth is beyond the now. Hence, "the whole in the untrue." And if this beyond that renders the now transcendeable is not to be betrayed, then hope must also be qualified. Therefore, in an alternate formulation articulated in a dialogue with Bloch, Adorno puts it this way: "Falsum—the false thing—index sui et veri. [The false is the sign of itself and the true.]"[37] This aphorism, which condenses the impetus of *Negative Dialectics*, is also expressed in a provocative and paradoxical formulation enunciated later in the same dialogue: "Actually I would think that unless there is no kind of trace of truth in the ontological proof of God, that is, unless the element of its reality is also already conveyed in the power of the concept itself, there could not only be no utopia but there could also not be any thinking."[38] To which Bloch retorted: "In hope, the matter concerns perfection, and to that extent it concerns the ontological proof of the existence of God. But the most perfect creature is posited by Anselm as something fixed that includes the most real at the same time. Such a tenant is not defensible. But what is true is that each and every criticism of imperfection, incompleteness, intolerance, and impatience already without a doubt presupposes the conception of, and longing for, a possible perfection."[39] I think that Adorno would have answered back, as he did several times throughout the dialogue, "*D'accord.*"

I would suggest that Adorno's and Horkheimer's reflections on religion can be provisionally summarized in the following way. First, enlightenment is catalyzed by religion. We cannot understand the critique of myth without understanding how religion itself, and in particular the Christian and Jewish traditions, are forms of demythologization. Second, religion, despite having accelerated the process of its own assimilation and secularization, is never divested of both its social and philosophical role: as the call to universality and the promise of an inextinguishable negativity that renders all claims to completeness and fulfillment questionable and partial. Third, while elements of criticism, or anamnesis, and utopian projecting might have migrated towards the aesthetic and the moral, religion remains both a reservoir and a compendium of humanity's most deeply felt injustices and yearned-for dreams of reconciliation. Fourth, insofar as critical theory is a bringing together of different research tools, which ought to allow for the use of reason against reason, its approach to religion is guided by a "methodological skepticism" that ought to render one ever vigilant to facile and glib dismissals of certain social phenomena. Religion is not to be dismissed simply because a certain school of sociology has discovered, given its methodological orientation, that religion has become functionally superfluous. Fifth, and finally, the Frankfurt School's critique of religion, which is less a rejection and more a reappropriation, refuses to answer in favor of one or the other side of the dyad: Athens or Jerusalem? One is unthinkable without the other. Reason is impossible without anamnesis, and memory remains ineffective if it were not married to universality: remembrance of what and for whom? memory of suffering by whom and for whom?[40]

The Linguistification of the Sacred as a Catalyst of Modernity

While the reception of Habermas by theologians and sociologists of religion continues to gain momentum,[41] his reception by philosophers as a philosopher of religion remains incipient.[42] Philosophers and social theorists in general have taken Habermas's pronouncements on religion in his *Theory of Communicative Action*, especially in volume 2,[43] and his sporadic and pointed criticisms against mysticism and messianism in *The Philosophical Discourse of Modernity*,[44] as definitive and representative of his general outlook. It would seem, from a quick and superficial reading of passages in these two works, that Habermas has put religion to rest, and has pronounced its theoretical and social-developmental death. In fact, a consensus has developed around the notion that Habermas's theory of the "linguistification of the sacred" entails the sublimation or *Aufhebung* of religion *tout court*. This misleading representation and conclusion about Habermas's positions on religion has made it undesirable, even unnecessary, to engage him any further as an insightful philosopher of religion.[45] This is most unfortunate, for if anything, Habermas has opened up a path for a renewed dialogue with religion, whether as a source of concepts or a fundamental element in lived experience. He has neither unequivocally rejected nor half-heartedly accepted calls for a turn to religion in an age of catastrophe. The point, as he writes, is "not to overcome modernity by having recourse to archaic sources, but to take specific account of the conditions of modern postmetaphysical thought, under which an ontotheologically insulated discourse with God cannot be continued."[46] The term "postmetaphysical" here carries conceptual weight, and it is not an empty rhetorical gesture. Postmetaphysical refers not just to a condition of philosophy, but also of religion. As Habermas makes explicit: "I do not believe that we, as Europeans, can seriously understand concepts like morality and ethical life, persons and individuality, or freedom and emancipation, without appropriating the substance of the Judeo-Christian understanding of history in terms of salvation. And these concepts are, perhaps, nearer to our hearts than the conceptual resources of Platonic thought, centering on order and revolving around the cathartic intuition of ideas.... But without the transmission through socialization and the transformation through philosophy of *any one* of the great world religions, this semantic potential could one day become inaccessible."[47]

Another factor that may have contributed to delaying the reception of Habermas as a philosopher who has contributed to our understanding of religion is certainly the very epochal and pointed character of his contributions. Every major work by Habermas has acted as a catalyst but also as a barometer of the *Zeitgeist*, registering its deepest fears and most cherished hopes.[48] Indeed the polemical and innovative character of Habermas's works, over the past forty years militates against trying to link Habermas's position with established and old-fashioned questions like What about religion? Further, the skewed reception of Habermas's work, especially in the United States, which sometimes detrimentally echoes throughout the world, has also prevented a cross-textual, cross-disciplinary reading of his work. This last factor is particularly surprising given the theoretical claims of Habermas's own research agenda. He has without equivocation continued the interdisciplinary research agenda that informed the Frankfurt School's critical theory.

In the following I will offer a reconstruction of those types of formulations and pronoucements made by Habermas's that trace out a historical-developmental, quasi-functionalist, in short phylogenetic, story of the rise and transformation, but not demise, of religion. This type of exegesis and reconstruction is necessary to dispel the misconception of an unambigous Habermasian rejection of religion. First, I want to illustrate that there have been modifications in Habermas's views on religion. Such variations have to do with the increase in nuance and sophistication of his theoretical model. At the same time, I would like to illustrate the extent to which Habermas has also continued to maintain questions concerning religion close to the center of his thought.[49]

A fuller, more appropriate analysis of Habermas's treatment of religion would have to complement the work here undertaken with what I would call its dialectical complement, namely Habermas's philosophical treatment of religion. Indeed, a parallel reconstruction and exegesis would need to be undertaken that traces those formulations and pronoucements made by Habermas that explicitly articulate how the semantic contents of religion (as well as its institutional dimension, I would say) remain inextinguishable and always still to be noninstrumentally appropriated. While the work I undertake here deals with Habermas the sociologist of religion, the missing dialectical complement would be one that deals with Habermas the philosopher of religion, in whose hands the philosophy of religion turns into the critique of religion. Indeed, such an extended analysis would demostrate how Habermas the philosopher of religion rescues, preserves, and transforms those views developed by the first generation of the Frankfurt School. While there are substantive differences between the two generations, I suggest that Habermas, for philosophical and cultural, as well as political reasons, has continued to make use of the critique of religion I briefly demarcated in the first section of this chapter. For the moment I will briefly mention the way in which Habermas has appealed during the *Historikerstreit* to the Benjaminian idea of anamnesis as not just a philosophical trope but even a civic duty.[50]

The debates about whether Habermas's turn toward the philosophy of language, analytic philosophy, the appropriation of certain motifs from Weber's functionalism and Luhmann's systems theory, and his severe criticisms of Adorno and Horkheimer have transformed him into an apostate, have had the unfortunate consequence of eclipsing the ways in which Habermas's thought has indeed inherited the spirit of the first generation of the Frankfurt School. In fact, the essays I have selected here, guided by Habermas's suggestions as well, ought to constitute evidence for this claim. The texts here selected speak eloquently to that inheritance by retaining its critical approach to religion, even to the extent of criticizing the religion projected by the first generation's critique of religion. In other words, Habermas remains true to the spirit of Horkheimer's and Adorno's critique of religion in his criticism of their own negative theology.

In the widely read and still classic text of 1968, written on the ocassion of Herbert Marcuse's seventieth birthday, Habermas already approaches the question of religion. This is a very important text for at least two reasons. First, because Habermas, vis-à-vis the work of Marcuse, seeks to elaborate a critical theoretical approach to the question of technology, in particular, and the growth of rationalization of society in general. Second, because here is made explicit, if not for the first time, at least in an extended and elaborated fashion, Habermas's own dissatisfaction with the Frankfurt School's traditional approach to the question of the rationalization of society. In this text, in fact, Habermas elaborates more extensively on the distinction between work and interaction, which he had announced in an essay from the same period: "Labor and Interaction: Remarks on Hegel's Jena *Philosophy of Mind*."[51] In this latter essay, Habermas pursues the missed opportunities in Hegel's early work, and how such a failure would have adverse effects in the development of Marx's own work. In the Marcuse essay, Habermas takes up his philosophical reflections from the angle of social theory. The intent behind the introduction of this distinction is dual. On the one hand, Habermas was to disentangle Marcuse's critical theory of technology and societal development from a host of aporias and self-contradictions that nullifed some worthy insights. On the other hand, Habermas wanted to rescue Weber's and Parsons's analysis from their subjectivistic and monological perspectives. Still, the unifying thrust of this distinction is to allow for an appropriate understanding of the logics that inform the rationalization of different modes of action. In this early sketch, "labor" refers to purposive action that brings together instrumental and/or rational choice. Such forms of action are guided by technical rules, or strategies of either maximization of benefits or minimization of costs. By "interaction," Habermas understands what he already called, in the late sixties, *communicative action*; that is, that type of action that is guided by binding *consensual norms*. Succinctly, as Habermas put it: "While the validity of technical rules and strategies depends on that of empirically true or analytically correct propositions, the validity of social norms is grounded only in the intersubjectivity of the mutual understanding of intentions and secured by the general recognition of obligations."[52] This analytical distinction actually corresponds to different social systems. Social systems, or societal contexts for interaction, differ and are differentiated on whether they are the locus for the predominance of one or the other mode of action. This mapping of modes of action to social systems allowed Habermas to distinguish between (1) the institutional framework of society or what he calls the lifeworld, and (2) the subsystems of purposive-rational, or instrumental, action. With this distinction to hand, Habermas proceeds to reconstruct Weber's theory of the rationalization of society with an eye, as well, to correcting the misguided appropriation of Weber by the first generation of critical theorists.

Max Weber's social theory is above all a theory of the phylogenesis of social systems and their corresponding forms of rationality. Weber's theory, as Habermas is going to make explicit in his *Theory of Communicative Action*, is a theory of society as a theory of rationality, which in turn must be specified as the theory of the differentiation of types of rationality, or typology of rationality. This much was already clear to the young Habermas in this early incursion into the reconstruction of historical materialism. In this early essay from 1968, thus, Habermas will offer a sketch of a succession of different developmental stages of human societies to match his analytical distinction between lifeworld and systems level. Habermas distinguishes among archaic, primitive, traditional, and modern or postconventional societies. Traditional societies differ from archaic or primitive societies in that traditional societies (1) have developed centralized ruling powers, (2) have divided vertically into socioeconomic casts or groups, and (3) have developed centralized worldviews to legitimate centralized powers and the distribution of social goods. But what is true about the distinction between archaic and traditional societies is also true of the distinction between traditional and modern societies. Their differences can be gauged by the asymmetry between the harnessing of productive forces and the dictates and goals of legitimation strategies of force and coercion, and how the latter are overtaken by the former. Differences in societal development are partly determined by the gap that develops between the extension and levels of sophistication in the subsystem of purposive-instrumental action and the legitimation of power.[53]

Indeed, the triumph of capitalism within modern societies has to do with its relative success at harmonizing and bringing into equilibrium the divergent trends of the expansion of subsystems of instrumental action and the legitimation of coercion. This is what Weber called the rationalization of the forms of interaction. In Habermas's view, however, it has to be made explicit that this rationalization is executed or brought about from "above" and "below." From below, by the very success of the subsystems of instrumental action that, with each gain, continue to expand vertically, taking over more and more subsystems of purposive or instrumental action. Progressively and ineluctably every major, and minor, structure of traditional society is brought under the logic of instrumental or strategic rationality. Simultaneously, but now as if from "above," worldviews, whether mythological or religious, lose their power and "cogency."[54] This rationalization from above is what Weber called secularization. This is made up of two aspects. On the one hand, traditional worldviews lose their power and status as myths, rituals, justifying metaphysics, and immutable traditions, as they are interiorized. In this view, secularization means subjectivification, or subjective relativization. On the other hand, secularization also means that such traditions, worldviews, rituals, legitimating metaphysics, and so forth, are transformed "into contructions that do both at once: criticize tradition and reorganize the released material of tradition according to the principles of formal law and the exchange of equivalents (rationalist natural law.)"[55] This is a pregnant formulation. Rationalization as secularization means that traditions, or world outlooks, themselves became the locus of contestation and innovation as well as the site for the preservation and transmission of tradition. There are no longer "traditional" worldviews that lag behind, as archaic remnants, which are not submitted to the court of rational self-justification. Tradition itself, be it religious or metaphysical, must be rationally justified. Hence the long history of theologizing and metaphysical speculation that accompies the modernization of world religions. Secularization, in short, means that religious as well as metaphysical outlooks became the site of their own delegitimation and relegitimation. Tradition is discovered as such at the very instant that it becomes open to reconfiguration and rational analysis. For this reason, Habermas notes, "ideologies are coeval with the critique of ideology."[56] Or, formulated in slightly different terms: The tradition of modernity is the critique of tradition for the sake of tradition.[57]

A slightly different version of such an orientation toward the modernity of religion is voiced in Habermas's 1973 work *Legitimation Crisis*.[58] Briefly put, the goal of this work was to translate the discourse about the contradictions of capitalism as it was articulated by historical materialism, into a discourse about the crises and deficits of the rational legitimation of modernized, secularized, rationalized systems of interaction and the increasingly weakened and demystified world outlooks. In this work, Habermas sought to offer his complement to Marxism and to classical Frankfurt School critical theory, in terms of politics and economics. How do we undertand the "contradictions" of a social totality when this totality itself is now conceptually dissected into two distinct levels, the lifeworld and the systems level? Both operate according to their own logics. Their development is dictated by their respective corporealizations of forms of reason, or modes of action. Further, if we understand society diachronically as a differentiated arrangement of types of rationality, then contradictions must now be rethought as crises or pathologies in the forms of rational abjudication and justification. Either insuficient rationalization or pathological rationalization. It is against this background of the systematic reformulation of the Marxist project of the critique of political economy into a critique of failed or pathological rationalizations of society that Habermas once again broaches the question of religion and, now explicitly, of God.

In the section entitled "The End of the Individual?" Habermas discusses the shipwrecking of worldviews on the shoals of the disjunction between the cognitive and social integrative functions of traditional worldviews. Indeed, at the minimum, one of the fundamental functions of religious and metaphysical worldviews was to integrate individuals into society, by offering bridges between individual and group identity, while offering a cognitive handle on the natural world.[59] With the rationalization of worldviews, from above, to use the language of his *Festschrift* essay for Marcuse, personal identity is now separated from group identity, and these in turn are made distinct from any cognitive management of the natural world. In this view, the rationalization of metaphysical and religious worldviews means that we must face our subjectivities and group alliances as contingent, for neither entails the other. At the same time, the intractability and resistance of the natural world before our own wills means that we must face our individual existences in the world as entirely contigent. We must face the world *disconsolately*, without warrants or guarantees. In this desolate world, bereft of unifying and meaningful mental or religious pictures, are we to surrender to technocracy, to disavow the links between truth and justice? And hence, in turn, is a universalistic morality to be reduced to its empty self-affirmation before the scientistic and objectifying self-understanding of contemporary humanity?[60]

Habermas speculates that an affirmative answer is not yet forthcoming, if only because of the "repoliticization" of the biblical tradition, as was particularly observable in the then emerging theological formulations of political theologians.[61] Such repoliticization, which entailed a leveling of the immanent/transcendent dichotomy, was not suppossed to be read as atheism. Instead, such "religious" revivals and modern reappropriations of the traditions, formulated from within but also heeding the calling of the times, are to be understood as modern reformulations of the very concept of God. Habermas writes: "The idea of God is transformed [*aufgehoben*] into a concept of a *Logos* that determines the community of believers and the real life-context of a self-emancipating society. 'God' becomes the name for a communicative structure that forces men [sic], on pain of a loss of their humanity, to go beyond their accidental, empirical nature to encounter one another *indirectly*, that is, across an objective something that they themselves are not."[62] Evidently, it would be anachronistic, although not illegitimate, to reread this incredible formulation in the language of the *Theory of Communicative Action*. God is the name for that substance that gives coherence, unity, and thickness to the lifeworld wherein humans dwell seeking to acknowledge each other as meaning-giving creatures. One may ask, paralleling this reinscription: Is this God the *Logos* of a community of "believers" (who are always believers only insofar as they speak, confess, and witness in a community of communication of biblical texts and truths), the same God that is now the communicative rationality of a community of arguers and vulnerable corporealities? And if we answer this question affirmatively, then how must we relate Habermas's reinscription of God to the tradition that sees God as the cipher of humanity's unactualized potentials? In this tradition, God is the name for a negative fiction of what humans should become but are always hindered from becoming by their own corporeality and finitude.

Another key textual point of reference that should be visited before we turn to the pivotal *The Theory of Communicative Action* is Habermas's synthesizing and synoptic 1976 introduction to his *Zur Rekonstruktion des Historischen Materialismus*,[63] "Historical Materialism and the Development of Normative Structures."[64] This introduction offers a map of Habermas's efforts to reconstruct historical materialism. The text it introduces is itself divided into four major sections: philosophical perspectives, identity, evolution, and legitimation. The introduction, therefore, undertakes the task of unifying what Habermas had been trying to accomplish during the early seventies, which succinctly and poignantly is summarized by him: To spell out the ways in which communication theory can contribute to understanding the learning processes that humanity has undergone not just in the dimension of objectivating and instrumentalizing thought, but also in the different dimensions of moral insight, practical knowledge, and consensual arbitration of social interaction. In short, Habermas sought to preserve the critical impetus of historical materialism by rearticulating its analysis of human history in terms of a theory of the acquisition of communicative competencies whose developmental logic can be analyzed as a process of rationalization, formalization, universalization, and abstraction. The idea, therefore, is to reconstruct the developmental logics of those processes of rationalization that have guided the internal differentiation of processes of identity constitution, social differentiation, and political legitimation. To accomplish this, Habermas draws out what he calls "homologies" between ontogenetic and phylogenetic developmental logics; such homologies are to be traced by comparing the developmental logics of the domains of ego and worldviews, on the one hand, and ego and group identities, on the other.[65]

Habermas is quick to qualify the conditions under which these homologies, or parallelisms, can be drawn. He spells out a long and detailed list of the kinds of reservations that must be heeded and specious parallelisms that might be illegitimately drawn. Nonetheless, Habermas goes on, certain homologies can be made explicit. Thus, we are able to discern within the ontogenesis of the cognitive capacities of individuals the following: the differentiation of temporal horizons, namely the differentiation between natural and subjective time; the articulation of the concepts of causality and substance. Similarly, mythological and religious worldviews admit of an analysis that makes explicit the development and acquisition of conceptual and logical differentiations. Myth, which corresponds to an early stage of human evolution, is incorporated within traditional societies in a functional manner. Myths are now supposed to legitimate the authority of the ruling structures. But at that very instant, myth turns into tradition by being assimilated within a temporal horizon. In other words, the very incorporation of myth within the social fabric of a differentiated social system leads to the catalyzing of myth into tradition, which in turn transforms itself into abstract principles upon which argumentative orders are grounded. In the parallel unfolding of logical structures, cognitive competencies, ego and group identities, myth and tradition never remain the same and are simply ossified. Just as the cognitive competencies and faculties of a human being can be understood as the acquisition of more decentered and self-reflexive learning abilities, worlviews, religious and metapysical systems are also caught in the flow of processes of desubstantialization, decentering and self-reflexivity. At the very moment that universalistic forms of interaction are being established through the triumph of capitalism and the bourgeois political revolutions of the eighteenth century, religious and metaphysical worldviews are simultaneously introjected and rendered reflexive.[66] The parallelism, however, is not simply a homology. There is a fundamental link. Ontogenesis must be understood as the unfolding of cognitive capacities which in fact are also learning abilities [*Lernfähigkeiten*]. A cognitive capacity is above all a way of learning. But such learning abilities must be, as Habermas notes, "latently" available in worldviews before they may be utilized socially, that is be "transposed into societal learning processes."[67] Enlightened subjects are not possible without enlightened worldviews, like those of the classical monotheistic religions of the Axial Age.[68]

Our chronological analysis of some key sections in Habermas's texts from the late sixties through the seventies should have left the clear impression that his project of a reconstruction of historical materialism entailed the salvaging of all kinds of insights from different fields. Viewed in this fashion, Habermas has remained true to the interdisciplinary project of the Frankfurt School. Practically, this has meant that Habermas has taken recourse to what seems to be prima facie antithetical approaches: Hegel, Marx, Gadamer, Adorno, Marcuse, Blumenberg, Koselleck, but also Piaget, Kohlberg, Luhmann, Weber, Durkheim, and Mead. Here we must recall that many of Habermas's books began as *Literaturberichte* (reports on the literature of a particular debate or field).[69] This approach should not be understood at all as a type of eclecticism or theoretical promiscuity. Instead, as we have noted thus far, Habermas wants to preserve Marx's insights into history and the pathogenesis of capitalism by translating them into the language of developmental logics and rationalization processes. The point was not to dissolve Marx into Weber, and historical materialism into systems theory, but rather to see whether both could be measured by the same standard; namely the question of humanity's differentiated unfolding, in which the development of cognitive competencies are matched by the development in social structures that both preserve and mobilize the learning abilities of human subjects. To this extent, Habermas's theoretical appropriations should be seen as *litmus tests* of the theories themselves. In Habermas's case theoretical reconstructions have a systematic intent in such a way that "for any social theory, linking up with the history of theory is also a kind of test; the more freely it can take up, explain, criticize, and carry on the intentions of earlier theory traditions, the more impervious it is to the danger that particular interests are being brought to bear unnoticed in its own theoretical perspective."[70]

On the question of Habermas's relationship to religion, we note that his analysis remains basically the same, albeit now formulated in terms of a detailed theory of communicative competencies and the symbolic acquisition of identity. Whereas in his earlier writings Habermas approached the question of the secularization (i.e., rationalization) of religious and metaphysical worldviews through the lens of Weber, Hegel, and his colleagues at Starnberg Klaus Eder and Rainer Döbert, in his *Theory of Communicative Action*, Habermas approaches this question through the lenses of Mead's and Durkheim's complementary theoretical models. Just as Habermas had found Hegel, Marx, and Marcuse wanting because of their failure to address the differentiated modes of action, namely instrumental and communicative, now Habermas finds Weber, Adorno, Parsons, and Luhmann also lacking because of their failure to address the question of the unfolding of modes of interaction, their corresponding domains of embodiment, and the acquisition of cognitive capacities in terms of a symbolic, communicative, linguistic understanding of reason and agency. The failures of these great thinkers, suggests Habermas, were to be remedied from within, namely, by making explicit what they already pressupposed tacitly. Here, again, Habermas has also remained faithful to the critical orientation of the Frankfurt School, that is, to think from within the very theoretical assumptions of a given analysis or conceptual orientation its own inadequacies.

More concretely, the fundamental question for Habermas in the late seventies became how we can explain the development of universal and normative structures as the development of linguistic and symbolic competencies. This is where Mead and Durkheim are introduced to play a pivotal role. The former allows Habermas to reconstruct his theory of individuation as a theory of language acquisition, which yields that subjectivity is posterior to an intersubjectivity that is co-originary with the acquisition of language. Mead turns into the Hegel and Kierkegaard of Habermas's new theory of subjectivity, or more accurately of communicative agency. Durkheim, on the other hand, allows Habermas to reconstruct the development of normative social order as the process of symbolic integration that is matched by social solidarity. Durkheim allows Habermas to translate Weber and Parsons's question about order into a question about the symbolic constitution of social solidarity and the symbolic integration of individuals into social groups. In tandem, Habermas must discuss the way in which worldviews, whether metaphysical or religious, are linguistified, that is rendered accessible to symbolically constituted agents through being opened up to discursive or linguistic treatment. Thus, in this expanded theoretical orientation, the separation between the profane and sacred corresponds to a split in the medium of communication, namely the slip that takes place between the propositional, expressive, and normative uses of language that correspond to objective nature, the social, and subjective worlds respectively.[71]

In order to accomplish his theoretical aims, Habermas must explain how religious and metaphysical worldviews, which at early or so-called archaic stages provided an analogical coordination between nature, humanity, and society, became a "drive belt that transforms the basic religious consensus into the energy of social solidarity and passes it onto social institutions, thus giving them a moral authority."[72] Religious worldviews, in fact, hasten the process of the sublimation of the compulsive power of terrifying divine power into the normative binding power of social norms. It is not that political or social power compels religion to surrender its grip over the cowered masses; rather, in as much as religion itself is ritualized and then made part of a tradition, which then is reflexively appropriated and rendered accessible to criticism, religion itself compels subjects to adopt universalizing and critical attitudes towards its own myths and theologemes. Habermas makes this explicit when he writes, and I must quote at length:

> The core of collective consciousness is a normative consensus established and regenerated in the ritual practices of a community of believers. Members thereby orient themselves to religious symbols; the intersubjective unity of the collective presents itself to them in concepts of the holy. This collective identity defines the circle of those who understand themselves as members of the same social group and can speak of themselves in the first-person plural. The symbolic actions of the rites can be comprehended as residues of a stage of communication that has already gone beyond in domains of profane social cooperation.[73]

Through a religious symbol, or a theologumenon, a community of believers, which is also a ritual community, constitutes itself as group. This clears up the linguistic space for the first-person plural of pronouncements. Simultaneously, this linguistic circumscription initiates the separation of the sacred from the profane. Everyday practice is desacralized. Religion, as belief and ritual (that is, practice) inaugurated a particular syntactical relation that in turn overtook it.[74] *Religion linguistifies the world, catalyzing the very dichotomies that in turn linguistify the sacred.* The power exercised by myth over humans is transformed into the noncoercive coercion of moral norms. The religious is not so much disposed and left behind but, rather, internalized in society; it allows for society to take place. The normative power harbored and protected within religious contexts is released through communicative action. "Only in and through communicative action can the energies of social solidarity attached to religious symbolism branch out and be imparted, in the form of moral authority, both to institutions and to persons."[75]

Only the disenchantment and disempowerment of the sacred domain through its linguistification leads to the release of the binding, normative power stored in its ritualistically accomplished normative agreements.[76] This also releases the rational potential implied in communicative action. For, the "aura of rapture and terror that emanates from the sacred, the *spellbinding* power of the holy, is sublimated into the *binding/bonding* force of criticizable validity claims and at the same time turned into an everyday occurrence."[77] The linguistification of the sacred leads to its dialectical assimilation and transformation. The compulsion exercised by the "wholly Other" turns into an everyday occurrence which we must live by in terms of our respect for the binding force of norms of action and moral maxims. Indeed, only a universalistic, deontic, moral outlook that corresponds to a postconventional moral outlook can appropriate the normative contents of religion: "Neither science nor art can inherit the mantle of religion; only a morality, set communicatively a flow and developed into a discourse ethics, can replace the authority of the sacred."[78]

After almost half a century of public intellectual and scientific work, Habermas's contribution is both impressive and humbling. Habermas has remained vital, creative, engaged, and most importantly attuned to the *Zeitgeist*, without sacrificing intellectual honesty and rigueur. There is no field that he has left untouched, and this includes religion, even if in this his reception has been mixed and skewed. As questions of pluralism, cross-cultural dialogue, fundamentalisms, reassessments of notions of inalienable rights and sacredness of life, religiously fueled conflicts, continue to press upon contemporary life, Habermas's insights into religion can offer a guide, and point of debate. In an age of so-called globalization, the "West" itself has been provincialized, rendered local and historically contingent. Globalization has meant that the West has now to give an account of itself, to others, as well as to itself. Giving such an account must begin, above all, with a discussion of the West's relationship to its religious identity.[79] It is against this background that Habermas's wide-ranging, systematic, sociologically and philosophically informed analyses of religion commend themselves. In the brief and focused reconstruction executed above, traces and points of entry for a thoughtful engagement were offered. At the very least, this reconstruction should make it more difficult to accept quick dismissals of Habermas's insights into religion. Habermas is certainly a secularist, but he is no antireligion *philosophe*. "As long as no better words for what religion can say are found in the medium of rational discourse, it [communicative reason] will even coexist abstemiously with the former, neither supporting it nor combating it."[80]

Postscript

This chapter was originally written as the introduction to a book of Habermas's writings on religion, theology, and the philosophy of religion—not something obvious to most Habermasians, most Frankfurt School critical theorists, or even critics of Habermas, except for some astute observers and good readers of German cultural history. A personal reminiscence is in order, however. I met Professor Habermas in the early nineties at Yale, thanks to Professor Richard Bernstein. Shortly thereafter, I came to Germany to write on Karl-Otto Apel and the origins of discourse ethics. Professor Apel had just retired, but I visited Professor Habermas, who very hospitably invited me to join his Monday seminar. It was customary to go for drinks and food at a Greek restaurant named Dionysius, and Habermas would join us. Of course, Habermas's seminar was a parliament of minds, a cosmopolitan gathering, and a stopover in Frankfurt if you were in Germany. Throughout the year I was there, scholars from all over Europe, the United States, Latin America, and Asia would be in residence for the semester, for weeks, or for a one-night visit. In that seminar I met people who to this day have remained close friends. After three or four hours of intense philosophical debate, in which everyone was everyone's peer, we all would relax by continuing to argue one or another particular philosophical point. As happens with large groups, smaller ones would form, and I was fortunate to sometimes end up talking with Habermas about the latest news. (He would sometimes share a letter or news from somewhere.) Mostly, however, it was just uncensored, immediate, friendly, philosophical banter. On a few occasions, we would ask Professor Habermas to share his opinions or views on a particular subject. On a few occasions, I asked him about religion and theology. Not only because of my background interests, but also because that year, which incidentally was his last before he became Emeritus, he was giving a series of lectures on the history of the concepts of rationality, from the ancients through late antiquity (Plotinus, in particular, whom he found fascinating), Aquinas, and of course the early moderns.

I had come to Frankfurt from New York City by way of the New School for Social Research (today it is called the New University), Frankfurt am Hudson, as some called the famous exile and Émigré School. I had come to the New School from Union Theological Seminar, after choosing the New School over Harvard Theological Seminary because of Dick Bernstein's powers of persuasion. My statement for Harvard laid out a research project on Habermas and theology, which I hoped to pursue with the Fiorenzas and Cornel West, although after a couple of years with Bernstein, Seyla Benhabib, Agnes Heller, and Reiner Schürmann, my interests turned more toward philosophy proper and American pragmatism (although I was already quite familiar with both traditions since my studies with Stephen Eric Bronner, a former student of Ernst Bloch). On one specific occasion Habermas spoke with me about Paul of Tarsus and his place in the Christian canon, and on another, on Existentialism as a form of witnessing. My questions and prodding were neither innocent nor vicarious. I had read almost everything Habermas had written by then, which is why I had to write on Apel, for Apel was the x-factor in Habermas's work. My intuition before I came to Germany and before I made the decision not to write on Habermas, as much as it pained me, was that my work would be more useful and important if I offered a hitherto unsuspected key to the Habermasian enigma (only Fred Dallmayr, in my view, understood the depth of Habermas's debt to Apel). I do not regret the decision, for through Apel I also discovered an amazing philosopher, whose contribution to German and continental philosophy have yet to be properly acknowledged in the United States.[81] Nonetheless, through my studies of Habermas I came to discover his longer-term and sustained preoccupation with religious themes. It is not necessary to rehearse what I documented in the present chapter, which was in fact my post facto prospectus for a book on Habermas and religion, in which I would have sought to weave and trace two (sometimes in conflict and tension) lines of analysis in Habermas's thinking about religion. While in this text I did profile these two lines of thinking, I failed to name them. Now, with hindsight, I would not hesitate to name one the "Benjaminian/Adornian stream," while the other can most appropriately and unequivocally be called the "Hegelian/Weberian stream." While the former stream aims to both rescue and preserve religion for the sake of enlightenment, lest enlightenment itself turn into religion, the latter can only see religion as a vestigial and useless organ, a stage of the self-recognition of mind itself, of a superseded stage in the evolution of society. The tensions in Habermas's work between Kant and Hegel, Rawls and Rorty, are very real, but so are the tensions between Durkheim and Weber, Hegel and Scholem, Kant and Adorno, as concerns the role of faith, belief, religion, piety, belief in the wholly other, and a form of solidarity that is neither a product of secular society nor even something that is replaced by it. While one stream suggests that later stages of social evolution presuppose the abolition and sublation of religion, the other recognizes that religion is an inexhaustible and incommensurable reservoir of conceptual as well as social resources.

The original version of this chapter—as the introduction to a book Habermas embraced with great enthusiasm and supported all the way, as is evident with the interview he wrote with me for the volume—really wanted to say one thing: Habermas's work on religion is just beginning, and whatever he said about religion in his *Theory of Communicative Action* is a digression, a detracting detour, and simply stands anomalously vis-à-vis a deeper current of his thinking. In this text, therefore, I intended to affirm that Habermas has deeper philosophical (and even personal and biographical) allegiances to what I called the Benjaminian/Adornian stream of thought on religion. Shortly after the Spanish version of this text appeared, in a volume with the same contents but with a different title, *Athens or Jerusalem*, I had the opportunity to visit Habermas at his home at Starnberg, outside Munich.[82] We went for a drive and a walk along the Starnberg Lake, with the Swiss Alps in the distance. Habermas spoke very animatedly about his preoccupation at the moment, namely on the challenge to secular societies by believers. He was also just finishing the long essay on the "Future of the Human Species," his philosophical engagement with the question of eugenics and cloning. Shortly thereafter Habermas received the Peace Prize of the German Book Trade (*Friedenspreis des Deutschen Buchhandels*), for which he gave his amazing speech "Faith and Reason."[83] Since that speech Professor Habermas has produced a series of essays that in more ways than one confirmed my analysis and intuitions. Most of these essays are now gathered in his book *Between Naturalism and Religion*.[84] One of the essays was prepared for an encounter with then Cardinal Ratzinger, now Pope Benedict XVI.[85] What is perhaps not unusual about these essays is the way in which they link up philosophical questions about the relationship between faith and religion with questions about the secular and constitutional democracies. The conceptual irritant or depth philosophical question, one with unmistakable practical consequences, is this: does the secular, rule-of-law state presuppose normative resources that are neither autochthonous to it nor can be secured by it? Or, alternatively, are secular, rights-based, constitutional states parasitic on nonsecular resources, resources that nourish the basic social solidarity that guarantees and enables a minimum acceptance of a secular order? The philosophical-theoretical aim, therefore is to offer insights into the virtues of constitutional and democratic forms of governance and sovereignty. In this way, these essays are of one same fabric with the last decade of his philosophical production. What is significant about them is the way in which they espouse and advance a philosophical position that is called "postsecular." Postsecular is neither a rejection of secularism nor its blithe embrace. Post-secular is the Habermasian answer to the Adornian/Horkheimerian imputation that enlightenment has reverted to myth through its idolatry of instrumental and calculative reason. Of course, it is also more than a response to an intra–Frankfurt School formulation about the pathologies of reason. Yet, what is decidedly noteworthy about these essays is the way in which they speak eloquently to what I called in my introduction *dialogical cosmopolitanism*. Unflinching and unwavering defenses of rationality, especially when it is matched to developmental narratives (i.e., modernity) that invidiously relegate some to undesirable stages, leave little space for dialogue and the speech act of the other, the religious other and other cultures whose path to modernity has been different from that experienced by many European nations. In these essays Habermas affirms the voice of the other, even the other of modernity, and invites us to learn from and with them.

In what follows I will to very quickly characterize what I take to be new in these essays of Habermas and how they enhance his cosmopolitanism in general. This characterization, additionally, will complement and update the present text, making it the more useful. I will suggest that there are two background figures against which Habermas is thinking in these recent essays on religion, in one case implicitly, and without naming names, and in another quite explicitly, naming names. The two figures are Richard Rorty and John Rawls. Habermas has been a keen and sympathetic reader of some of Rorty's work.[86] He is also aware of Rorty's antireligious stance, which is made very explicit when Habermas writes about him: "Rorty advocates a strictly secular conception of politics. He opposes a political-theological self-understanding that crystallizes around the concept of sin."[87] Habermas has also been a sympathetic critic of Rawls, with whom he engaged in important exchanges that have left their indelible mark on Habermas's own conceptualization of politics in general and deliberative democracy in particular.

In one well-known review essay, Rorty refers to "religion as a conversation stopper."[88] There he argues: "I take the point of Rawls and Habermas, as of Dewey and Peirce, to be that the epistemology suitable for such a democracy [a pluralistic one] is one in which the only test of a political proposal is its ability to gain assent from people who retain radically diverse ideas about the point and meaning of human life, about the path to private perfection. The more such consensus becomes the test of a belief, the less important is the belief's source."[89] More recently Rorty has voiced the view that "the advantage of getting rid of the Falwells is worth the risk of getting rid of the Kings. But I [Rorty] have no knock-down argument to bring to bear. I just suspect that the continued existence of the churches is, by and large, more of a danger than a help to the rise of global democratic society."[90] One of the unmistakable marks of Rorty's work is that he has drawn a sharp distinction between the private and public spheres. Rorty exhorts us to consign our quest for utopia, the sublime, and perfection to the former, while in the latter we ought to pursue solidarity and justice, with the aim of expanding our loyalties, at the very least seeking to lessen suffering in this realm. Unapologetic and all the way down secularism is another name for what Rorty calls irony, the stance that we must adopt in the face of the groundlessness of our beliefs, identities, and principles. This is why Rorty believes religion is a conversation stopper, for forcing people to heed our religious notions is one way in which we seek to impose our private dreams on others and thus allow our personal quests for the sublime to colonize the public realm. Alternatively, an ironic—that is to say enlightened—attitude is one that leaves religion at home, and off the public square, precisely so that we all can gather and talk about what concerns us communally.

I suspect that Habermas finds this stance to be emblematic of how secular liberals feel about religion, but one that also is sociologically and philosophically untenable. Habermas's work has been from its inception inflected by and suffused with hermeneutical sensibilities and approaches. We are also familiar with his famous differentiation between the lifeworld and systems level. Additionally, Habermas has articulated the entwinement between justice and solidarity. More recently, Habermas has argued that the moral stance is itself an ethical commitment. In short, Habermas's work is structurally inoculated to what one can call a hermeneutical vivisection of the social agent such as the one that is performed by a Rortyan disjunction between the private and public realms. While Rorty is willing to wager incoherence, so long as the alleged neutrality of the public world remains intact, Habermas is unwilling to dissect the living tissue that links public and private existence. To ask someone to cease and desist talking about religion is to ask them to silence vital private and public sources and elements of their identity.

If Rorty remains unnamed in Habermas recent works on religion, Rawls does not. Chapter 5 of *Between Naturalism and Religion*, entitled "Religion in the Public Sphere: Cognitive Presuppositions for the 'Public Use of Reason' by Religious and Secular Citizens,"[91] takes up Rawls's treatment of religion. In an incisive way Habermas underscores the virtues of the Rawlsian approach by sketching it against the background of the self-understanding of rule-of-law state. This self-understanding is one that relied on natural reason, that is to say, on the ability of citizens to make public use of reason to justify their law making. In the same way that appeals to natural reason led to the rationalization, and eventual secularization, of natural law into human rights, natural law also led to the uncoupling of the state from church authority. It is important to note here that according to Habermas's reading, this process of decoupling and secularization was instigated from within religion itself. Another important factor that must be considered when studying the self-understanding of rule-of-law states is that they owe their historical emergence to the religious wars of the sixteenth century. Thus, a process that was partly initiated from within required an additional push in order to bring peace among warring confessions and creeds within states and among states. Consequently, the rule-of-law state emerged from two different but complementary processes: on the one hand, the secularization of the state, and on the other, the quest for a rational transparency and accountability of state power. In this way, the rule-of-law state was now able to generate legitimacy from within its own procedures of adjudication and juridification.

It is against this historical and conceptual genealogy of the rule-of-law state that Habermas places Rawls's achievements. In Habermas's reading, Rawls allows us to see how the democratic and constitutional state (forms of the rule-of-law state) achieve new levels of legitimacy through two components: the equal participation of all citizens, which then allows for the polity to understand itself as legislator; and, through "the epistemic dimension of a deliberation that grounds the presumption of rationally acceptable outcomes."[92] These two sources of democratic legitimation in turn become sources for indispensable political virtues. As Habermas writes: "It is precisely the conditions for the successful participation in the shared practice of democratic self-determination that define the ethics of citizenship: For all their ongoing dissent on questions of worldviews and religious doctrines, citizens are meant to respect one another as free and equal members of their political community. And on this basis of civic solidarity when it comes to contentious political issues they are expected to look for a way to reach a rationally motivated agreement—they owe one another good reasons."[93] Habermas concludes that Rawls's approach entails that the liberal understanding of the state demands the separation of church and state, which must be accepted by all nominations seeking to accommodate themselves to that polity, and additionally, a restricted and restrictive understanding of the use of public reason is also presupposed.

In this text, Habermas entertains some severe criticisms of Rawls's views on religion. In general, however, he seems to agree with some of those critics who argue that Rawls's understanding of the public use of reason prejudicially burdens religious members of a democratic polity. This prejudicial treatment in fact hoists on religious citizens duties and responsibilities that may create what Habermas calls "undue" mental and psychological burdens. Additionally, Habermas argues that the refusal to allow in the public square what he refers to as "nontranslated religious utterances" can lead to a deleterious homogenization of the rich cacophony of public voices that are indispensable to the process of democratic deliberation. As Habermas writes, concluding his critique of Rawls:

> The liberal state has an interest in unleashing religious voices in the political public sphere, and in the political participation of religious organizations as well. It must not discourage religious persons and communities from also expressing themselves politically *as such*, for it cannot know whether secular society would not otherwise cut itself off from key resources for the creation of meaning and identity. Secular citizens or those of other religious persuasions can under certain circumstance learn something from religious contributions.... Religious traditions have a special power to articulate moral intuitions, especially with regard to vulnerable forms of communal life.[94]

Yet, as Habermas advocates that a liberal state cannot for its own sake and that of its citizens unduly burden them with contrary and even self-denying duties, he also recognizes that allowing religious voices to be heard and uttered in the public square unleashes a dual process of learning. Secular and nonsecular citizens are put in the process of having to translate for each other their reasons. Here the rational transparency of the rule-of-law state acts as dual catalyst: both secular and nonsecular forms of thinking are required to offer reason. In other words, reason is not the sole property and presumption of the secular citizen or legislator. Neither religious citizens nor secular citizens have a privileged hold on reason. Both are commanded to undergo complementary "learning processes." It is this nonsecular presumption of reason that Habemas calls a post-secular stance, one that, additionally, converges with what he calls postmetaphysical thought. For Habermas, then, postmetaphysical and postsecular are two sides of one same process of the enlightenment of reason that in its humility and openness to its other—faith—prevents itself from reverting to myth. Postmetaphysical and postsecular reason is enlightened reason that is neither presumptuous nor self-satisfied with its own security. As he writes succinctly and beautifully: "Postmetaphysical thought is prepared to learn from religion, but remains agnostic in the process. It insists on the difference between the certainties of faith, on the one hand, and validity claims that be publicly criticized, on the other; but it refrains from the rationalist presumption that it can itself decide what part of the religious doctrines is rational and what part irrational."[95] Philosophy cannot replace religion, even as it translates its semantic potentials. Religion in turn cannot replace philosophy, even as it is an irreducible and inexhaustible resource of normative ideals. Both must coexist in mutual regard, without derisive contempt or self-defeating dismissal. In the introduction to this book I defined dialogical cosmopolitanism as the convergence of hermeneutical humility and hermeneutical solicitude. I also intimated there that Habermas's work is an exemplar of such a cosmopolitanism. The writings on religion that I just discussed make such commitment become the most evident and unquestionable. A postmetaphysical and postsecular stance is one that dispossesses itself of strong metaphysical and rational presuppositions that hinder and discourage dialogue across cultures and traditions. It is certainly an attitude that invites us to a pedagogy of reason itself, from unsuspected sources.

9

Which Pragmatism? Whose America?

On Cornel West

Introduction

Pragmatism has once again become a worthy and formidable philosophical movement, after having been eclipsed during most of the twentieth century[1]. Yet, the revival and rescue of pragmatism is linked to some of the same reasons that have made poststructuralism, deconstruction, postmodernism, and postcolonial theory the vogue of the academy and the talk of highbrow journalism. So, the revival is neither fortuitous nor adroitly forced. There is a logic to it. Indeed, there is a strong family resemblance between pragmatism's rejection of foundationalism, logocentrism disguised as a philosophy of consciousness, a strong concept of theory and philosophy, a correspondence theory of truth, a museumlike theory of language (in which there are things, and language just names them, like labels on diaramas in museums), and similar rejections by deconstruction, postmodernism, and related philosophical and literary criticism currents. Such convergences and elective affinities have been explored with great acuity and perspicacity by writers like Rorty, Bernstein, Fraser, and West.[2] What has not been analyzed and made explicit is that underlying the various projects of the re-functioning and renaissance of pragmatism, whether as simple neopragmatism or prophetic pragmatism, is the project of the reconstitution and reframing of national identity. Curiously, many have noted that there is a relationship between the projects of the total critique of reason and the critism of the West.[3] The postmodern critique has been assimilated to a critique of the West as such. The idea is that the totalitarism of the West is rooted in the totalitarianism of monological and instrumental reason, at which is aimed the deconstructive onslaught of postmodern criticisms. Such criticism arose from two sources: internally, from the

This chapter first appeared in George Yancy, ed., *Cornel West: A Critical Reader* (Malden, MA: Blackwell, 2001), 83–102.

demise of Western credibility and claim to historical privilige due to the horrors of the holocaust and two bloody World Wars; and externally, from the decolonizing countries that had suffered Western colonialism. To what extent, it should be asked, is the revival of pragmatism related to these crises and critiques of the "West," and the internal and external criticisms of the United States, who unquestionably has taken over the civilizing project of the West? Pragmatism emerged during the middle of the nineteenth century partly as a response to the question, What has the United States become, and what should it become after a traumatic and devastating Civil War? Today, when "American" philosophers reach back to nineteenth-century pragmatism as an autochthonous philosophical tradition, they do so in order to partly and sometimes covertly answer the question, what has the United States become, and what should it become after at the end of a century and the beginning of a new one? In other words—and this is the core of these reflections—how American pragmatism is reconstructed and portrayed, which figures are foregrounded and given prominence, and what philosophical importance is attached to specific insights and arguments seeks to develop and project a new national imaginary, that is, a new image of the nation. To use West's language, we might say that which America we are able to visualize and project depends on which genealogy we trace. Which pragmatism, thus, also means, which America?

The title of this chapter therefore is to be taken as suggesting that there is a deep link between these two questions, that to attempt to answer one is, in a very unequivocal sense, to attempt to answer the other. The vision that we may posses of what "America" was, is, and should become, informs and guides our reconstructions and interpretations of its intellectual biography. By the same token, how we reconstruct and interpret the history of this intellectual, philosophical, and cultural inheritance will give a very concrete content to our own anticipatory and prospective images of who we are and who we would like to become. It is precisely this entwinement that reveals itself in the contemporary debates concerning, let us say, Robert Westbrook's reading of Dewey, or John Smith's, in contrast to Richard Rorty's; or in the much broader debate between Richard Rorty's privately ironic and publicly solidaristic neopragmatism and Cornel West's publicly and privately prophetic pragmatism.[4] This subterranean connection between how we reconstruct our so-called autochthonous philosophical inheritance and what we claim we have become as a nation, as a country, and as a culture that faces very unique problems, is precisely what is revealed in the debate about the canon and the debilitating, disempowering, fetichisizing, and alienating images therein projected, legitimated, and made hegemonic. In this chapter, therefore, I argue that Cornel West's "genealogy of pragmatism" be read not just as a quaint philosophical and exegetical or history-of-ideas project. Rather, West's project should be read as a profound intervention in the national project and discourse about what and how it should define itself.

Further, I want to argue that West's reading is not just politically charged but also philosophically astute; that is, the sugesstion is that West's reconstruction of North American pragmatism is philosophically constructive because it furthers the insights of classical pragmatism. And finally, this chapter hopes to offer warrants for the arguments that West's reconstruction of pragmatism offers us a "more useful" image of our intellectul traditions. In order to accomplish these goals, I proceed by way of a reconstruction of Cornel West's intellectual itinerary and then I conclude with the discussion of four key rubrics that typify West's creative contribution to the rescue, renewal, and transformation of American pragmatism.

The Making of a Public Intellectual and the Project of Prophetic Pragmatism

Cornel West unquestionably has emerged as one of the most important public intellectuals in contemporary United States.[5] His rise to prominence can only be appropriately understood when contrasted with that of Richard Rorty. Earlier, Rorty seemed to occupy the place that West has assumed. The *New York Times Sunday Magazine*, for instance, dedicated its front page to Rorty, with a lengthy and sympathetic profile.[6] This profile, however, placed Rorty within the narrow horizon of intrauniversity struggles and transformations. Rorty is an apostate professor, a rebellious and disillusioned one, who tells of the crises internal to his own field. While announcing the obsolescence and anachronism of a particular form of doing philosophy, Rorty calls for the transformation of the profession and its revitalization by means of a turn to certain elements within American's philosophical traditions. Rorty's intellectual biography and his recent rise to prominence in the intellectual life of "North Atlantic" cultures, then, must be understood as the history of the crisis of an institution, namely professional philosophy, and of a particular philosophical tradition, namely analytic philosophy, the professional philosophy that has been hegemonic in most philosophy departments at least since World War II, and the philosophies of science, mind, and language that evolved from it. Rorty's rise to prominence, at the same time, must also be understood against the background of the overall "crises" of upper—and one should also include secondary—education within the United States. It is not without surprise, or incidental, that within the last decade we have had the similar rise to prominence of conservative intellectuals like Bloom and Hirschman, who bewail the disintegration of cultural standards brought about by the inclusion of the barbarians within the sacred halls of the parthenon of United States's intellectual life, while on the left, as well, intellectuals like Russel Jacoby, who for different reasons also bemoan the institutionalization of left intellectuals whereby these are domesticated into professional academics. The "multiculturalism," the "canon," and "why Johnny can't add," debates have to do with the crises of the educational system in the United States. In short, we need to keep in mind the plethora of institutional and societal crises out of which Rorty arises. In another context, under different goals, it would perhaps be more relevant and pertinent to attempt a richer profile of the "thick" web of economic, social, political, and cultural factors and events that have conditioned the appearance of cultural phenomena like Rorty, Bloom, Hirschmann, and Jacoby. I would suggest that this picture, rich in tones and thick in consistency, would have to start, at least, with the inclusion within the academy of an unprecedented number of minorities (i.e., blacks, women, Hispanics, Asians, etc.), the decline of the United States as a world empire, the deep and unhealed wound of the catastrophic failure in Vietnam, the return of the "Other America" in Michael Harrington's words, the conservative dismantling of the welfare state (which affected the structures of education to the point that higher education is turning more and more into a class privilege), and the attack on democratic structures, or nominal presuppositions of its working principles, by the conservative elites (I am here thinking of Ronald Reagan's Iran-Contra Affair, the unconstitutional and undeclared war on Nicaragua, the Invasion of Panama, and later, G. W. Bush's Iraq war, which was waged on the deceitful and coercive deployment of power at the international level through the United Nations. More than twenty years, in short, of conservative rule that have left a seriously undermined and politicized judiciary, a splintered legislative, and an overgrown and overpowering executive) and the transformation of United States economy from industry to a highly technical and service-oriented economy. Indeed, the elitism of a conservative government, a depoliticized body politic, the increasing demand for justice and inclusion by minorities, the struggles over the canon, and the similar struggles for the development of nonracist, noneurocentric curricula, and thus over what elements are included in the definition of our self-identity as citizens of the United States, as well as the need to meet the challenge of Japan and a postindustrial economy are all one within the fabric that also determines the rise of intellectuals like Rorty, Hirschman, Bloom.

Cornel West's case is, if not entirely different, at least one that cannot be easily subsumed under the internal dynamics of the crises of a particular institution or philosophical tradition. In contrast to Rorty, for instance, who has published most of his books with academic presses, Cornel West has published with popular and left presses such as Pantheon, which generally published left liberal materials, South End Press, Monthly Review Press, Courage Press, and even Africa World Press, as well as the religious presses Orbis Books and Westminster Press. Similarly, although West received a philosophy PhD from Princeton University, 1980, he has taught for most of his professional career in either religion departments or in theological schools (i.e. Union Theological Seminary, Yale Divinity School, Princeton University, and Harvard). West has been no outsider, but by no means has he been an insider who needs to renounce and denounce a moribund institution. Most importantly, and in stark contrast to Rorty, West has been what in Gramscian terminology we call an "organic intellectual." The use of this denomination for West is warranted by his close ties to the African American churches. In addition, West has been active in Democratic Socialists of America (DSA—the socialist conference that takes place yearly in New York), and has participated in all kinds of locally based protest movements. West moves comfortably between the different dimensions and aspects of the North American public sphere: he can preach in the morning, teach a seminar on Wittgenstein, Heidegger, and Dewey in the afternoon, talk to a group of workers on the history of the labor movement in the United States, and spend the evening playing jazz with his music buddies. All of West's talents, at the same time, come to bear on his interventions in any public situation. As against Rorty who would like to retreat behind the postfeminist realization that the private and the public are always codetermining and overdetermining each other, West wants to mobilize private experience, which is always shot through with the public, in order to transform a public which has frozen and petrified into particular modes and forms of injustice, and dehumanization.

In any event, what I am trying to delineate very sketchily is the extent to which Rorty and West are different, while also keeping in mind how both emerge from the same constellation of societal problems that presently confront United States citizens. Later, after we have gone over some aspects of West's work, these contrasts will become more evident, and perhaps we will be able to see in greater detail how West's work is important in how it contributes to a self-understanding by and of the United States that is not reflected in or refracted through Rorty's work.

In order to obtain a substantive but not exhaustive characterization of West's work, I would like to focus on two of his major works. These two works mark the two major points of transition and solidification in West's own development. There are at least four other books that merit close discussion but that in my analysis—since they are collections of essays, speeches, and reviews—can only indirectly contribute to our understanding of West's philosophical and intellectual program. Furthermore, I do not discuss the books produced during the nineties, mostly because they are applications of his insights and approach rather than departures and transformations in his basic intellectual and philosophical orientation. In any event, I will refer to them only in order to illustrate the cogency and coherence of West's project.

First, we need to note that Cornel West received his PhD from Princeton in 1980, where he submitted his dissertation "Ethics, Historicism and the Marxist Tradition." This dissertation has since been published under the title *The Ethical Dimensions of Marxist Thought*.[7] Very succinctly, in this work West sets out to demonstrate how Marx made a metaphilosophical move by means of which he overcame the classical form of doing philosophy. This metaphilosophical move consisted, in West's view and under the influence of Rorty who was his professor at Princeton, in turning away from ontological, epistemological, and metaphysical questions toward historical, social, and ethical issues. West proceeds to show, through exegeses of Marx's *1844 Manuscripts*, the *German Ideology*, and his minor historical writings, how Marx was not interested in developing a grand system of philosophy that would set aright all prior philosophical systems. Marx was interested in thick historical narratives from the perspective of the need to transform social reality. Marx's social analytics had the concrete goal of empowering historical subjects to engage in the historical transformation of situations in which these same subjects are rendered inhuman. For West, above all, Marx's social analytics was a moral judgment on a dehumanizing world that demanded its abolition and transformation.

It is with Kautsky, Engels, and Lukács that Marx's metaphilosophical move of evading Platonist-Kantian-Hegelian–type philosophy gets disarmed and his historical views become frozen systems. It is only with Gramsci that we see a return to the fundamental insights of Marx. Gramsci, in this sense, will become the true inheritor of the Marxist move that abolishes philosophy by transforming it into localized sociocultural criticism and engaged political practice. This view of Gramsci will become permanent in West's thought.

Between 1980 and 1982, when his next major work was published (*Prophesy Deliverance!*) West worked on a series of essays on the relationship between the black theology of liberation and Marxism. These essays, however, were subsumed within *Prophesy Deliverance!*, as we will see. Nevertheless, it is important to keep in mind that this work emerges in many ways out of the discussions and debates around black liberation theology that took place in the context of West's first and early teaching years at Union Theological Seminar, where James H. Cone (author of *Black Theology and Black Power* [1969]), James M. Washington (editor of Martin Luther King Jr.'s speeches and writings), James Forbes (who was senior preacher at Riverside Church in Manhattan), and where Gustavo Gutierrez, Enrique Dussel, and many other theologians of liberation have taught. West was also a member of the editorial collective of *Social Text*, where he interacted with Jameson, Aranowitz, and other Marxist thinkers. In short, the context is one where black religiosity, black liberation theology, Latin American liberation theology, postmodern, postcommunist Marxism intersect and overlap.

Prophesy Deliverance! is an ambitious, rich, challenging, and systematic work whose primary dual question is What are the tasks for Afro-American thought, and what are the intellectual, philosophical, cultural, religious, and historical sources that Afro-American thought can take recourse to in order to address these tasks as they present themselves to the Afro-American in contemporary United States? The task, in fact, of Afro-American thought becomes that of discovering, reconstructing, and rescuing its own sources. This project, in other words, is archeological, destructive, reconstructive, and constructive. For West, two of the major sources of Afro-American thought are, first, prophetic Christian thought and religiosity, and, second, American pragmatism: Christianity because it combines the fundamental principle of self-realization, self-actualization, with the deeply ingrained awareness of the dynamic between tragedy and triumph. Christianity, viewed by West through the lens of black Baptist evangelical Protestantism, is primarily a theodicy, that is, the perennial question after the origins of evil and suffering, and the tentative answer that God will redeem all suffering. It goes without saying that it is through this lens that slaves read Christianity, namely, primarily as a theodicy. From this perspective, then, slaves were able to transform Christianity into a gospel of rebellion and liberation. Christianity as theodicy, as opposed to Christianity as theogony, or cosmogony, or the like, can thus be understood as a type of optimism tempered by healthy skepticism and a long memory of defeat and failure. American pragmatism is a major source because it rejected Cartesianism, its ontological dualism and intellectual individualism, and its obsession with epistemology for a form of agency born out of intersubjectivity, and the reconceptualization of knowledge as a societal and communal affair. Above all, for West, the pragmatist's dethroning of epistemology meant the transformation of philosophy into an ethical practice of critique. To a certain extent, we may say, these two complementary sources related to a complementary division of labor. If prophetic Christianity, sobered by the theodicy perspective, contributes to the constructive function of Afro-American thought, American pragmatism contributes to its destructive function. One develops the prospective dimensions of the intellectual tradition, while the other helps undermine any kind of philosophical vision that would challenge or place in question the prospective project. Later this division of labor will not be as severe or parcelled. West will move to a reading of pragmatism that places it already within the Christian tradition. Pragmatism will be read by West more clearly and distinctly as a form of second- and third-wave romanticism, which will also bring it into a closer vicinity to Marxism, another variant of romanticism.

For West, there cannot be a serious and in-depth understanding of the tasks of Afro-American thought without an understanding of the historical situation in which Afro-Americans find themselves today, and the genesis of that situation. In this context, West suggests a periodization that attempts to provide us with a historical panorama filled with historical upheavals and major dynamics. In West's historical canvas we have, first, the age of Europe that lasts approximately from 1492 through 1945, second, the end of modernity as a consequent of the end of the age of Europe, and third, the rise of dispersive and critical practices under the rubric of postmodernism. Part and parcel of these periods, more or less, are the dissolution of industrial provinciality and the challenge to the overweening confidence in the supremacy and coherence of Western humanism, as well as the deployment of postindustrial cosmopolitanism and the development of complementary inclusionary practices, demanded and attained, if only partially, by the exploding third world and the empowered and embattled subjectivities of hitherto marginalized and occluded selves.

Of greatest importance in this historical canvas that West paints is the character of postmodernity. West paints it in broad strokes in the following manner. First, the crisis of science, brought about by its pyrrhic victory, epitomized in two bloody and devastating world wars, the atom bomb, and the unleashment of ecological devastation and waste. This crisis, notes West, resembles the crisis of the church that was catalyzed by the Enlightenment. Second, with the deligitimation of Western humanism and the rise of relativistic historicism, the cultural atmosphere of Europe gets saturated by paganism, skepticism, cynicism, fatalism, and hedonism. Third, the continuance and deepening of the attacks on the Cartesian and Kantian primacy of the subject. It is against this broadly characterized historical background that we need to understand the possibility for the development of a viable Afro-American thought tradition that addresses itself to its historical situation. In other words, it is precisely against the background of the twilight of Western humanism and the emergence of a discourse of Otherness that Afro-American thought makes its bid for self-identity and relevance.

Consonant with this historical periodization is West's genealogy of modern racism. Neither unsophisticated Marxist economic determinism nor broad cultural views will do in the task of understanding modern racism. One of the tasks, in fact, of Afro-American thought is to develop a set of analytical tools that will allow the Afro-American thinker, in particular, and society, in general, to explore the multiple levels at which racism is elaborated, produced, deployed, legitimated, and sedimented into sets of cultural norms and practices that permeate the entire social fabric. It is with this in mind that West rejects these unilateral, abstractive, insufficient perspectives and opts for the development of his own, one that he calls a "genealogical perspective." This perspective, or methodology, above all, asks the question after the conditions of possibility of a particular set of discursive practices and their accompanying structures. Here West takes Foucault as his teacher. Given this understanding of genealogy, West proceeds to ask, What are the structures of modern racial discourses, what are their grammars, how do they constitute the domains within which they locate their racialized subject-objects? In West's understanding of discursive practices, one must include not only metaphors, notions, categories, and norms, but also the social structures that serve as the institutional space for the articulation of the former. West's genealogies, then, also attain greater "thickness" when they addresses themselves to the historical, economic, political, and social causes and effects of these discursive practices and institutions. These metaphors, norms, categories, and their corresponding institutions have been conditioned and are circumscribed by three major historical events: First, the scientific revolution; second, the Cartesian transformation of philosophy; third, the classical revival, or what Bernal has refereed to as the "creation of the Greek" aesthetic myth. With science there emerges the primacy of evidence and observation that harmonizes and complements the Cartesian preoccupation with epistemological representability, which in turn also coordinate and harmonize with the dominance of the ocular within Greek aesthetic ideals. In short, modern discourses of raciality must be understood under the rubric of the hegemony of ocularity, representability, scientificity, and the hegemony of the Greek aesthetic ideal imposed by a return to Greece as a cultural model for beauty of a particular type, proportion, moderation, and so forth. The convergence of these historical currents give rise to what West calls "the normative gaze." In a second stage in the development of modern racism, there appear, as concomitants of the "normative gaze," phrenology and physiognomy, pseudosciences that, in any event, came to receive the widest support even by the most avid defenders of the Enlightenment: Hegel, Kant, Hume, and others. What Cornel West is arguing is that racism is not an aberration of modernity but, rather, its sine qua non, its logical outcome and not one of its pathologies.

Given this periodization of modernity and postmodernity, and this genealogy of modern racism, West proceeds to develop a typology of Afro-American responses to the experience of racism. In this typology, curiously, West presents himself as a internal but nevertheless serious and uncompromising critic of his own tradition(s), and in the process of characterizing these different responses, his own counterproposal is adumbrated. West speaks of four major traditions: the exceptionalist, the assimilationalist, the marginalist, and the humanist.[8]

The exceptionalist tradition lauds the uniqueness, particularity, and exceptionality of Afro-American culture and personality. This exaltation might assume either strong or weak forms depending on the emphasis and nature of the exceptional character of the Afro-American. West faults this tradition for romanticizing Afro-American experience and culture. At the same time, West also sees the origins of this type of cultural position in the emergence of a black bourgeoisie for which the primary question was that of their own cultural identity. In their hypostatization of a cultural nucleus that is representative of all suffering black humanity, the rising petit bourgeois is able to conceal its own class mobility, a class mobility that nevertheless leaves untouched, or barely calls into question, the overall structure of racism. To this tradition there belong DuBois, James Weldon Johnson, and Martin Luther King.

The assimilationalist tradition began from the opposite proposition of the exceptionalist tradition. It considers Afro-American culture inferior, a liability, a product of pathology and underdevelopment. This self-image is one of hate, shame, and fear. This perspective elaborates a sociological analysis that tries to explain the superstition, ignorance, self-hatred, and fear that plague Afro-American culture as consequences of institutional racism.

It was this type of analysis that provided the intellectual framework for the legal and political argumentation for civil rights during the decades of the forties, fifties, and sixties. This tradition rejects en toto Afro-American culture and calls for complete assimilation. To this tradition there belong people like Franklin Frazier.

The marginalist tradition, like the assimilationalist tradition, posits Afro-American culture to be constraining, confining, restrictive, and disabling, evidently as a consequence of the history of slavery and institutional racism. In contrast, however, whereas the assimilationalist tradition performed its critique of Afro-American culture from a sociological perspective, sensitive to historical determination, the marginalist tradition seems to read the negativity of Afro-American culture through the existentialist, ontological, metaphysical constructs. To this tradition there belong Richard Wright and Charles Chesnut.

The Humanist Tradition begins with the taken-for-granted humanity of Afro-Americans and sees their culture as both rich and varied, but also filled with profound insights into humanizing attitudes. Instead of seeing Afro-American culture as an opiate, it sees it as a balm that heals, a repository of memories of struggle and hopes of liberation, and also a great testament for all humanity of the struggles against all inhumanity. This tradition, above all, values the cultural gains made by Afro-Americans, despite all the odds, without romanticizing their experience, seeing them as products of humans interacting in history, in their own situations. In this sense, the projects for liberation and transformation can be and must be read through the very cultural documents left behind by Afro-Americans. The question of identity, too, can be addressed only through a serious engagement with Afro-American cultural traditions. To this tradition belong Ralph Ellison, Zora Neale Hurston, Langston Hughes, and others. Without question it is to this tradition that Cornel West himself subscribes, the one he feels closest to.

Finally, West proceeds to delineate a history of the development of black theology of liberation and what this has to say to both prophetic Christianity and progressive Marxism. In this last section, then, after he has given us characterizations of why, methodologically and substantially, Marxism and Christianity share many goals, and presupposition, and after he has sketched a history of black liberation theology itself, West gives more substance to his own project of developing an autochthonous intellectual tradition that sets out to discover both what its sources and tasks are.

After this work, West continued to develop his notion of prophetic criticism through a series of essays and reviews, in which the major themes are Marxism, the Afro-American experience, religion and contemporary social criticism, and especially Afro-American contemporary culture, which includes music, movies, and letters. We can say then that the first three quarters of the eighties was the period in which West was primarily concerned with the development of a productive and mutually fruitful discourse between, above all, two major traditions: prophetic Christianity, as best expressed in Afro-American religiosity, and progressive Marxism, as best expressed in the thought of Gramsci, Jameson, and Williams. It is within the context of this encounter that we must place West's concern with postmodernity. Indeed, in many ways, postmodernism has a place within West's thought only as long as it is conceptualized as contributing to the methodological expertise and dexterity of deep and thick deconstructive and destructive practices that elaborate narratives and analytics of both struggle and oppression. Postmodernism is internal to Marxist critiques and is already a cultural presupposition of the cultural projects of modern Afro-American subjectivity. To this period belong the collection of essays *Prophetic Fragments*,[9] *Keeping the Faith: Philosophy and Race in America*,[10] and the book he coauthored with bell hooks, *Breaking Bread*.[11] This last book is noteworthy because in it Cornel West opens himself wholeheartedly to the problem of sexism within the Afro-American community, in general, and the gender blind spot in his own work, which up to then had priviliged black male intellectuals. This entire book, a collection of conversations between bell hooks and Cornel West, represents the execution of a public critical pedagogy, the living out of an ideal that both West and hooks have espoused for as long as they have been public intellectuals.

With West's next major work *The American Evasion of Philosophy: A Genealogy of Pragmatism*,[12] the focus changes, but not the project. As we already saw above, West considers pragmatism to be one of the main sources for a critical and prophetic criticism. In his early work, however, West only dealt with pragmatism tangentially and not as extensively as he had dealt with the other two major sources, namely prophetic Christianity and progressive Marxism. In this major work of interpretative cultural criticism and history, West sets out to rescue by means of an avowedly political and ideological genealogy the most important intellectual and philosophical tradition that the United States has given birth to. West is clear and honest about the nature of his project; namely that it is a project that has to be understood against the background of our particular postmodern situation, which includes not only the internal crises of the academy, the crises of the left, but also the much more important national identity crisis. This crisis affects Afro-Americans as much as other members of the body politic, although it is clear that the point of entry into this crisis for West is precisely his belonging to the Afro-American community. With this in mind, West hopes to engage in a project of cultural reinterpretation and rescue so as to intervene directly and effectively in the mobilization of autochthonous cultural resources that would address this crisis in cultural identity. For West, this tendentious look at the history of American pragmatism is far from being an academic pursuit. It is, above all, a political gesture, one which has his project as a background. As West puts it, it is a political interpretation that hopes not to be ideological in the pejorative sense.[13]

Inasmuch, then, as West is primarily interested in rendering evident the cultural resources that gravitate around what is considered to be the most unique intellectual tradition of the United States, he reaches back to Emerson in whom West locates the origins of that particular set of cultural, philosophical, temperamental attitudes that characterized most broadly but specifically American pragmatism. In Emerson, whose "The American Scholar" is said to have been a declaration of intellectual independence for the United States, West discovers the formulations that will be again and again taken up by later North American thinkers as their guide. Emerson, according to West, elaborates a concept of the self that is at the center of the North American imperial self, namely, the protean, exceptional, creative, courageous, voluntaristic, independent, self. This self is also characterized by its idealism and experimentative character. Emerson also rejects tradition so as to free the exceptional American individuality to engage in its own project of creation. West, at the same time, is careful to note that this self that must struggle against the market but, nonetheless, inasmuch as it lives from provocation, can easily align itself with the forces of the marketplace. The protean, imperial self can also fall into an anthrophagy; it literally feeds off other people. Abstractly, the consequences of this mobile and creative self, as West notes pointedly, can lead to a kind of antihierarchism, egalitarism, and populist democracy. In the concrete, however, it leads to elitism, to a disregard for the common person and an unexpected classism. But, most important, is Emerson's "evasion" of philosophy, that is, that "he skillfully refuses (1) its quest for certainty and its hope for professional, i.e., scientific, respectability; (2) its search for foundations. It is from this refusal that the sensibilities and sentiments of future American pragmatism emerge."[14]

American pragmatism emerges, in West's account, when the Emersonian evasion of philosophy has to be justified within the professional parameters of academic philosophy. It is this evasion that Peirce, James, and Dewey, the classical philosophers of American pragmatism, are said to be justifying and explaining to their academic colleagues. Peirce, for instance, is read as carrying on one of the most devastating critiques of classical philosophy by means of a critique of Cartesianism. Above all, Peirce champions an intersubjective notion of the self (if not at least of knowledge), and a transformation of the scientific enterprise into a communal project. Here, Peirce, in West's view, is said to be also reaching to the same kind of religious and emotive sources that lay behind Emerson, namely a certain form of pietistic Christianity. Love, community, and the scientific method are woven in Peirce's thinking so as to provide us a view of the world in which both our knowledge and the order of the cosmos are assumed to be on a path of convergence.

In contrast to Peirce, James emerges as the thinker of individuality and subjectivity. James's concern with cultural and experiential issues, to which he brings to bear the methodological insights he credited Peirce for having discovered, makes him into the great popularizer of pragmatism. West creates an interesting parallel between Peirce and James. If the former gave greater primacy to convergence, harmony, oneness, and synthesis, the latter gave greater primacy to individuality, creativity, diversity, and plurality. Above all, also, these differences are temperamental. Peirce was interested in logic, mathematics, science, and the scientific method, to which he contributed in such significant ways that even today we are still discovering the importance of his contributions. James, on the other hand, was interested in religion, psychology, culture, and the constitution of subjective experience and its effects of practical life.

American pragmatism, however, comes of age with Dewey, his greatest representative. West links this coming of age of pragmatism in Dewey with the particular historical juncture in which Dewey operates. This is the time when the United States is emerging in the world scene as a world power. In this sense, the United States is confronted with a new role. It must both open itself to Europe in a new and unprecedented manner and at the same time articulate its own cultural identity.[15] The most important contribution and further articulation of pragmatism that Dewey makes is to bring to the Emersonian concern with futurity, creativity, individuality, and power the European discovery of historicity. In contrast, then, to Emerson, who thought of conditionedness in individualistic and subjective terms, and Peirce, who thought of conditionedness in terms of fallibilism and revisability of scientific theories and scientific knowledge in general, Dewey came to think of conditionedness in terms of historical contingency, that is, in terms of historical projects and processes. In short, Dewey introduces to pragmatism, via his early Hegelianism and later via his concern with the consequences of Darwinism for science, a fully historical consciousness, a deep sense of contingency and historical fallibility. This will affect Dewey's perception not only of the fundamental issues with which philosophy concerns itself, but it will also affect his very conception of philosophy. According to West, with Dewey, pragmatism finally reaches the consequences of the Emersonian evasion of philosophy. For it is with Dewey that philosophy becomes a type of social criticism in which philosophical problems are societal problems, in which philosophical systems express particular social values, goals, concerns, and historical situations. In this way, the role of the philosophers is to engage philosophical problems as social problems and not as parts of ahistorical thought systems. West calls this final "metaphilosophical" move, first made by Emerson and now concluded by Dewey, a "regicide." Dewey dethrones and beheads philosophy. For Dewey attacks—just as Peirce had attacked the Cartesian preoccupation with total doubt and self-evident truths—the obsession with epistemology and its corollary, subjectivism, or the experience of the subject without the horizon of its possibility. In Dewey's move, then, the autarchic self, the epistemology industry, as Rorty will later call it, and the hegemony of science are all challenged and demystified. With this critique there also comes the critique of philosophy as the arbiter of truth and objectivity, rationality, and normativity. Philosophy is finally dethroned, and in that sense it has been sublated, superseded into a type of social criticism with practical intent (as Habermas will talk about his own project of universal pragmatics).

For this genealogy of American pragmatism, West claims Sidney Hook, W.E.B. DuBois, C. Wright Mills, Reinhold Neibuhr, and Lionel Trilling. The tradition continues, now challenged, broadened, put on the defensive but still as a subtext, as a general horizon, a general set of presuppositions. In West's mind, Sidney Hook, who was a student of Dewey and one of his points of contact with American left thought, contributes to pragmatism by historicizing tragedy. In contrast to Dewey, who had already historicized pragmatism's meliorism and optimism, Hook historicizes Emerson's concern with evil. Hook, as a thinker deeply aware of the Marxist critique of capitalism and, in general, of a thick understanding of the material constraints on human creativity, gives a substantive twist to Emersonian theodicy. DuBois, a student of James, and Dilthey, in West's opinion, contributes to pragmatism by providing Americans with thick narratives of the struggles for liberation and democracy in the United States. DuBois's *Black Reconstruction*, for instance, is taken to be an exemplary work in that it shows the possibility for individuals to assume a democratic character and how that same character can be thwarted and suppressed by the weight of history itself. C. Wright Mills, who wrote his dissertation on the rise of the social sciences, the institutionalization of social criticism and research, and pragmatism, concerned himself similarly with the constraints on democracy. Mills was concerned, throughout all of his work, with the possibility for true democracy in a society that has organized itself around principles that lead it in the opposite direction—that is, in the direction of elitism, political apathy, technocracy, and oligarchy. Trilling, one of the first Jews to be allowed into the academy, is said to have contributed to pragmatism inasmuch as he was interested in literature as a means to develop cultural consensus. For Trilling, just as for Matthew Arnold, the tradition of Western literature was the repository of Western humanism in which mass cultures and mass democracies can find the moral and cultural resources to confront popular kitsch and totalitarian simplemindeness.[16] Trilling, in West's view, would be the pragmatic equivalent of Lukács, the Marxist literaty critic, minus the Stalinism—or Williams without the unequivocal thrust in the masses.

After this broad historical view on the effects of pragmatism in the general cultural life of the United States, West turns to pragmatism's fate within philosophy as an academic discipline. The story of pragmatism within the philosophical profession is one both of decline and resurgence, or rediscovery. West notes three major factors as being the causes for the decline of pragmatism. First, there was pragmatism's unprofessionalism, which made it anathema to the overall turn toward professionalism and respectability within the academy. Second, there was the wave of European emigrants who brought with them logical positivism, analytical philosophy, and very specialized concerns with logic, mathematics, and science. Third, the overall turn in philosophy toward the question of logic, which was originally initiated by Russell and Whitehead. Obviously one must can take issue with all of these factors. Obviously, one may challenge each one of these factors as influencing the so-called decline of pragmatism. One may even challenge the whole narrative of a decline of pragmatism, as Richard J. Bernstein has done in an extremely insightful essay on the metanarratives of pragmatism.[17] The other side of West's narrative is the metanarrative of the hegemony of analytical philosophy, which in turn has come under attack. Nonetheless, the point is that the classical pragmatism associated with James and Dewey, and partly with Mead, was eclipsed by the formalism and rigorism of analytical philosophy. It is for this reason that West portrays the period between the fifties and seventies as a stage of decline and occlusion but also a period of preparation and ferment. To this period belong, in West's narrative, principally Quine and Rorty, who, from within the analytic tradition, began a process of dismantlement and criticism that will, if not augur, at least prepare the ground for the arguments that will allow the revival of pragmatism in the eighties in the work of critics and philosophers like Nancy Fraser, Richard J. Bernstein, and Cornel West himself. Cornel West's political and contentious rereading of American pragmatism closes with analyses of Antonio Gramsci, Roberto Unger, and Michel Foucault. The goal, however, in looking at these foreign figures (an Italian, an Americanized Brazilian, and a Frenchman), is to highlight the contemporary challenges of how and why committed cultural criticism is possible; why we must and can still believe in the power of the people to rule themselves, and why if social theory is to be at the service of their cause they must contribute to the demystification of the false necessity of historical inevitability; and why forms of criticism of power and genealogies of regimes of control cannot and should not lead into a mere negative, nihilistic, and anarchistic type of great refusal. In short, the challenges concern the viability of tradition, the possibility of criticism, and the need for engaged praxis that is guided by visions of transformation that are not based on the hypostatization of false ideals, which have at the same time dispensed with historical and metaphysical certainties.

Achieving a New America: Tragedy, Memory, and Hope

As Richard J. Bernstein put it: "There is not only a conflict of narratives, but *a fortiori*, a conflict of metanarratives. There are better and worse narratives and metanarratives. And we can give good reasons in support of our claims for what is better."[18] A central thesis of this chapter is that Cornel West's metanarrative of pragmatism is not just one among many such metanarratives, but that it is one of the best ones. And that "good reasons" can be offered for such a claim. I will devote this last section to this task.

It is quite clear that West is a great synthesizer, very much like Habermas and Rorty are also synthesizers. He fuses creatively and insightfully not just particular figures but also traditions: Emerson, Dewey, DuBois, Trilling, Unger, and Gramsci; but also American social democracy, romantic Marxism, ethically motivated postmodernism, black liberation theology, politically engaged literary criticism. In contrast to Rorty, and much like Habermas, West has a foothold in different public spheres: the black church, political activism on behalf of the oppressed, excluded, and exploited. He is no mere academic, just as he is clearly not simply a preacher. This infuriates and perplexes many, as it also makes him highly attractive and seductive to many. To some Cornel West's hybridity (professor, church speaker, media celebrity, political advisor, etc.) makes him defacto suspect and unreliable. To many more, however, this is what makes him especially unique, relevant, and important in the contemporary context. But, what is this new context? After the end of the age of Europe, the end of the American century, the end of decolonization, and the begining of postoccidentalism, postorientalism, and postmoderism, it is the time for beginnings. We are beyond the "end of" and the "posts." We are at the historical juncture in which we are in need of new visions and new projects. We are also at a particular juncture in the history of American public spaces. On the one hand, the American university is poised for major transformations. The end of the cold war is beginning to register as the privatization of higher education and research. On the other hand, the rise of the infotainment sector, to use Benjamin Barber's phrase, has meant the hypercorporatization of mass media and the concomitant commodification of popular culture, in levels unimaginable by the Frankfurt School theorists. These factors are combined with a general crises of the disciplines and areas of investigation that were housed in the ivory tower. The crises of both the West and the American empire has registered itself in the interminable and trenchant debates about the future of the social sciences.[19] Another way of putting it is that the provincializing of Europe and the globalization of finance capitalism has meant that the disciplinary regimes that crystallized around such hegemonies are cracking under the power of external contestation and their own obsolescence. All of this, of course, at the very moment that obscene levels of capital accumulation in fewer hands is matched by growing levels of poverty in major cities and across the land of the brave, free, racially segregated, and empoverished masses of a nation that peddles itself as the pinnacle of history. We live in a social situation that is framed by new forms of empoverishment, as the welfare state is rolled back and the dynamics of racial apportionment shift with the influx of newer minorities. While race has not ceased to be a determinant in the political economy of the nation, Hispanics and Asians are shifting and modifying the character of this discourse. This, in broad strokes, is the contemporary context, and it is against it that Cornel West's prophetic pragmatism offers itself as a "better" metanarrative of pragmatism, which is nevertheless, a narrative about "America."

In Cornel West's prophetic pragmatism we find articulate at least four elements or themes: First, tragedy; second, political, existential, and spiritual engagement as committed praxis; third, anamnestic and historical situatedness; and fourth, posthumanistic, postuniversalistic cosmopolitanism. Each one of these themes or elements rescues, synthesizes, and reformulates elements from classical pragmatism and makes them speak to us in the context of postimperial United States. With respect to the first, it does not need too much elaboration. One of the key ideas in West's prophetic pragmatism is the foregrounding the idea of tragedy, of misery, of evil and defeat[20]—not so as to undermine the idea of the amelioration and positive transformation so central to pragmatism, but precisely so as to temper and inform that sense of progress and hope. In West's view, the protean and Adamic character of the Emersonian pragmatist needs to be tempered by a profound sense of tragedy, of the inevitability of defeat and retreat behind accomplishments won at great pains and suffering. Tragedy is the name we give to fallibilism in history. There are no guarantees and, furthermore, our best dreams will flounder on the shoals of historical resistance. Second, the quest for transformation, which is always guided by a dual vision that looks forward while never forgetting past defeats, can result in a mass movement only if it is able to combine political with spiritual and existential engagement. This means that a viable mass democratic movement can succeed only if it speaks to the existential fears, dreams, and hopes of the people as they are gathered up and preserved in a community's spiritual yearnings. As West does not tire of repeating, the culture of the oppressed is "deeply religious."[21] This culture of the oppressed is not just a palliative or opiate of the people; it is a compendium of memories and a pedagogical resource. Communities are empowered by their religious traditions, especially when these are prophetic and critical. Third, West speaks of the power of remembrance, or anamnesis, to keep us on track. How do we know we are going the right way when we have no guarantees either from reason or history, that is, when we have dispensed with all metaphysical and historical alibi? "Subversive memory" provides this guidance.[22] Subversive memory is memory of danger, a memory of past suffering, of past defeat, but also of past triumph and success. And as such, subversive memory can serve as both a negative and positive point of reference. "Memory without hope is blind, hope without memory is empty" could be one of the central aphorisms of West's prophetic pragmatism.[23] Evidently, if tragedy is what deflates all exorbitant claims to success or possibility for change, then anamnesis provides both guidance and impetus. Fourth, and finally, West offers the countours of a postuniversalistic cosmpolitanism that is based on the recognition of differences but does not seek to assimilate them or neutralized them with the acid of procedural homogenization so central to political liberalism. In contrast with Rorty, West does not speak of an abstract "we" that too easily can be confused with a type of tribal ethnocentrism. West localizes himself as a critic of American culture who speaks from the subversive memory of black Americans and who takes sides with the oppressed throughout the world. At the same time, he continues to provincialize himself in a gesture of solidarity with all those people who have suffered the underside of European modernity, and the riches and poverty of the American century. West speaks on behalf of the Enlightenment and its political bequest—not as a great past accomplishment but as something still to be achieved. In this sense, I think that Cornel West's type of cosmopolitanism is fueled not by abstract or procedural universalism, or a dehistoricized, deflated, and contingent "we," but is instead energized by a universality of diversity, or better, to use Walter Mignolo's terms, a diversality: the imperative of establishing a broader "we" on a greater appreciation, recognition, preservation, and respect for differences. For such differences are not only a challenge but also a source of creativity and hope.

Inasmuch as West has reread pragmatism in order to offer warrants for his prophetic pragmatism, then I think he has done a great service to both pragmatism and the broader U.S. society. "Pragmatism" is the American word for a sense of moral outrage combined with a sense of hope and belief in the power of people to redeem and transform themselves. If academics reject Cornel West's revitalization of this unique American gospel, the worse for them. In an age in which Americans are forging a new identity it is important to remember, as Rorty put it with respect to the political left, that the "moral identity" of our country's we is yet to be achieved.[24] But how can that moral identity be established if we also forget all the past injustices and suffering that weigh so heavily on the shoulders of so many Americans? Prophetic pragmatism is hope that refuses to forget. It is the name of a form of critical pedagogy on the side of the oppressed. It is what results when we do what Rorty, again, described so well in his review of West's *The American Evasion of Philosophy*; namely, replace the reality-appearance distinction with one that juxtaposes instead "between the oppressor's descriptions of what is going on and the oppressed's descriptions, unsupplemented by the claim that the oppressed are on the side of the *really* real."[25] In the euphoria of the moment, speaking for and with the oppressed may strike many as out of tune and even un-American. But West's pragmatism rescues for most contemporary Americans that dream that was so central to so many paradigmatic Americans—Douglass, Day, Geronimo, Lincoln, the Grimke sisters, King, Parks, Steinem, Chavez, and many others—the dream of justice for the oppressed, exploited, and excluded. For them, America remains an ideal, something still to be achieved.[26]

NOTES

Introduction

1. See Dwight N. Hopkins's essay "The Religion of Globalization" in Dwight N. Hopkins, Lois Ann Lorentzen, Eduardo Mendieta, David Bastone, eds., *Religions/Globalizations: Theories and Cases* (Durham, NC: Duke University Press, 2001).
2. Theodor W. Adorno, *Negative Dialectics* (New York: Seabury, 1973), 147.
3. Theodor W. Adorno, *Negative Dialectics*, 320.
4. See Martin Jay's *Marxism and Totality: The Adventures of a Concept from Lukács to Habermas* (Berkeley/Los Angeles: University of California Press, 1984).
5. See Eduardo Mendieta, "Communicative Freedom, Citizenship, and Political Justice in the Age of Globalization: On Seyla Benhabib's *The Claims of Culture*" *Philosophy and Social Criticism* 31. 7 (2005): 739–52.
6. See Eduardo Mendieta, "Plantations, Ghettos, Prisons: United States Racial Geographies," *Philosophy and Geography* 7.1 (February 2004): 43–59. See also my interview with Angela Y. Davis, "Politics and Prisons: An Interview with Angela Davis," *Radical Philosophy Review* 6.2 (2003): 163–78.
7. Martin W. Lewis and Kären E. Wigen, *The Myth of Continents: A Critique of Metageography* (Berkeley/Los Angeles/London: University of California Press, 1997).
8. See Edward W. Said, "Traveling Theory" in Edward W. Said, *The World, the Text, and the Critic* (Cambridge: Harvard University Press, 1983), 226–47.
9. Arjun Appadurai, *Modernity at Large: Cultura Dimensions of Globalization* (Minneapolis: University of Minnesota Press, 1996), 31. See also Pierre Bourdieu, "The Social Conditions of the International Circulation of Ideas" in Richard Shusterman, ed., *Bourdieu: A Critical Reader* (Malden: Blackwell, 1999), 220–28; and Pierre Bourdieu, *Pascalian Meditations* (Stanford: Stanford University Press, 2000).
10. See Martin Heidegger, *Being and Time* (New York: Harper and Row, 1962), 62. The passage I have in mind reads: "*Phenomenological truth (the disclosedness of Being) is veritas transcendentalis.* Ontology and phenomenology are not two distinct philosophical disciplines among others. These terms characterize philosophy itself with regard to its object and its way of treating that object. Philosophy is universal phenomenological ontology, and takes its departure from the hermeneutics of Dasein, which, as an analytic of *existence*, has made fast the

guiding-line for all inquiry at the point where it *arises* and to which it *returns*." 62, German 28.

11. Theodor Adorno, *Minima Moralia: Reflections from Damaged Life* (London: Verso, 1974), 39. See also the wonderful essay by Edward W. Said, "Reflections on Exile" in Edward W. Said, *Reflections on Exile and other Essays* (Cambridge: Harvard University Press, 2000), 173–86.
12. Eduardo Mendieta, "Chronotopology: Critique of Spatiotemporal Regimes" in William S. Wilkerson and Jeffrey Paris, eds., *New Critical Theory: Essays on Liberation* (Lanham, MD: Rowman and Littlefield, 2001), 175–200.
13. See my introduction to Enrique Dussel, *Beyond Philosophy: Ethics, History, Marxism and Liberation Theology*, ed. Eduardo Mendieta (Lanham, MD: Rowman and Littlefield, 2003), 1–20.
14. Enrique Dussel, *Ética de la Liberación en la edad de la globalización y de la exclusion* (Madrid: Editorial Trotta, 1998). See my review, "Ethics for an Age of Globalization and Exclusion," *Philosophy and Social Criticism* 25.2 (1999): 115–21.
15. I develop this reading in "Religion as Critique: Theology as Social Critique and Enlightened Reason," my introduction to Eduardo Mendieta, ed., *The Frankfurt School on Religion* (New York/London: Routledge, 2004), 1–17.
16. Jürgen Habermas, *Religion and Rationality: Essays on Reason, God, and Modernity*, edited and with an introduction by Eduardo Mendieta (Cambridge, UK: Polity, 2002).
17. Jürgen Habermas, *Israel o Atenas: Ensayos sobre religion, teologia y racionalidad* (Madrid: Editorial Trotta, 2001).
18. See my interview with Jürgen Habermas, "Wege aus der Weltunordnung" in *Blatter für Deutsche und internationale Politik* 1.04 (January, 2004): 27–46. For the English translation see "America and the World: A Conversation with Jürgen Habermas," *Logos* 3.3 (Summer 2004), available on line at: http://www.logosjournal.com/habermas_america.htm
19. Eduardo Mendieta, "What Can Latinas/os Learn from Cornel West? The Latino Postcolonial Intellectual in the Age of the Exhaustion of Public Spheres," *Nepantla: Views from the South* 4.2: 305–25.
20. See Gerhard Schweppenhäuser, *Ethik nach Auschwitz: Adornos negative Moralphilosophie* (Hamburg: Argument-Verlag, 1993).
21. Martha Nussbaum, *For Love of Country?* Ed. Joshua Cohen for *Boston Review* (Boston: Beacon, 2002), 11–14. This book, which contains Nussbaum's original essay, also contains responses and critiques by sixteen other major scholars (such as Elaine Scarry, Benjamin Barber, Kwame Anthony Appiah, Michael Walzer, Sessila Bok, Judith Butler, Emmanuel Wallerstein, and many others) and a response by Nussbaum to them. This is an outstanding little book.
22. New York: Norton, 2006.
23. Kwame A. Appiah, *Cosmopolitanism: Ethics in a World of Strangers* (New York: Norton, 2006).
24. Appiah, *Cosmopolitanism*, 151.
25. Appiah, *Cosmopolitanism*, 152–53
26. Walter Mignolo, "The Many Faces of Cosmo-polis: Border Thinking and Critical Cosmopolitanism," *Public Culture* 12.3 (Fall 2000): 721–48.
27. Mignolo, "The Many Faces of Cosmo-polis," 744.
28. Mignolo, "The Many Faces of Cosmo-polis," 744.
29. Judith Butler, "Universality in Culture" in Martha Nussbaum, *For Love of Country?* 45–52, citation at 49. Butler develops more extensively her views on universality in the book coauthored with Žižek and Laclau, *Contingency, Hege-*

mony, Universality: Contemporary Dialogues on the Left* (London/New York: Verso, 2000).

30. See Celina María Bragagnolo, "Deprovincializing the West: How the Rest Globalizes the West," forthcoming in Gary Backhaus and John Muringi, eds. *Interfacing Globalization and Colonialism* (forthcoming).
31. Butler, "Universality in Culture," 45.
32. Lorenzo C. Simpson, *The Unfinished Project: Toward a Postmetaphysical Humanism* (New York/London: Routledge, 2001), 92.
33. Amartya Sen, "Democracy and Its Global Roots: Why Democratization is Not the Same as Westernization," *The New Republic* 229.4, 629 (October 6, 2003): 28–35, citation at 35. See also part four of his recent collection of essays, Amartya Sen, *The Argumentative Indian: Writings on Indian History, Culture and Identity* (New York: Farrar, Straus and Giroux, 2005).

Chapter 1. Philosophizing Globalizations

1. See for instance A. T. Kearney's globalization index in *Foreign Policy*, "Measuring Globalization: Who's Up, Who's Down?" *Foreign Policy* (January/February 2003): 60–72. I refer to *Foreign Policy*'s globalization index, not because I take it to be an accurate or even tell-tale type of indicator, but only because it gives a modicum of insight into the different ways in which globalization can be measured. Later in this chapter I will talk about the types of indexes that the World Bank, or Worldwatch came up with, which in turn have been contested by independent researchers, who argued that the indicators and indexes help to conceal the ways in which developing societies are in fact not developing, but undeveloping digging themselves deeper into cycles of enduring inequality.
2. Jeremy Black, *Maps and History: Constructing Images of the Past* (New Haven/London: Yale University Press, 1997).
3. J. B. Harley, *The New Nature of Maps: Essays in the History of Cartography* (Baltimore/London: Johns Hopkins University Press, 2001).
4. The thinker who has most consistently worked on the epistemological challenges of globalization to social science in general, and to philosophy in particular, is without a doubt Immanuel Wallerstein. See these two books in particular: *The End of the World as We Know It: Social Science for the Twenty-First Century* (Minneapolis: University of Minnesota Press, 1999) and *The Uncertainties of Knowledge* (Philadelphia: Temple University Press, 2004). See also the by-now classic Gulbenkian Commission report: *Open the Social Sciences: Report for the Gulbenkian Commission on the Reconstruction of the Social Sciences* (Stanford: Stanford University Press, 1996).
5. There are "only globalizations"—if only because there are so many ways of trying to make sense, to organize our ways of knowing this globalized world. In fact, I have developed a typology of theories of globalization, all clearly proffering different pictures and analyses of the world. See Eduardo Mendieta, "Society's Religion: The Rise of Social Theory, Globalization, and the Invention of Religion" in Dwight N. Hopkins, Lois Ann Lorentzen, Eduardo Mendieta, and Davi Batstone, eds. *Religions/Globalizations: Theories and Cases* (Durham, NC: Duke University Press, 2001), 46–65.
6. See United Nations Centre for Human Settlements (Habitat), *Cities in a Globalizing World: Global Report on Human Settlements 2001* (London/Sterling, VA: Earthscan, 2001).

7. See Eugene Linden, "The Exploding Cities of the Developing World" in Patrick O'Meare, Howard D. Mehlinger, and Matthew Krain, eds., *Globalization and the Challenges of a New Century* (Bloomington: Indiana University Press, 2000), 406–15.
8. Mike Davis, "Planet of Slums: Urban Involution and the Informal Proletariat" *New Left Review* 25 (March–April, 2004): 5–34.
9. See the wonderful discussion of the class dimensions of this acceleration of time by Zygmut Bauman, *Globalization: The Human Consequences* (New York: Columbia University Press, 1998), 6–26.
10. See James N. Rosenau, *Distant Proximities* (Princeton: Princeton University Press, 2003), especially chapter 11: "The Information Revolution: Both Powerful and Neutral," 257–72.
11. The terms "horizon of expectation" and "space of experience" come from Reinhart Koselleck, *Futures Past: On the Semantics of Historical Time* (Cambridge, MA: MIT Press, 1985), 267–88.
12. See James N. Rosenau, *Distant Proximities: Dynamics beyond Globalization* (Princeton: Princeton University Press, 2003).
13. See Fernand Braudel, *The Mediterranean and the Mediterranean World in the Age of Phillip II* (New York: Harper and Row, 1976), 20–21; and Fernand Braudel, *Las Ambiciones de la Historia* (Barcelona: Critica, 2002 [1997]), chapter 3.
14. I take E. P. Thompson's germinal essay "Time, Work-Discipline and Industrial Capitalism," first published in 1967, to have inaugurated something like a political economy of time production-consumption-disciplining. See E. P. Thompson, *Customs in Common: Studies in Traditional Popular Culture* (New York: New Press, 1991), 352–403.
15. James Gleick, *Faster: The Acceleration of Just About Everything* (New York: Pantheon, 1999).
16. Gerhard Dorn-Van Rossum, *History of the Hour: Clocks and Modern Temporal Orders* (Chicago/London: University of Chicago Press, 1996). See also Arno Borst, *The Ordering of Time: From Ancient Computus to the Modern Computer* (Chicago: University of Chicago Press, 1993).
17. Alfred W. Crosby, *Ecological Imperialism: The Biological Expansion of The Europe, 900–1900* (Cambridge: Cambridge University Press, 1986).
18. Vandana Shiva, *Biopiracy: The Plunder of Nature and Knowledge* (Boston: South End, 1997).
19. See Alfred W. Crosby, Jr., *The Columbian Exchange: Biological and Cultural Consequences of 1492* (Westport, CT: Greenwood, 1972), especially chapters 3 and 6.
20. See Manuel Castells, *The Rise of the Network Society*, vol. 1, *The Information Age: Economy, Society and Culture*, second edition (Malden, MA: Blackwell, 2000 [1996]), especially chapters 6 and 7.
21. See Ranajit Guha, *History at the Limit of World History* (New York: Columbia University Press, 2002).
22. See Gayatri Chakravorty Spivak, *A Critique of Postcolonial Reason: Toward a History of the Vanishing Present* (Cambridge, MA: Harvard University Press, 1999).
23. Peter Galison and David J. Stump, eds., *The Disunity of Science: Boundaries, Contexts, and Power* (Stanford: Stanford University Press, 1996).
24. Peter Galison, "Material Culture, Theoretical Culture, and Delocalization" in Joan W. Scott and Debra Keates, eds., *Schools of Thought: Twenty-five Years of*

Interpretative Social Science (Princeton: Princeton University Press, 2001), 179–93.

25. See Dipesh Chakrabarty, *Provincializing Europe* (Princeton: Princeton University Press, 2000); see also Anthony Pagden, ed., *The Idea of Europe: From Antiquity to the European Union* (Cambridge: Cambridge University Press, 2001).
26. Couze Venn, *Occidentalism: Modernity and Subjectivity* (London: Sage, 2000).
27. Ian Buruma and Avishai Margalit, *Occidentalism: The West in the Eyes of Its Enemies* (New York: Penguin, 2004).
28. Bill McKibben, *The End of Nature* (New York: Anchor, 1999 [1989]).
29. Klaus Eder, *The Social Construction of Nature* (London: Sage, 1996).
30. Roland Robertson, *Globalization: Social Theory and Global Culture* (London: Sage, 1992), 173–74.
31. See Kwame Anthony Appiah, "Whose Culture Is It?" *New York Review of Books* 52.2 (February 9, 2006): 38–41.
32. See Arjun Appadurai, *Modernity at Large: Cultural Dimensions of Globalization* (Minneapolis: University of Minnesota Press, 1996), especially the discussion in chapter 3: "Global Ethnoscapes: Notes and Queries for a Transnational Anthropology."
33. See table in Alfred W. Crosby Jr., *The Columbian Exchange: Biological and Cultural Consequences of 1492*, 216, table 4.
34. Saskia Sassen, *Guests and Aliens* (New York: New Press, 1999)
35. See Seyla Benhabib's excellent treatment of this question: *The Rights of Others: Aliens, Residents, Citizens* (Cambridge: Cambridge University Press, 2004).
36. World Bank, *World Development Report 2000/2001* (New York: Oxford University Press, 2001), 3, my italics.
37. Ibid., 3.
38. Ibid., 6.
39. World Bank, *World Development Report 2003* (New York: Oxford University Press, 2003), 2.
40. Ibid., 7.
41. Mike Davis, *Planet of Slums* (London/New York: Verso, 2006).
42. I explored Davis's claims further in "The Axle of Evil: SUVing through the Slums of Globalizing Neoliberalism," *City* 9.2 (July 2005): 195–204.
43. Worldwatch Institute, *State of the World 2001* (New York: Norton, 2001), 7.
44. Paul Ehrlich and Anne Ehrlich, *One with Nineveh: Politics, Consumption, and the Human Future* (Washington/Covelo/London: Island Press/Shearwater, 2004), 24.
45. From Hilary French, *Vanishing Borders: Protecting the Planet in the Age of Globalization* (New York/London: Norton, 2000), 11.
46. This is from the 2001 report on *Ecological Footprint of Nations* by the Redefining Progress's Sustainability Program (www.Redefiningprogress.org/publications/ef1999.pfd.
47. Vandana Shiva, *Water Wars: Privatization, Pollution, and Profit* (Boston: South End, 2002), 1.
48. Paul Ehrlich and Anne Ehrlich, *One with Nineveh: Politics, Consumption, and the Human Future* (Washington/Covelo/London: Island Press/Shearwater, 2004), 40. See also Richard Petrella, *The Water Manifesto: Arguments for a World Water Contract* (London/New York: Zed, 2001).
49. Vandana Shiva, *The Violence of the Green Revolution: Third World Agriculture, Ecology and Politics* (London/New Jersey: Zed, 1991).

50. Andrew Kimbrell, ed. *Fatal Harvest: The Tragedy of Industrial Agriculture* (Washington/Covelo/London: Island, 2002).
51. The green revolution has been another form of ecological imperialism, but its twenty-first century effects could be catastrophic. See Eduardo Mendieta, "Imperial Gardens: Ecological Imperialism and the Re-Seeding of the New World" in Gary Backhaus and John Murungi, eds., *Ecoscapes: Geographical Patternings of Relations* (Lanham, MD: Lexington, 2006), 1–16.
52. I am paraphrasing Peter Manning's powerful and accurate picture: "Farming is . . . an annual artificial catastrophe, and it requires the equivalent of three or four tons of TNT per acre for a modern American farm. Iowa's fields require the energy of 4,000 Nagasaki bombs every year." "The Oil We Eat: Following the Food Chain Back to Iraq" *Harper's Magazine* 308.1845 (February, 2004), 39.
53. McNeill, *Something New Under the Sun: An Environmental History of the Twentieth-Century World* (New York: Penguin, 2000), 224, note 77.
54. Manning, "The Oil We Eat: Following the Food Chain Back to Iraq," *Harper's Magazine* 308.1845 (February, 2004), 44.

Chapter 2. Invisible Cities

I want to thank Bob Catterall for encouraging me to write this chapter and for his comments on early versions of it. I also want to thank Lois Ann Lorentzen and Nelson Maldonado Torres, who read it with great care and made substantive suggestions, corrections, and criticisms that have helped me to better understand my own project. I also want to thank Enrique Dussel, Jürgen Habermas, Walter Mignolo, and Santiago Castro-Gómez, with whom I have discussed many of the ideas here developed, and who have given me impetus to continue along this line with their own pioneering works.

Chapter epigraph is from Italo Calvino, *Invisible Cities* (New York: Harcourt Brace Javanovich, 1974), 69.

1. John Rennie Short et al., "From World Cities to Gateway Cities: Extending the Boundaries of Globalization Theory," *City: Analysis of Urban Trends, Culture, Theory, Policy, Action* 4.3 (November 2000): 317–40; Lawrence Grossberg, "Speculations and Articulations of Globalization," in *Polygraph* 11 (1999): 11–48; and Michael Veseth, *Selling Globalization: The Myth of the Global Economy* (Boulder/London: Rienner, 1998).
2. David Held and Anthony McGrew, *The Global Transformations Reader: An Introduction to the Globalization Debate* (Cambridge, UK: Polity, 2000); and David Held et al., *Global Transformations: Politics, Economics, and Culture* (Stanford: Stanford University Press, 1999).
3. See Saskia Sassen, *Territory, Authority, Rights: From Medieval to Global Assemblages* (Princeton: Princeton University Press, 2006), *Cities in a World Economy*, second edition (Thousand Oaks: Pine Forge, 2000); *Guests and Aliens* (New York: New Press, 1999); *Globalization and Its Discontents: Selected Essays* (New York: New Press, 1998); *Losing Control? Sovereignty in an Age of Globalization* (New York: Columbia University Press, 1996); and *The Global City: New York, London, Tokyo* (Princeton: Princeton University Press, 1991).
4. David Harvey, *The Condition of Postmodernity: An Enquiry into the Origins of Cultural Change* (Cambridge, MA: Basil Blackwell, 1989).
5. Martin E. Marty and R. Scott Appleby, eds., *The Fundamentalism Project*, 5 vols. (Chicago: University of Chicago Press, 1991–1995).

6. See Dwight N. Hopkins et al., eds., *Religions/Globalizations* (Durham, N.C.: Duke University Press, 2001); Max Stackhouse and Peter J. Paris, eds., *God and Globalization*, vol. 1, *Religion and the Powers of the Common Life*, vol. 2, *The Spirit and the Modern Authorities* (Harrisburg: Trinity, 2000–2001); and Peter Beyer, *Religion and Globalization* (London: Sage, 1994).
7. See José Casanova, *Public Religions in the Modern World* (Chicago: University of Chicago Press, 1994); Niklas Luhmann, *Die Religion der Gesellschaft* (Frankfurt: Suhrkamp, 2000); and Eduardo Mendieta, "Society's Religion: The Rise of Social Theory, Globalization, and the Invention of Religion" in Hopkins et al., *Religions/Globalizations* (Durham, N.C.: Duke University Press, 2001).
8. Saskia Sassen, *Cities in a World Economy,* 2000, 143, emphasis added.
9. Molly O'Meara, *Reinventing Cities for People and the Planet* (Worldwatch Paper 147, June 1999), 5.
10. State of the World's Cities 1999—Cities in a Globalizing World, *http://www.urbanobservatory.org/swc1999/cities.html*
11. United Nations Development Programme, *Human Development Report 1998* (New York: Oxford University Press, 1998), 2–4.
12. Daniel D. Luria and Joel Rogers, *Metro Futures: Economic Solutions for Cities and Their Suburbs* (Boston: Beacon, 1999); Kenneth Jackson, *Crabgrass Frontier: The Suburbanization of the United States* (New York: Oxford University Press, 1985); and Douglass S. Massey and Nancy A. Denton, *American Apartheid: Segregation and the Making of the Underclass* (Cambridge: Harvard University Press, 1993).
13. Henri Lefebvre, *Le Droit a la ville* (Paris: Éditions Anthropos, 1969).
14. Martin Heidegger, *Being and Time* (Albany, NY: State University of New York Press, 1996), 30.
15. Anthony Giddens, *The Constitution of Society* (Cambridge: Polity, 1984); and Giddens, *Social Theory and Modern Sociology* (Stanford: Stanford University Press, 1987).
16. See Martin Heidegger, *The Question Concerning Technology and Other Essays* (New York: Harper and Row, 1977).
17. Fredric Jameson, "Notes on Globalization as a Philosophical Issue" in Fredric Jameson and Masao Miyoshi, eds., *The Cultures of Globalization* (Durham, NC: Duke University Press, 1998).
18. Manuel Castells, *The Information Age: Economy, Society and Culture*, vol. 1, *The Rise of the Network Society*; vol. 2, *The Power of Identity*; and vol. 3, *End of Millenium* (Malden, MA/Oxford, UK: Blackwell, 1996–1998).
19. Karl Jaspers, *The Origin and Goal of History* (New Haven: Yale University Press, 1953).
20. Amartya Sen, *Development as Freedom* (New York: Knopf, 1999).
21. Jeremey Rifkin, *The Biotech Century: Harnessing the Gene and Remaking the World* (New York: Tarcher/Putnam, 1998).
22. Kristin Dawkins, *Gene Wars: The Politics of Biotechnology* (New York: Seven Stories, 1997).
23. Vandana Shiva, *Stolen Harverst: The Hijacking of the Global Food Supply* (Cambridge, MA: South End, 1999); *Biopiracy: The Plunder of Nature and Knowledge* (Boston: South End, 1997); and *The Violence of the Green Revolution: Third World Agriculture, Ecology and Politics* (London/New Jersey: Zed, 1991).
24. *National Geographic* (August 1999), "Global Culture."
25. Scott Lash and John Urry, *Economies of Signs and Spaces* (London: Sage, 1994); Jean Baudrillard, *For a Critique of the Political Economy of the Sign* (St. Louis,

MO: Telos, 1981); and Donald M. Lowe, *The Body in Late-Capitalist USA* (Durham, NC: Duke University Press, 1995).

26. Marc Lappé and Britt Bailey, *Against the Grain: Biotechnology and the Corporate Takeover of Your Food* (Monroe, ME: Common Courage, 1998); and Jeremey Rifkin, *The Biotech Century*, 1998.
27. George Kubler, *The Shape of Time: Remarks on the History of Things* (New Haven and London: Yale University Press, 1962); Gregory Benford, *Deep Time: How Humanity Communicates across Millenia* (New York: Avon, 1999); Martin Heidegger, *The Concept of Time* (Oxford, UK/Cambridge, MA: Blackwell, 1992); and Norbert Elias, *Time: An Essay* (Cambridge, MA: Blackwell, 1992).
28. Immanuel Wallerstein, *Unthinking Social Science: The Limits of Nineteenth-Century Paradigms* (Cambridge, UK: Polity, 1991).
29. Paul Heelas, Scott Lash, and Paul Morris, eds., *Detraditionalization: Critical Reflections on Authority and Identity* (Cambridge, MA: Blackwell, 1996).
30. Sir Peter Hall, *Cities in Civilization* (New York: Pantheon, 1998).
31. Eric Hobsbawm, *The Age of Extremes* (New York: Pantheon, 1994), 289.
32. Vandana Shiva, *Monocultures of the Mind: Perspectives on Biodiversity and Biotechnology* (London/New York: Zed, 1993).
33. See Zygmut Bauman, *Globalization: The Human Consequences* (New York: Columbia University Press, 1998), 53–54.
34. Jürgen Habermas, *The Postnational Constellation: Political Essays* (Cambridge, MA: MIT Press, 2001); and Paul Kennedy, *Preparing for the Twenty-First Century* (New York: Random House, 1993).
35. See David Harvey, *Space of Global Capitalism: Towards a Theory of Uneven Geographical Development* (New York/London: Verso, 2006).
36. Mike Featherstone, *Undoing Culture: Globalization, Postmodernism and Identity* (London: Sage, 1995).
37. Sassen, *Globalization and Its Discontents*, 1998, xx.
38. Habermas, *The Postnational Constellation*, 2001, 39.
39. José Ortega y Gasset, *The Revolt of the Masses* (Notre Dame: University of Notre Dame Press, 1985).
40. Johannes Fritsche, *Historical Destiny and National Socialism in Heidegger's "Being and Time"* (Berkeley/Los Angeles: University of California Press, 1999).
41. Christopher Lasch, *The Culture of Narcissism: American Life in an Age of Diminishing Expectations* (New York: Warner, 1979).
42. Zygmut Bauman, "Postmodern Religion?" in Paul Heelas, ed., *Religion, Modernity and Postmodernity* (Cambridge, UK: Blackwell, 1998); Ulrich Beck, *Was ist Globalisierung?* (Frankfurt am Main: Suhrkamp, 1997); Anthony Giddens, *The Consequences of Modernity* (Cambridge: Polity, 1990); and Habermas, *The Postnational Constellation*, 2001.
43. Enrique Dussel, *Ética de la Liberación en la edad de globalización y de la exclusión* (Madrid: Editorial Trotta, 1998).
44. Anthony D. King, *Urbanism, Colonialism, and the World Economy: Cultural and Spatial Foundations of the World Urban System* (London: Routledge, 1990); and Sassen, *Guests and Aliens*, 1999.
45. Arjun Appadurai, *Modernity at Large: Cultural Dimensions of Globalization* (Minneapolis: University of Minnesota Press, 1996).
46. Daniel Bell, *The Cultural Contradictions of Capitalism* (New York: Basic, 1976), 29.
47. Alfred North Whitehead, *Science and the Modern World* (New York: Macmillan, 1925), 141.

48. Martin Kenney, *The University Industrial Complex* (New Haven: Yale University Press, 1986); and Stanley Aronowitz, *The Knowledge Factory: Dismantling the Corporate University and Creating True Higher Learning* (Boston: Beacon, 2000).
49. Anthony Giddens, *The Constitution of Society* (Cambridge: Polity, 1984); and Anthony Giddens, *Social Theory and Modern Sociology* (Stanford: Stanford University Press, 1987).
50. David Rothenberg, *Hand's End: Technology and the Limits of Nature* (Berkeley: University of California Press, 1993).
51. Gabriel Brahm Jr. and Mark Driscoll, eds., *Prosthetic Territories: Politics and Hypertechnologies* (Boulder: Westview, 1995).
52. Donna Haraway, *Simians, Cyborgs, and Women: The Reinvention of Nature* (New York: Routledge, 1991).
53. Katherine N. Hayles, *How We Became Posthuman: Virtual Bodies in Cybernetics, Literature, and Informatics* (Chicago: University of Chicago Press, 1999).
54. Manuel Castells, *The Information Age: Economy, Society and Culture*, vol. 1, *The Rise of the Network Society* (Malden, MA/Oxford, UK: Blackwell, 1996), 65.
55. Theodor W. Adorno, "The Idea of Natural History," *Telos* 60 (1984): 31–42.
56. Niklas Luhmann, *Die Religion der Gesellschaft* (Frankfurt: Suhrkamp, 2000), 118.
57. Luhmann, *Die Religion der Gesellschaft*; and Roland Robertson and William R. Garrett, eds., *Religion and Global Order: Religion and the Political Order* (New York: Paragon, 1991).
58. Eduardo Mendieta, "Introduction" in Jürgen Habermas, *Religion and Rationality: Essays on Reason, God, and Modernity* (Cambridge, UK: Polity, 2002).
59. William C. Placher, *The Domestication of Transcendence: How Modern Thinking about God Went Wrong* (Louisville, KY: Westminster, 1996); and Jürgen Habermas, *Postmetaphysical Thinking: Philosophical Essays* (Cambridge, MA: MIT Press, 1992).
60. Erik Barnouw, *Tube of Plenty: The Evolution of American Television* (New York: Oxford University Press, 1990).
61. Jürgen Habermas, *The Inclusion of the Other: Studies in Political Theory* (Cambridge, MA: MIT Press, 1998).
62. Michael Hardt and Antonio Negri, *Empire* (Cambridge, MA: Harvard University Press, 2000), 413.
63. Werner Hamacher, "One 2 Many Multiculturalisms" in *Violence, Identity, and Self-Determination*, Hent de Vries and Samuel Weber, eds. (Stanford: Stanford University Press, 1997).
64. Roland Robertson, "Globalisation or Glocalisation?" *The Journal of International Communication* 1.1 (1994): 33–52.
65. Karl Marx, "Toward a Critique of Hegel's Philosophy of Right: Introduction" in Karl Marx, *Selected Writings*, ed. Lawrence H. Simon (Indianapolis/Cambridge: Hackett, Inc., 1994), 28.

Chapter 3. From Modernity, through Postmodernity, to Globalization

1. Werner Hamacher, "One 2 Many Multiculturalisms" in *Violence, Identity, and Self-Determination*, ed. Hent de Vries and Samuel Weber (Stanford: Stanford University Press, 1997), 295–96.

2. Santiago Castro-Gómez, *Crítica de la razón latinoamericana* (Barcelona: Puvill, 1996), Hermann Herlinghaus and Monika Walter, eds., *Posmodernidad en la periferia: Enfoques latinoamericanos de la nueva teoria cultural* (Berlin: Langer, 1994); and John Beverly, José Oviedo, Michael Aronna, eds., *The Postmodernism Debate in Latin America* (Durham/London: Duke University Press, 1995).
3. See the classic study by Michael Köhler, "'Postmodernismus': ein begriffsgeschichtlicher Ueberblick," *Amerikastudien* 22.1 (1977): 8–18; the discussions by Wolfgang Welsch, *Unsere postmoderne Moderne* (Weinheim: Acta Humaniora, 1988); and Hans Bertens, *The Idea of the Postmodern: A History* (London/New York: Routledge, 1995).
4. See Jean-François Lyotard, *The Postmodern Condition: A Report on Knowledge* (Minneapolis: University of Minnesota Press, 1984 [1979]).
5. Enrique Dussel, *The Underside of Modernity: Apel, Ricoeur, Rorty, Taylor, and the Philosophy of Liberation* (Atlantic Highlands, NJ: Humanities, 1996).
6. See the fascinating and enlightening discussion by Ann Douglass, "Periodizing the American Century: Modernism, Postmodernism, and Postcolonialism in the Cold War Context" in *Modernism/Modernity* 5.3 (1998), 71–98. See also my discussion of postmodernity as an epochal marker and its relationship to Latin America specifically: Eduardo Mendieta, "La Geografía de la Modernidad: Los Regimenes spacio-temporales de la Modernidad" in *Cuadernos Americanos—Nueva Epoca* 67 Enero-Febrero, vol. 1 (1997): 238–55.
7. Welsch, *Unsere postmoderne Moderne* (1988).
8. See the divergent approaches to the question of postmodernity in Bertens, *The Idea of the Postmodern* (1995); Barry Smart *Postmodernity* (London/New York: Routledge, 1993); and Zygmut Bauman, the don of postmodern sociology, *Intimations of Postmodernity* (London/New York: Routledge, 1992); as well as Scott Lash, *The Sociology of Postmodernism* (London/New York: Routledge, 1990).
9. The classical work from an economic angle is David Harvey, *The Condition of Postmodernity* (Oxford/Cambridge: Blackwell, 1989), which was partly anticipated by Daniel Bell, *The Coming of Post-Industrial Society* (New York: Basic, 1973).
10. This type of analysis is to be found in Linda Hutcheon, *The Poetics of Postmodernism* (London/New York: Routledge, 1988); Andreas Huyssen, *After the Great Divide: Modernism, Mass Culture, Postmodernism* (Bloomington/Indianapolis: Indiana University Press, 1987); and some works by Jameson, who pursues aesthetic theory under the guise of cultural Marxism. See Fredric Jameson, *The Political Unconscious: Narrative as Socially Symbolic Art* (Ithaca, NY: Cornell University Press, 1981), and *Postmodernism, or the Cultural Logic of Late Capitalism* (Durham, NC: Duke University Press, 1990). See also the works by Albrecht Wellmer, as well as Peter Bürger. With respect to Latin America, see Santiago Colás, *Postmodernity in Latin America: The Argentine Paradigm* (Durham, NC: Duke University Press, 1994); Neil Larsen, *Reading North by South: On Latin American Literature, Culture, and Politics* (Minneapolis: University of Minnesota Press, 1995); and John Beverly, "The Politics of Latin American Postmodernism" in Beverly, *Against Literature* (Minneapolis: University of Minnesota Press, 1993), 103–23.
11. Durcilla Cornell, *The Philosophy of the Limit* (New York: Routledge, 1992).
12. The classical point of reference is, of course, Jürgen Habermas, *The Philosophical Discourse of Modernity: Twelve Lectures* (Cambridge, MA: MIT Press, 1987); but see also Gianni Vattimo, *The End of Modernity: Nihilism and Hermeneutics of Postmodern Culture. Parallax: Re-visions of Culture and*

Society (Baltimore: Johns Hopkins University Press, 1988); and Robert B. Pippin, *Modernism as a Philosophical Problem: On the Dissatisfaction of European High Culture* (Cambridge: Blackwell, 1991).

13. Jean Baudrillard, *In the Shadow of the Silent Majorities . . . or The End of the Social and Other Essays* (New York: Semiotexte, 1983).
14. See Stuart Hall et al., *Modernity: An Introduction to Modern Societies* (Cambridge, MA: Blackwell, 1995); as well as Edward Said, *Orientalism* (London: Chatto and Windus, 1978) and *Culture and Imperialism* (London: Vintage, 1993); and Ato Quayson, *Postcolonialism: Theory, Practice or Process?* (Cambridge: Polity, 2000). See also all the works by Ramón Grosfoguel.
15. Tzvetan Todorov, *The Morals of History* (Minneapolis: University of Minnesota Press, 1995); Agnes Heller, *Can Modernity Survive?* (Berkeley: University of California Press, 1990); and A. Heller, *A Theory of Modernity* (Malden, MA: Blackwell, 1999).
16. John Beverly, José Oviedo, and Michael Aronna, eds., *The Postmodernism Debate in Latin America* (Durham/London: Duke University Press, 1995), 4.
17. Ann Douglass, "Periodizing the American Century: Modernism, Postmodernism, and Postcolonialism in the Cold War Context," *Modernism/Modernity* 5.3 (1998): 71–98.
18. Zygmut Bauman has been one of the few theorists of postmodernity to make this explicit. See Zygmut Bauman, *Legislators and Intepreters: On Modernity, Postmodernity, and Intellectuals* (Cambridge: Polity, 1987). With respect to the Latin American case, the by-now classic point of reference is Santiago Castro-Gómez, *Crítica de la razón latinoamericana* (Barcelona: Puvill, 1996).
19. The following discussion is guided by Jameson's acute reflections on the plurality of ideological positions on the postmodernism debate. See Jameson, "The Politics of Theory: Ideological Positions in the Postmodernism Debate," *New German Critique* 33 (Fall 1984): 53–66. My knowledge of these different positions is informed above all by the work of Santiago Castro-Gómez, and the collections by Beverley, Oviedo, and Aronna (1995); and Hermann Herlinghaus and Monika Walter, eds., *Posmodernidad en la periferia: Enfoques latinoamericanos de la nueva teoria cultural* (Berlin: Langer, 1994). In an unfortunately protracted volume, which dates in composition back to 1995, Pedro Lange-Churión and Eduardo Mendieta attempt to broaden the perspective into this growing canon. See Pedro Lange-Churión and Eduardo Mendieta, eds., *Latin America and Postmodernity: A Contemporary Reader* (Amherst, NY: Humanity, 2001).
20. Adrienne Rich, *Blood, Bread, and Poetry: Selected Prose 1979–1985* (New York: Norton, 1986), 212.
21. For one of the most careful and insightful discussions on all of these questions see Jorge J. E. Gracia's seminal text, *Hispanic/Latino Identity: A Philosophical Perspective* (Malden, MA: Blackwell, 1999).
22. Edmundo O'Gorman, *The Invention of America: An Inquiry into the historical nature of the New World and the Meaning of its History* (Bloominton: Indiana University Press, 1961).
23. Note how this chronology differs from Jürgen Habermas's *The Philosophical Discourse of Modernity: Twelve Lectures* (Cambridge, MA: MIT Press, 1987), and how it is also guided by Anthony Gidden's formulations in *The Consequences of Modernity* (Cambridge: Polity, 1990). Compare also Enrique Dussel, *The Underside of Modernity: Apel, Ricoeur, Rorty, Taylor, and the Philosophy of Liberation* (Atlantic Highlands, NJ: Humanities, 1996), and "Beyond Eurocentrism: The World-System and the Limits of Modernity" in Fredric Jameson

and Maso Myoshi, eds., *The Cultures of Globalization* (Durham, NC: Duke University Press, 1998), 3–31.

24. Charles Taylor, *The Sources of the Self* (Cambridge: Harvard University Press, 1989) and *The Ethics of Authenticity* (Cambridge: Harvard University Press, 1992).
25. Jorge J. E. Gracia, *Hispanic/Latino Identity: A Philosophical Perspective* (Malden, MA: Blackwell, 1999).
26. Dussel, *The Underside of Modernity* (1996) and Dussel, "Beyond Eurocentrism" (1998).
27. Said, *Orientalism* (1978) and *Culture and Imperialism*, 1993.
28. Dussel, "Beyond Eurocentrism" (1998).
29. This entire discussion in guided and informed by the work of David Harvey. See Harvey, *Social Justice and the City* (Oxford, UK: Blackwell, 1975), *The Condition of Postmodernity* (Oxford/Cambridge: Blackwell,1989), and *Justice, Nature and the Geography of Difference* (Cambridge, MA: Blackwell, 1996).
30. Edward W. Soja, *Postmodern Geographies: The Reassertion of Space in Critical Social Theory* (London/New York: Verso, 1989).
31. I develop this interpretation of (post)modernity in my essays "Modernity and Postmodernity as Challenges to Discourse Ethics. An Ethics of Planetary Coresponsibility in an Age of Suspect Foundationalism and Rhetorical Relativism" in Amós Nascimento, ed., *A Matter of Discourse: Community and Communication in Contemporary Philosophies* (Brookfield, VT: Ashgate, 1997), 219–42; "Postmodernidad y Transmodernidad: una búsqueda esperanzadora del tiempo," *Universitas Philosophica* 27.14 (Diciembre 1996): 63–86; "The Geography of Utopia: Modernity's Spatio-Temporal Regimes," Spanish translation in *Cuadernos Americanos–Nueva Época* 67 (Enero–Febrero): 238–55; "The Othering of the Other: Santiago Castro-Gómez's Critique of Latin American Reason," *Dissens: Revista Internacional de Pensamiento Latinoamericano* 3 (1997): 117–23. Spanish in *Cuadernos Americanos* 11.6 (March–April 1997): 76–86; "Whose Modernity, Which Postmodernity? Latin America and the Crisis of the West," *Latino Review of Books* 2.3 (Winter 1996–97): 20–23. The philosophical framework is spelled out in Eduardo Mendieta, "Chronotopology: Critique of Spatio-Temporal Regimes" in Jeffrey Paris and Wilkerson William, eds., *New Critical Theory: Essays on Liberation* (New York: Rowman and Littlefield, 2001), 175–97.
32. Mendieta, "Chronotopology," and Soja, *Postmodern Geographies*, 1989.
33. Roland Robertson, *Globalization: Social Theory and Global Culture* (London: Sage, 1992), and "Globalisation or Glocalisation?" *Journal of International Communication* 1.1 (1994): 33–52.
34. Mendieta, "Whose Modernity, Which Postmodernity? Latin America and the Crisis of the West," *Latino Review of Books* 2.3 (1997): 20–23.
35. Beverley, et al., *The Postmodernism Debate in Latin America* (1995).
36. Niklas Luhmann, *The Differentiation of Society* (New York: Columbia University Press, 1982), and *La Ciencia de la Sociedad* (México: Anthropos, Universidad Iberoamericana, Iteso, 1996).
37. David Batstone et al., *Liberation Theologies, Postmodernity, and the Americas* (New York/London: Routledge, 1997).
38. Chantal Mouffe, ed., *Deconstruction and Pragmatism: Simon Critchley, Jacques Derrida, Ernesto Laclau and Richard Rorty* (London/New York: Routledge, 1996).

39. The seminal work to turn on this is Manuel Castells's three-volume theoretical and empirical tour de force, *The Information Age: Economy, Society and Culture* (Malden, MA: Blackwell, 1997). See also Nick Dyer-Witheford, *Cyber-Marx: Cycles and Circuits of Struggle in High Technology Capitalism* (Urbana/Chicago: University of Illinois Press, 1999).
40. Ulrich Beck, *Risikogesellschaft: Auf dem Weg in eine andere Moderne* (Frankfut am Main: Suhrkamp Verlag, 1986).
41. Manuel Castells, *The Information Age: Economy, Society and Culture* (Malden, MA: Blackwell, 1997).
42. Jean Baudrillard, *Simulacra and Simulation* (Ann Arbor: The University of Michigan Press, 1994).
43. Scott Lash and John Urry, *The End of Organized Capitalism* (Cambridge: Polity, 1987).

Chapter 4. Remapping Latin American Studies

1. Domingo Sarmiento, *Life in the Argentine Republic in the Days of the Tyrants, or Civilization and Barbarism* (New York: Hafner Library Classics, 1868).
2. Román de la Campa, *Latinamericanism* (Minneapolis: University of Minnesota Press, 1999).
3. Carl E. Pletsch, "The Three Worlds of the Division of Social Scientific Labor, circa 1950–1975," *Comparative Studies in Society and History* 23 (1981): 574.
4. Immanuel Wallerstein, "What Are We Bounding, and Whom, When We Bound Social Research?" *Social Research* 62.4 (1995): 839–56.
5. *Open the Social Sciences: Report of the Gulbenkian Commission on the Restructuring of the Social Sciences* (Stanford: Stanford University Press, 1996).
6. See *Open the Social Sciences*, 103–105.
7. Gayatri Chakravorty Spivak, *A Critique of Postcolonial Reason: Toward a History of the Vanishing Present* (Cambridge, MA: Harvard University Press, 1999).
8. Eric Wolf, *Europe and the People without History* (Berkeley: University of California Press, 1997).
9. Enrique Dussel, *Etica de la Liberación en la edad de la Globalización y la de la Exclusión* (Madrid: Editorial Trotta, 1998).
10. Jacques Derrida, *El Lenguaje y las instituciones filosoficas* (Barceolona: Ediciones Paidos, 1995).
11. See Walter Mignolo, *Global Designs, Local Histories* (Princeton: Princeton University Press, 2000); and Edgardo Lander, "Eurocentrism and colonialism in Latin American Social Thought," *Nepantla: Views from South* 1.3 (2001): 519–32.
12. See Franz Hinkelammert, *El Huracán de la Globalización* (San José: DEI, 1999); "El Proceso Actual de Globalización y los Derechos Humanos" in Joaquin Herrera Flores, ed., *El Vuelo de Anteo: Derechos Humanos y Crítica de la Razón Liberal* (Bilbao, España: Editorial Desclée de Brouwer, 2000), 117–28, and "La inversión de los derechos humanos: el caso de John Locke" in Herrera Flores, *El Vuelo de Anteo*, 79–114.
13. Spivak cited in Bart Moore-Gilbert, *Postcolonial Theory: Contexts, Practices, Politics* (London: Verso, 1997), 101.
14. Ibid., 102.

Chapter 5. The Emperor's Map

The title makes a reverential bow to two figures and forms of thought. First, to Jorge Luis Borges, and in particular to a fascinating vignette or quasi story, which appears in his collection *A Universal History of Infamy* (New York: Dutton, 1979 [1935]), which I will quote, since in quintessential Borgesian style, it is pithy but profoundly telling: "In that Empire, the craft of Cartography attained such Perfection that the Map of a Single providence covered the space of an entire city, and the Map of the Empire itself an entire Province. In the course of Time, these Extensive maps were found somehow wanting, and so the College of Cartographers evolved a Map of the Empire that was of the same Scale as the Empire that coincided with it point for point. Less attentive to the Study of Cartography, succeeding Generations came to judge a map of such Magnitude cumbersome, and, not without Irreverence, they abandoned it to the Rigors of sun and Rain. In the western Deserts, tattered fragments of the Map are still to be found, Sheltering an occasional Beast or beggar; in the whole Nation, no other relic is left of the Geographic Disciplines" (142, *translation slightly altered*). What Borges here calls the craft of cartography, which appears as one of the geographic disciplines, reminds me of the relationship between "globalization" and "metatheory." No matter how detailed our data about the "global" world, these "facts" and "statistics" only make sense within a theory about what is worth counting and documenting, correlating and mapping onto a graph. All of this, however, presupposes a metatheory about the direction of history, the flows of peoples, cultures, technologies, money, and ideas. One day, not too long from now, all that will remain of contemporary "geographic disciplines" will be the tattered and worn fragments of so many theories of globalization. The other point of reference is Franz Hinkelammert, who wrote a book in Spanish with the title *El mapa del Emperador: Determinismo, Caos, Sujeto* [*The Emperor's Map: Determinism, Chaos, Subject*] (San Jose, Costa Rica: Editorial Dei, 1996). Hinkelammert is a profoundly original and important Latin American thinker who has been writing about economy philosophically and theologically for the past thirty years. Hinkelammert has been dealing with neoliberal economy as both a philosophy and a theology, in which the old philosophemes of determinism, freedom, and the Cartesian, Lockean, Hobbesian, and Smithian economic and epistemic subject are given new mystifications and are fetishized to new levels of idolatry.

Chapter epigraph from Terry Eagleton, *Ideology: An Introduction* (London: Verso, 1991), 222–223.

1. For incisive analysis of these terms and their variegated uses see Manfred B. Steger, *Globalism: The New Market Ideology* (Lanham, MD: Rowman & Littlefield, 2002); see also Ulrich Beck, *What Is Globalization*? (Cambridge, UK: Polity, 2000).
2. See Walter Mignolo, "Latin American Social Thought and Latino/as American Studies" *APA Newsletter on Hispanic/Latino Issues in Philosophy*, 100.2 (Spring 2001): 105–12; Walter Mignolo, *Global Designs, Local Histories* (Princeton: Princeton University Press, 2000); and Walter Mignolo, "Are Subaltern Studies Postmodern or Postcolonial? The Politics and Sensibilities of Geo-Cultural Locations," *Subaltern Studies in the Americas*, special issue of *Dispositio/n*, ed. José Rabasa, Javier Sanjínes C., and Robert Carr, 19.46 (1994 [1996]): 45–71.
3. For a discussion of my use of chronotope and an extensive bibliography see Eduardo Mendieta, "Chronotopology: Critique of Spatio-Temporal Regimes" in

New Critical Theory: Essays on Liberation, Jeffrey Paris and William Wilkerson, eds. (New York: Rowman and Littlefield, 2001), 175–97.

4. Edward S. Said, *Orientalism* (New York: Vintage, 1979).
5. Octavio Ianni, *Enigmas de la modernidad-mundo* (Mexico: Siglo 21 editores, 2000), 76.
6. Samuel P. Huntington, *The Clash of Civilizations and the Remaking of the World Order* (New York: Simon and Schuster, 1996).
7. Arturo Ardao, *América Latina y la latinidad* (México: Universidad Nacional Autónoma de México, 1993).
8. This first type of Latinamericanism should be more properly demarcated by two dates: first, the pronouncement of the Monroe Doctrine in 1823, and, second, its institutionalization in 1948 with the founding of the Organization of American States. This type of *Kulturkampf* Latinamericanism, furthermore, should be seen as being internally punctuated by the 1910 Mexican Revolution. This revolution, which in Paz's words gave rise to modern Mexico and from which spring the romantic and historicist intellectual currents that have fueled most intellectual Latinamericanism, also registered in the United States imaginary, as was documented by John Reed's committed revolutionary journalism. See Robert A. Rosenstone's biography *Romantic Revolutionary: A Biography of John Reed* (New York: Knopf, 1975), especially chapter 10: "Mexico." See also Christopher P. Wilson, "Plotting the Border: John Reed, Pancho Villa, and *Insurgent Mexico*" in *Cultures of United States Imperialism*, Amy Kaplan and Donald E. Pease, eds. (Durham, NC: Duke University Press, 1993), 340–61. Yet, the revolutionary romanticism that the Mexican Revolution inspired in the left-leaning sectors of U.S. society was to be transferred over to Russia, and later to the Spanish anarchists.
9. José Enrique Rodo, *Ariel* (Austin: University of Texas Press, 1988).
10. José Martí, *Nuestra America* (Caracas, Venezuela: Biblioteca Ayacucho, 1977).
11. A very valid, nay necessary, question that this sentence raises is "which Europe?" At the risk of overextending my analysis in this chapter, I would claim that there is not one Europe, just as there is not one Latin America. Europe is an ideal, an idea, and an ideology. There have been many Europes, and their histories have either been erased or relegated to the dustbin of history, or they have become salient and orienting. One may talk about the Europe of the sixteenth century, with Spain as its colonial and imperial center, or the seventeenth-century Europe of the Netherlands, etc. The history of Europe can be written as the history of the succession of different imperial and colonial powers, with their respective series of civilizing missions. See Anthony Pagden, ed., *The Idea of Europe: From Antiquity to the European Union* (Cambridge, UK: Cambridge University Press, 2002). A classical study on this issue is Denys Hay, *Europe: The Emergence of an Idea* (Edinburgh: Edinburgh University Press, 1957).
12. Domingo Sarmiento, *Life in the Argentine Republic in the Days of the Tyrants, or Civilization and Barbarism* (New York: Hafner Library Classics, 1868).
13. Pedro Henriquez Ureña, *La Utopia de America* (Caracas, Venezuela: Biblioteca Ayacucho, 1978), 8–11.
14. Leopoldo von Ranke, *History of the Latin and Teutonic Nations (1494 to 1514)* (London: Bell, 1909 [1824]).
15. See Noam Chomsky et al., *The Cold War and the University: Toward an Intellectual History of the Postwar Years* (New York: New Press, 1997), especially Immanuel Wallerstein's contribution, pages 195–231.

16. Carl E. Pletsch, "The Three Worlds of the Division of Social Scientific Labor, circa 1950–1975," *Comparative Studies in Society and History* 23.4 (1981): 565–90.
17. Román de la Campa, *Latinamericanism* (Minneapolis: University of Minnesota Press, 1999); and Jean Franco, *The Decline and Fall of the Lettered City* (Cambridge, MA: Harvard University Press, 2002).
18. For work that develops this line of analysis see David Batstone, Eduardo Mendieta, Lois Ann Lorentzen, and Dwight N. Hopkins, eds., *Liberation Theologies, Postmodernity, and the Americas* (New York: Routledge, 1997).
19. For my use of "occidentalism" see Fernando Coronil, "Beyond Occidentalism: Toward Nonimperial Geohistorical Categories," *Cultural Anthropology* 11.1 (1996): 52–87.
20. The U.S. counterpart, and ideal dialogue partner, to this fourth type of Latinamericanism is what has been called the "New Americanists." These are a critical wing of American studies that has sought to redirect and restructure the way we study the cultures of the United States by deconstructing three types of absences, as Amy Kaplan elaborates them: "the absence of culture from the history of U.S. imperialism, the absence of empire from the study of American culture; and the absence of the United States from the postcolonial study of imperialism." Amy Kaplan, ""Left Alone with America" in *Cultures of United States Imperialism*. Amy Kaplan and Donald E. Pease, eds. (Durham, NC: Duke University Press, 1993), 3–21, quote at 11. This entire book should be read as the manifesto of the New Americanists.
21. Samuel P. Huntington, *The Clash of Civilizations and the Remaking of the World Order*, 304.
22. The reader should also consult the special issue of *Latin American Perspectives* on *Globalization and Globalism in Latin America: Contending Perspectives*, ed. Richard L. Harris, 127, 29.6 (November 2002).
23. See Hernando de Soto, *The Other Path: The Invisible Revolution in the Third World* (New York: Harper and Row, 1989), and his other recent bestseller *The Mystery of Capital: Why Capitalism Triumphs in the West and Fails Everywhere Else* (New York: Basic, 2000). For Cardoso's views, see the essay by Geisa Maria Rocha, "Neo-Dependency in Brazil," *New Left Review* 16 (July–August, 2002): 5–33. See also Theotônio dos Santos, "The Theoretical Foundations of the Cardoso Government: A New Stage of the Dependency Theory Debate" *Latin American Perspectives* 98, 25.1 (Nov. 1998): 53–70.
24. See David Rock, "Racking Argentina," *New Left Review* 17 (September–October, 2002): 55–86.
25. Rocha, "Neo-dependency in Brazil," 30–31.
26. On Lula's electoral win, see Kenneth Maxwell, "Brazil: Lula's Prospects," *New York Review of Books* 49.19 (December 5, 2002): 27–30.
27. Roland Robertson, "Globalization Theory 2000+: Major Problematics" in *Handbook of Social Theory*, George Ritzer and Barry Smart, eds. (London: Sage, 2001), 458–71.
28. Immanuel Wallerstein et al., *Open the Social Sciences: Report of the Gulbenkian Commission on the Restructuring of the Social Sciences* (Stanford: Stanford University Press, 1996).
29. John Urry, *Sociology beyond Societies: Mobilities for the Twenty-first Century* (London/New York: Routledge, 1999).
30. See Immanuel Wallerstein, *The End of the World as We Know It: Social Science for the Twenty-first Century* (Minneapolis/London: University of Minnesota

Press, 1999), and part 2 of his collected essays, Immanuel Wallerstein, *The Essential Wallerstein* (New York: New Press, 2000).

31. For a fascinating reading of the Zapatistas's theoretical break-through see Walter Mignolo, "The Zapatistas's Theoretical Revolution: Its Historical, Ethical, and Political Consequences," *Review* 25.3 (2002): 245

Chapter 6. Beyond Universal History

I would like to thank Linda Martín Alcoff, Santiago Castro-Gómez, and Martin Woessner for their insightful comments.

1. The classic statement of this insight is to be found in Marshall G. S. Hodgson's "In the Center of the Map: Nations See Themselves as the Hub of History" in Marshall G. S. Hodgson, *Rethinking World History: Essays on Europe, Islam, and World History*, ed. with an introduction and conclusion by Edmund Burke III (Cambridge: Cambridge University Press, 1993), 29–34. See also Lewis Martins and Kären E. Wigen, *The Myth of Continents: A Critique of Metageography* (Berkeley: University of California Press, 1997).
2. These words appear in Adrienne Rich, "Notes toward a Politics of Location" in *Blood, Bread, and Poetry: Selected Prose 1979–1985* (New York/London: Norton, 1986), 212.
3. The "West" is to be taken as signaling a set of representations and not a "real" geographical entity. One of the central themes of this chapter is precisely how the "West" comes to constitute its identity through the practices of historical representation. What I want to underscore is the need to question our practices of narrating the history of the world as a means to privileging certain ways of representing and constituting the "West" that at the same time entail the erasure of other geohistorical markers and entities. For a succinct but precise presentation of this issue see Thomas C. Patterson, *Inventing Western Civilization* (New York: Monthly Review, 1997).
4. See Karl Löwith, *Meaning in History* (Chicago: University of Chicago Press, 1949).
5. See Immanuel Wallerstein et al., *Open the Social Sciences: Report of the Gulbenkian Commission on the Restructuring of the Social Sciences* (Stanford: Stanford University Press, 1996), especially chapter 2.
6. See J. M. Blaut, *The Colonizer's Model of the World: Geographical Diffusionism and Eurocentric History* (New York/London: Guilford, 1992), especially the first two chapters. See also Samir Amin, *Eurocentrism* (London: Zed, 1989).
7. For the idea of "cluster of absences" see Bryan S. Turner, *Marx and the End of Orientalism* (London: Croom Helm, 1986), 81, quoted in Andre Gunder Frank, *ReOrient: Global Economy in the Asian Age* (Berkeley/Los Angeles/London: University of California Press, 1998), 17.
8. See Manfred Kossok, "From Universal History to Global History" in Bruce Mazlish and Ralph Buultjens, eds., *Conceptualizing Global History* (Boulder/San Francisco/Oxford: Westview, 1993), 93–111. See also Gilbert Allardyce, "Toward World History: American Historians and the Coming of the World History Course," *Journal of World History* 1.1 (1990), 23–76.
9. See William H. McNeill, *Mythistory and Other Essays* (Chicago/London: University of Chicago, 1986), chapter 6: "Lord Acton," 109–24.
10. See William McNeill, "Basic Assumptions of Toynbee's *A Study of History*" in *Mythistory and Other Essays*, 125–46.

11. See Arnold Toynbee, *The World and the West* (New York/London: Oxford University Press, 1953).
12. William H. McNeill, *The Rise of the West: A History of the Human Community* (Chicago: University of Chicago Press, 1963).
13. See William H. McNeill, "The Rise of the West after Twenty-five Years," *Journal of World History* 1.1:1–21. See also R. I. Moore, "World History" in Michael Bentley, ed., *Companion to Historiography* (London/New York: Routledge, 1997), 941–59.
14. My argument is similar to that made by Frederick Buell, although aimed at a different group of theorists, Buell argues acutely that globalization has become a nationalist postnationalist discourse. He writes: "I am taking the position that the demise of the nation has been greatly exaggerated and that the recent U.S. culture is characterized less by insurgent postnationalism (however much it is being invoked now by dissident-progressive cultural movements) than by the invention of a new breed of cultural nationalism—a form of cultural nationalism for postnational circumstances." "Nationalist Postnationalism: Globalist Discourse in Contemporary American Culture," *American Quarterly* 50.3 (September 1988): 548–91, at 550. I go further than Buell and argue that globalization has become the discourse of the West that replaces the already exhausted discourses on modernity/postmodernity. Still, Buell offers a historicization of the rise of discourses about globalization within American culture that is insightful and indispensable.
15. I think the proliferation of these discourses about globalization has reached already such levels of differentiation and complexity that we are in need of a typology. I have ventured such a typology in "Society's Religion: The Rise of Social Theory, Globalization, and the Invention of Religion," Dwight Hopkins, Lorentzen, Batstone, Mendieta, eds., *Religions/Globalizations* (Durham, NC: Duke University Press, 2001). There I have argued that theories of globalization can be divided into three types: (1) Monometastructural (like Wallerstein, Amin, Barber, etc.), (2) Matrix Rearrangement and Differentiation (like Robertson, Turner, and Appadurai), (3) Metatheoretical Reflexivity (Luhman, Münch, Clark). Given what I argue in the present chapter, I think that Dussel should be put under the third type of theories of globalization. Further, I find the typology offered by Held, McGrew, Goldblatt, and Perraton pedagogically useful but not perspicacious. See their impressive work *Global Transformations: Politics, Economics and Culture* (Stanford: Stanford University Press, 1999).
16. Richard J. Barnet and John Cavanagh, *Global Dreams: Imperial Corporations and the New World Order* (New York: Simon and Schuster, 1994). See also their nice summary of their work in Mazlish and Buultjens, eds., *Conceptualizing Global History*.
17. Benjamin R. Barber, *Jihad vs. McWorld: How Globalism and Tribalism Are Reshaping the World* (New York: Ballantine, 1995).
18. Barber, *Jihad vs. McWorld*, 24.
19. See his collection of essays epynomously subtitled after the classic essay "The Cultural Logic of Late Capitalism," *Postmodernism, or The Cultural Logic of Late Capitalism* (Durham, NC: Duke University Press, 1991).
20. Fredric Jameson, "Notes on Globalization as a Philosophical Issue" in Fredric Jameson and Masao Miyoshi, eds., *The Cultures of Globalization* (Durham, NC: Duke University Press, 1998), 54–77.
21. Arjun Appadurai, *Modernity at Large: Cultural Dimensions of Globalization* (Minneapolis: University of Minnesota Press, 1996).
22. Malcom Waters, *Globalization* (New York: Routledge, 1995).

23. Jürgen Habermas, *Die postnationale Konstellation: Politische Essays* (Frankfurt am Main: Suhrkamp Verlag, 1998), the essays under the second part: "Die postnationale Konstellation," two of which have already appeared in translations. "Aus Katastrophen lernen? Ein zeitdiagnostischer Rückblick auf das kurze 20. Jahrhundert" has appeared in *Constellations: An International Journal of Critical and Democratic Theory* 5.3 (September 1998): 307–20; "Zur Legitimation durch Menschenrechte" has appeared in *Philosophy and Social Criticism* 24.2/3 (April, 1998), 157–71.
24. Appropriately Habermas has circumscribed his reflections on globalization within the horizon of Europe's fate in light of European unification and the disintegration of the Soviet Union. At the same time, this is certainly disappointing in its narrowness. What is an otherwise brilliant phenomenological description of the physiognomy of modernity, turns into a hypostatization of Europe's experience of it. Compare Habermas's recent collection of *Kleine polistische Schriften*, his *Die Normalität einer Berliner Republik* (Frankfurt: Suhrkamp, 1995), and *Vergangenheit als Zukunft* (Zürich: Pendo-Verlag, 1990).
25. See Habermas, "Remarks on Legitimation through Human Rights," *Philosophy and Social Criticism* 24.3/4 (April 1998): 167.
26. See Niklas Luhmann, *Die Gesellschaft der Gesellschaft*, 2 vols. (Frankfurt am Main: Suhrkamp, 1997). See also his recently translated *Observations on Modernity*, trans. William Whobrey (Stanford: Stanford University Press, 1998).
27. Martin Albrow, *The Global Age: State and Society beyond Modernity* (Stanford: Stanford University Press, 1997). Albrow sees globalization as entailing the end of modernity, or of a particular type of discourse about society that we have come to associate with it.
28. Roland Roberton, *Globalization: Social Theory and Global Culture* (London: Sage, 1992).
29. See Robertson, *Globalization*, 25–31.
30. Robertson, *Globalization*, 100.
31. Robertson, *Globalization*, 130.
32. Here Robertson seems to be in agreement with some of the world-systems theorists like Wallerstein and Frank. Yet, the world system propounders connect the world-system to the emergence of capitalism in such a way that globalization is the imposition of a global capitalist system since 1492. Andre Gunder Frank has began to take distance from this capitalistic-eurocentric perspective. See Andre Gunder Frank and Barry K. Gills, "The Five Thousand Year World System" in Andre Gunder Frank and Barry K. Gills, eds., *The World System: Five Hundred Years or Five Thousand Years?* (New York: Routledge, 1993); see also Andre Gunder Frank, *ReOrient: Global Economy in the Asian Age*. A recent intervention in the discourse about a world-systems approach is the fascinating work by Robert P. Clark, *The Global Imperative: An Interpretative History of the Spread of Humankind* (Boulder: Westview, 1997). Whereas Wallerstein, Frank, and Amin write the history of the world system in terms of center-periphery, accumulation-expropriation, etc., Clark pivots his narrative around the notion of entropy.
33. Robertson, *Globalization,* 133.
34. The clear cases of self-conscious attempts at theorizing globalization in historical terms are the world-systems theorists as well as the Annales School historians: Wallerstein, Frank, as well as Braudel, Chaunu, and others.
35. Enrique Dussel, *Ética de la Liberación en la edad de globalización y de la exclusión* (Madrid: Editorial Trotta, 1998). See my review essay "Ethics for an Age of Globalization and Exclusion" in *Philosophy and Social Criticism* 25.2: 115–21.

36. Ulrich Beck, Anthony Giddens, and Scott Lash, *Reflexive Modernization: Politics, Tradition and Aesthetics in the Modern Social Order* (Stanford: Stanford University Press, 1994). See also Ulrich Beck, *Was ist Globalisierung? Irrtümer des Globalismus—Antworten auf Globalisierung* (Frankfurt: Suhrkamp, 1998). Note that this book appears in the series edited by Beck himself that carries the name of "Edition Zweite Moderne" (Second Modernity Edition).
37. See the excellent essay by Michael Geyer and Charles Bright, "World History in a Global Age," *American Historical Review* (October 1995): 1034–60. See also the introduction to Mazlinsh and Buultjens, *Conceptualizing Global History*, and Andre Gunder Frank, "A Plea for World System History," *Journal of World History* 2.1 (Spring 1991): 1–28.
38. See K.-O. Apel, "The Problem of Justice in a Multicultural Society: The Response of Discourse Ethics" in Richard Kearney and Mark Dooley, eds., *Questioning Ethics: Contemporary Debates in Philosophy* (London/New York: Routledge, 1999), and "Globalization and the Need for Universal Ethics" (Manuscript, 1998).
39. See Jürgen Habermas, *The Inclusion of the Other: Studies in Political Theory*, Ciaran Cronin and Pablo De Greiff, eds. (Cambridge: MIT Press, 1998), especially chapters 1, 3, 4, and 8, as well as the already-cited *Die postnationale Konstellation. Politische Essays.*
40. Enrique Dussel, *Ética de la Liberación en la edad de globalización y de la exclusión*, 21. All translations from this work are mine.
41. Dussel, *Ética de la Liberación en la edad de globalización y de la exclusión*, 621.
42. Ibid.
43. These arguments have been more extensively elaborated by Dussel in *The Underside of Modernity: Apel, Ricoeur, Rorty, Taylor and the Philosophy of Liberation*, ed. and trans. Eduardo Mendieta (Atlantic Highlands, NJ: Humanities, 1996). See also "Beyond Eurocentrism: The World System and the Limits of Modernity" in Jameson and Miyoshi, eds., *The Cultures of Globalization*, 3–31; and Enrique Dussel, *The Invention of the Americas: Eclipse of "The Other" and the Myth of Modernity*, trans. Michael D. Barber (New York: Continuum, 1995).
44. While the *Ética de la Liberación* contains the most succinct version of this Dusselian narrative, it is by no means the first time he has offered it. In fact, this history of ethicities has been a recurrent theme of Dussel's work. It begins with his earliest works, such as *El humanismo semita. Estructuras intencionales radicales del pueblo de Israel y otros semitas* (Buenos Aires: EUDEBA, 1969), this book was finished in 1964; *El dualismo en la antropología de la cristiandad. Desde los orígenes hasta antes de la conquista de América* (Buenos Aires: Ed. Guadalupe, 1974), this book was finished in 1968; *El humanismo helénico* (Buenos Aires: EUDEBA, 1975). This book was first written in 1961 and was published in 1975, but remained unavailable due to a censure by the Videla dictatorship. There is a wonderful collection of Dussel's essays on the topic of Latin America in world history and the elaboration of his notion of mythicoethical cores of civilizations: Enrique Dussel, *Oito Ensaios: Sobre cultura Latino-Americana e Libertacao*, trans. Sandra Trabucco Valenzuela (Sao Paulo: Paulinas, 1997). On the chronology of Dussel's works see his recent autobiographical essay, "Autopercepción intelectual de un proceso histórico," *Revista Anthropos: Huellas del Conocimiento* 180 (September–October, 1998): 13–36. This issue of the prestigious Spanish magazine *Anthropos* is dedicated to Dussel's work. See also Hans Schelkshorn, *Ethik der Befreiung: Einführung in die Philosophie Enrique Dussels* (Vienna: Herder, 1992).

45. See Roger Burbach, Olando Núñez, and Boris Kagarlitsky, *Globalization and Its Discontents: The Rise of Postmodern Socialism* (London: Pluto, 1996), especially chapter 1: "New World Disorder."
46. See the excellent collection by Jennifer Turpin and Lois Ann Lorentzen, eds., *The Gendered New World Order: Militarism, Development, and the Environment* (New York: Routledge, 1996).
47. See Samir Amin, *Capitalism in the Age of Globalization* (London/New York: Zed, 1996).
48. Cornel West, "The Moral Obligations of Living in a Democratic Society" in David Batstone and Eduardo Mendieta, eds., *The Good Citizen* (New York/London: Routledge, 1999), 6.
49. See Hans-Peter Martin and Harald Schumann, *The Global Trap: Globalization and the Assault on Prosperity and Democracy*, trans. Patrick Camiller (London: Zed, 1997), 1ff.

Chapter 7. Politics in an Age of Planetarization

Chapter epigraph is from Enrique Dussel, *Introducción a la filosofía de la liberación* (Bogotá: Editorial nueva américa, 1979), 198.

1. For biographical details see Dussel's autobiographical essay "Autopercepción intelectual de un proceso histórico," *Revista Anthropos* 180 (Sept.–Oct. 1998): 13–36; and the introduction to Linda Martín Alcoff and Eduardo Mendieta, eds., *Thinking from the Underside of History: Enrique Dussel's Philosophy of Liberation* (Lanham, MD: Rowman & Littlefield, 2000).
2. See in particular the essays gathered in Enrique Dussel, *América latina, dependencia y liberación* (Buenos Aires: García Cambeiro, 1974). As Dussel notes repeatedly throughout his magisterial five-volume ethics—*Para una ética de la liberación latinoamericana*, 3 vols., (Buenos Aires: Siglos 21, 1973), *Filosofía ética latinoamericana*, 4 (Bogotá: USTA, 1979), and *Filosofía ética latinoamericana*, 5 (Bogotá: USTA, 1980)—the challenge was not just the inappropriateness of the methods, which not only neglected but contributed to the exclusion of Latin American or, for that matter, all non-Western thought traditions, but also the lack of sources and materials. For this reason, Dussel's volumes on ethics contained lengthy reconstructions of what he calls Latin American pedagogic, erotics, politics, and archeology, each one dealing with a separate moment of the analectics. So, erotics deals with the analectical relationship between men and women; pedagogic, with the analectical relationship between parent and child; politics with the analectical relationship of brother to brother; and archeology, with the analectical relationships between cultures and worlds of meaning that have met and clashed in the so-called New World.
3. Enrique Dussel, *Para una ética de la liberación latinoamericana*, 3 vols. (Buenos Aires: Siglos 21, 1973).
4. Emmanuel Levinas, *Totality and Infinity: An Essay on Exteriority*, trans. Alphonso Lingis (Pittsburgh: Duquesne University Press, 1969).
5. Enrique Dussel and D. E. Guillot, *Liberación Latinoamericana and Emmanuel Levinas* (Buenos Aires, Editorial Bonum, 1975), 7.
6. Dussel, *Para una ética de la liberación latinoamericana*, 1973.
7. For a discussion of the philosophy of liberation see Horacio Cerutti, *Filosofía de la liberación latinoamericana* (México: FCE, 1983); and Hans Schelskorn, *Ethik der Befreiung. Eine Einführung in der Philosophie Enrique Dussels* (Freiburg:

Herder, 1992). Liberation philosophy is a heterogeneous current with figures as different as Bondy and Zea, and Scannone and Cerutti himself.

8. Eugen Kogon, *The Theory and Practice of Hell: The German Concentration Camps and the System behind Them* (New York: Berkeley, 1960).
9. For the following see Dussel, in particular volume 4 of the *Filosofía ética latinoamericana [Latin American Philosophical Ethics]* (Bogotá: USTA, 1979), as well as Enrique Dussel, *Introducción a la filosofía de la liberación* (Bogotá: Editorial nueva américa,1979), and *La producción teórica de Marx. Un comentario de los Grundrisse* (México: Siglo 21, 1985).
10. In the context of this chapter, I will not address the unsubstantiated and misleading criticisms that impute on Dussel's thinking an uncritical and slovenly nationalism and populism. It would take too long to demonstrate that Dussel's references to the nation, pueblo, and class, are overdetermined by contexts of relations vis-á-vis their hegemonic others. Thus, for instance, when Dussel refers to the symbolics of Latin American peoples (pueblos), which needs to be rescued and studied, he does so in light of the dominant national bourgeoisie whose orientation was toward Europe and whose ethos was industrial and military modernization. At the same time, however, Dussel realizes that a pueblo is neither homogenous nor historically stable. A people, as a people, also alterizes others, its others: women, indigenous populations, other ethnicities, etc. It is truly unfortunate how the readings and commentaries of certain scholars can totally derail the reception of a thinker, and this has been the sorry case of Enrique Dussel's so-called populism and fideism. For a discussion of some of these criticisms, see Linda Martín Alcoff's wonderful essay on Dussel and Foucault in Linda Martín Alcoff and Eduardo Mendieta, eds. *Thinking from the Underside of History: Enrique Dussel's Philosophy of Liberation* (Lanham, MD: Rowman and Littlefield, 2000); see also Michael D. Barber, *Ethical Hermeneutics: Rationalism in Enrique Dussel's Philosophy of Liberation* (New York: Fordham University Press, 1998).
11. Dussel, *La producción teórica de Marx. Un comentario de los Grundrisse* (México: Siglo 21, 1985); *Hacia un Marx desconcido. Un comentario a los Manuscritos del 61–63* (México: Siglo 21, 1988); and *El último Marx (1863–1882) y la liberación latinoamericana* (México: Siglo 21, 1990).
12. Ander Gunder Frank, *Latin America: Underdevelopment or Revolution* (New York: Monthly Review, 1970).
13. Emmanuel Wallerstein,. *The Capitalist World Economy* (Cambridge: Cambridge University Press, 1979); and Samir Amin, *Accumulation on a World Scale: A Critique of the Theory of Underdevelopment* (New York: Monthly Review, 1974).
14. The earliest, and already fairly substantive, formulations of the principles and structure of discourse ethics can be found in Karl-Otto Apel, *Transformation der Philosophie*, 2 vols., (Frankfurt: Suhrkamp, 1973), partly translated in Karl-Otto Apel, *Towards a Transformation of Philosophy*, trans. Glyn Adey and David Frisby (London: Routledge Kegan and Paul, 1980)) and Karl-Otto Apel, *Diskurs und Verantwortung. Das Problem des Übergangs zur postkonventionellen Moral* (Frankfurt: Suhrkamp, 1988).
15. Enrique Dussel, *Para una ética de la liberación latinoamericana*, 3 vols., (Buenos Aires: Siglos 21, 1973), *Filosofía ética latinoamericana,* vol. 4 (Bogotá: USTA, 1979), and *Filosofía ética latinoamericana,* vol. 5 (Bogotá: USTA, 1980).
16. Enrique Dussel, *La producción teórica de Marx. Un comentario de los Grundrisse* (México: Siglo 21, 1985); *Hacia un Marx desconcido. Un comentario a*

los Manuscritos del 61–63 (México: Siglo 21, 1988); and *El último Marx (1863–1882) y la liberación latinoamericana* (México: Siglo 21, 1990).

17. Enrique Dussel, *Ética de la Liberación en la edad de globalización y de la exclusión* (Madrid: Editorial Trotta, 1998).
18. See Eduardo Mendieta, "Ethics for an Age of Globalization and Exclusion," *Philosophy and Social Criticism* 25.2 (1999): 115–21, for an extended review of this work.
19. Enrique Dussel, *The Underside of Modernity: Apel, Ricoeur, Rorty, Taylor and the Philosophy of Liberation* (Atlantic Highlands, NJ: Humanities, 1996).
20. For a summary of the *Ethics of Liberation*, see Enrique Dussel, "Principles, Mediations and the 'Good' as Synthesis (From 'Discourse Ethics' to 'Ethics of Liberation')," *Philosophy Today* 41 (Supplement 1997): 55–66.
21. See Jürgen Habermas, *The Theory of Communicative Action*, 2 vols., trans. Thomas McCarthy (Boston: Beacon, 1984–1987); *The Philosophical Discourse of Modernity: Twelve Lectures*, trans. Frederick G. Lawrence (Cambridge, MA: MIT Press, 1987); *Moral Consciousness and Communicative Action*, trans. Christian Lenhardt and Shierry Weber Nicholsen (Cambridge, MA: MIT Press, 1990); and *Postmetaphysical Thinking: Philosophical Essays*, trans. William Mark Hohengarten (Cambridge, MA: MIT Press, 1992).
22. See Enrique Dussel, "Principles, Mediations and the 'Good' as Synthesis (From 'Discourse Ethics' to 'Ethics of Liberation')," *Philosophy Today* 41 (Supplement 1997): 55–66.
23. Enrique Dussel, *Philosophy of Liberation*, trans. Aquila Martinez and Christine Morkovsky (Maryknoll: Orbis, 1985).
24. Ibid.
25. Dussel, *The Underside of Modernity*, 1996.
26. Enrique Dussel, *1492 El encubrimiento del otro. Hacia el origen del mito de la Modernidad* (Madrid: Ed. nueva utopia, 1992).
27. As Dussel untiringly notes, what we call political science used to be called political philosophy, which in turn was another name for practical philosophy, or ethics. Politics, like economics, jurisprudence, aesthetics, and of course ethical philosophy, are the practical part of philosophy.
28. Dussel, *Ética de la Liberación en la edad de globalización y de la exclusion*, 1998.
29. Compare also with Pierre Bourdieu, *Pascalian Meditations* (Stanford: Stanford University Press, 2000).
30. See Franz Hinkelammert, *Crítica de la razón utópica* (San José, Costa Rica: DEI, 1990 [1984]).
31. Notwithstanding Dussel's criticisms of Rawls in the present text, as well as in the ethics of 1998, I think that Rawls's maximin principle is in accordance with this thesis. Freedom and participation in civil rights should be maximized as the adverse effects of all distributions of social goods is minimized for those most affected in the population. See John Rawls, *Theory of Justice* (Oxford: Clarendon, 1971).

Chapter 8. The Linguistification of the Sacred as a Catalyst of Modernity

I want to thank Santiago Castro-Gómez, Martin Matustik, Matthias Fritsch, and Reyes Mate for their comments on earlier versions of this chapter. I also want to thank the anonymous readers for Polity Press, whose suggestions substantively improved this text.

1. See Jürgen Habermas, "A Genealogical Analysis of the Cognitive Content of Morality" in his *The Inclusion of the Other: Studies in Political Theory* (Cambridge, MA: MIT Press, 1998), 3–46.
2. Albert Schweitzer, *The Quest for the Historical Jesus: A Critical Study of Its Progress from Reimarus to Wrede*, trans. W. Montgomery (London: Black, 1936), 1.
3. Theodor W. Adorno, *Negative Dialectics*, trans. E. B. Ashton (New York: Continuum, 1983), 365.
4. Michael Löwy, *Redemption and Utopia: Jewish Libertarian Thought in Central Europe: A Study in Elective Affinity*, trans. Hope Heaney (Stanford: Stanford University Press, 1992).
5. Gershom Scholem, *On Jews and Judaism in Crisis: Selected Essays*, ed. Werner J. Dannhauser (New York: Shocken, 1976), 287.
6. In addition to the already mentioned works, we need to add Michael Löwy, *On Changing The World: Essays in Political Philosophy, from Karl Marx to Walter Benjamin* (New Jersey/London: Humanities, 1992), and Reyes Mate, *Memoria de Occidente. Actualidad de pensadores judíos olvidados* (Barcelona: Editorial Anthropos, 1997).
7. See Anson Rabinbach, "Between Enlightenment and Apocalypse: Benjamin, Bloch and Modern German Jewish Messianism," *New German Critique* 34 (Winter 1985): 78–124. See also the extended discussion of the relationship between Jews and Germans in Richard Wolin's important book *Heidegger's Children* (Princeton: Princeton University Press, 2001), especially the first chapter "The German-Jewish Dialogue: Way Stations of Misrecognition."
8. See Löwy, *Redemption and Utopia*, 34.
9. See the excellent essay by Zygmunt Bauman, "Exit Visas and Entry Tickets: Paradoxes of Jewish Assimilation," *Telos* 77 (Fall 1988): 45–77.
10. Anson Rabinbach, "Between Enlightenment and Apocalypse," 87.
11. See Rudolf J. Siebert, *The Critical Theory of Religion: From Universal Pragmatic to Political Theology* (Berlin/New York/Amsterdam: Mouton, 1985). See also the short studies gathered in Wilhelm Schmidt, ed., *Die Religion der Religionskritik* (München: Claudius Verlag, 1972); Edmund Arens, Ottmar John, Peter Rottländer, *Erinnerung, Befreiung, Solidarität: Benjamin, Marcuse, Habermas und die politische Theologie* (Düsseldorf: Patmos Verlag, 1991); see also Edmund Arens, "Interruptions: Critical Theory and Political Theology between Modernity and Postmodernity" in David Batstone et al., *Liberation Theologies, Postmodernity, and the Americas* (New York: Routledge, 1997), 222–42.
12. See Rudolf J. Siebert, *Horkheimer's Critical Sociology of Religion: The Relative and the Transcendent* (Washington, DC: University Press of America, 1979), see also the excellent introduction to the Spanish translation of some of Horkheimer's writings on religion by Juan José Sánchez, in Max Horkheimer, *Anhelo de Justicia: Teoría crítica y religión*, edición de Juan José Sánchez (Madrid: Editorial Trotta, 2000).
13. The works of Rudolf Siebert, Michael Löwy, Reyes Mate, and José Mardones are substantive contributions in the direction of an exclusive study of the critique of religion by the Frankfurt School. While Siebert's is oriented toward philosophy and, in particular, Hegel's philosophy of religion, Löwy's is oriented toward the elective affinity of Judaism and libertarian utopianism in the early part of the twentieth century.
14. See the interview with Helmut Gumnior, "Die Sehnsucht nach dem ganz Anderen" in *Gesammelte Schriften*, vol. 7, 398.
15. Adorno, *Negative Dialectics*, 397.

16. Martin Jay, *The Dialectical Imagination: A History of the Frankfurt School and the Institute for Social Research 1923–1950* (Boston/Toronto: Little, Brown, 1973), xii.
17. See Löwy, *Redemption and Utopia*, 127. Lukács used the expression with reference to F. Dostoyevsky.
18. Scholem, *On Jews and Judaism in Crisis*, 46.
19. On Walter Benjamin's thinking from the standpoint of theology and Judaism see the following sources: Susan Buck-Morss, *The Origin of Negative Dialectics: Theodor W. Adorno, Walter Benjamin, and the Frankfurt Institute* (New York: Free Press, 1977), and her *The Dialectics of Seeing: Walter Benjamin and the Arcades Project* (Cambridge, MA: MIT Press, 1989); Peter Szondi, "Hope in the Past: On Walter Benjamin" *Critical Inquiry* 4.3 (Spring 1978): 491–506; Rolf Tiedemann, "Historical Materialism or Political Messianism? An Interpretation of the Theses 'On the Concept of History,'" *Philosophical Forum* 15.1–2 (Fall–Winter 1983–1984): 71–104; Christian Lenhardt, "Anamnestic Solidarity: The Proletariat and Its *Manes*," in *Telos* 25 (Fall 1975): 133–54. On Ernst Bloch, see Gerard Raulet, "Critique of Religion and Religion as Critique: The Secularized Hope of Ernst Bloch," *New German Critique* 9 (Fall 1976): 71–85; Richard H. Roberts, *Hope and Its Hieroglyphs: A Critical Interpretation of Ernst Bloch's Principle of Hope* (Atlanta: Scholars, 1989); and of course Jürgen Habermas's essays on both Walter Benjamin and Ernst Bloch in his *Philosophical-Political Profiles*, trans. Frederick G. Lawrence (Cambridge, MA: MIT Press, 1983).
20. Although one may argue that toward the end of his life, after his return to Germany, Max Horkheimer exacerbated his preoccupation and statements about religion. As my friend Martin Matustik suggested to me, there might be a correlation between Horkheimer's political conservatism and his religious mysticism. It is true that Horkheimer became almost virulently conservative. Some of his statements make him sound like a religious fundamentalist; for instance, he opposed the pill, abortion, and I suspect also the hedonism and libertinage of the New Left.
21. See the numerous aphorisms on religion, Christianity, Judaism, theology, and so on, in Max Horkheimer, *Dawn and Decline: Notes 1926–1931 and 1950–1969*, trans. Michael Shaw (New York: Seabury, 1978).
22. Max Horkheimer, "Theism and Atheism" [1963] in *Critique of Instrumental Reason*, trans. Matthew J. O' Connell et al. (New York: Continuum, 1974), 47–48. Now in *Gesammelte Schriften, Band 7: Vorträge und Aufzeichnungen 1949–1973*, Herausgegeben von Gunzelin Schmid Noerr (Frankfurt am Main: S. Fischer Verlag, 1985), 173–86.
23. Horkheimer, *Gesammelte Schriften*, Band 7, 276.
24. This has already been done in Spanish. See the wonderful collection of Max Horkheimer's writing on religion: Max Horheimer, *Anhelo de Justicia: teoría crítica y religión*, edición de Juan José Sánchez (Madrid: Editorial Trotta, 2000).
25. See Max Horkheimer, *Critique of Instrumental Reason*, 113; and *Gesammelte Schriften*, vol. 7, 387.
26. Horkheimer, *Dawn and Decline*, 239. Tellingly, this sentence written toward the end of his life is to be found in the section entitled "The Difference between Critical Theory and the Idea of Faith."
27. See Arnold Künzli, "Irrationalism of the Left" in Judith Marcus and Zoltán Tar, eds., *Foundations of the Frankfurt School of Social Research* (New Brunswick, NJ: Transaction, 1984), 133–54.
28. Walter Benjamin, *The Arcades Project*, trans. Howard Eiland and Kevin McLaughlin (Cambridge: Belknap, 1999), 471. In the citation format of the Passagen-Werk, N7a,7.

29. Theodor W. Adorno and Walter Benjamin, *The Complete Correspondence 1928–1940*, ed. Henri Lonitz, trans. Nicholas Walker (Cambridge, MA: Harvard University Press, 1999), 108.
30. Theodor W. Adorno, *Critical Models: Interventions and Catchwords*, trans. Henry W. Pickford (New York: Columbia University Press, 1998), 139.
31. See Adorno's discussion of the relationship between metaphysics and theology in his lectures from 1965. Theodor W. Adorno, *Metaphysics. Begriff und Probleme (1965) Nachgelassene Schriften. Band 14* (Frankfurt am Main: Suhrkamp Verlag, 1998), 9–22.
32. On Adorno and religion, see Rudolf J. Siebert, "Adorno's Theory of Religion," in *Telos*, 58 (Winter 1983–1984): 108–14; and Wayne Whitson Floyd Jr., *Theology and the Dialectics of Otherness: On Reading Bonhöffer and Adorno* (Lanham/New York/London: University Press of America, 1988)
33. Adorno, *Negative Dialectics*, 400.
34. Ibid., 401–402.
35. Adorno, *Critical Models*, 142.
36. Adorno, *Minima Moralia*, 98.
37. See "Something's Missing: A Discussion between Ernst Bloch and Theodor W. Adorno on the Contradictions of Utopian Longing" in Ernst Bloch, *The Utopian Function of Art and Literature. Selected Essays*, trans. Jack Zipes and Frank Mecklenburg (Cambridge, MA: MIT Press, 1988), 12.
38. Ibid, 16.
39. Ibid., 16.
40. See Reyes Mate, "Thinking in Spanish: Memory or Logos?" *Nepantla: Views from the South* 2.2 (Fall 2001), 274–64; see also chapter 3, "Dreaming up Solidarity: Feminist Witnessing and the Community of the *Ought to Be*" in Drucilla Cornell's *Legacies of Dignity* (New York: Palgrave, 2002).
41. See Edmund Arens, ed., *Habermas und die Theologie: Beiträge zur theologischen Rezeption, Diskussion und Kritik der Theorie kommunkativen Handelns* (Düsseldorf: Patmos Verlag, 1989); Edmund Arens, Ottmar John, Peter Rottländer, *Erinnerung, Befriung, Solidarität: Benjamin, Marcuse, Habermas und die politische Theologie* (Düsseldorf: Patmos, 1991); Edmund Arens, ed., *Kommunikatives Handeln und christlicher Glaube. Ein theologischer Diskurs mit Jürgen Habermas* (Paderborn: Ferdinand Schöningh, 1997); Helmut Peukert, *Science, Action, and Fundamental Theology*, trans. James Bohman (Cambridge, MA: MIT Press, 1984); Don S. Browning and Francis Schüssler Fiorenza, eds., *Habermas, Modernity, and Public Theology* (New York: Crossroad, 1992). See the following works for extended applications of Habermas's theories to theology: Paul Lakeland, *Theology and Critical Theory: The Discourse of the Church* (Nashville: Abingdon, 1990); and Jens Glebe-Moller, *A Political Dogmatic* (Philadelphia: Fortress, 1987).
42. See the works by Rudolf Siebert, which unfortunately remain hardly accessible because of their demanding Hegelian language.
43. See for instance, the essays gathered in *Habermas, Modernity, and Public Theology*, already cited above. See also Donald Jay Rothberg, "Rationality and Religion in Habermas's Recent Work: Some Remarks on the Relation between Critical Theory and the Phenomenology of Religion," *Philosophy and Social Criticism* 11 (1986): 221–46; Klaus-M Kodalle, "Zur religionsphilosophischen Auseinandersetzung mit Jürgen Habermas's 'Theorie des kommunikativen Handelns,'" *Allgemeine Zeitschrift für Philosophie.* 12 (1987): 39–66; Ludwig Nagl, "Aufhebung der Theologie in der Diskurstheorie? Kritische Anmmerkungen zur Religionskritik von Jürgen Habermas" in Herta Nagl-Doceckal, ed., *Ueber-*

lieferung und Aufgabe. Festschrift für Erich Heintel (Wien: Wilhelm Braumüller Verlag, 1982), 197–213; Anne Fortin-Melkevik, "The Reciprocal Exclusiveness of Modernity and Religion among Contemporary Thinkers: Jürgen Habermas and Marcel Gauchet" in Claude Geffré and Jean-Pierre Jossua, eds., *The Debate on Modernity: Concilium 1992.6* (London: SCM, 1992), 57–66.

44. I am refering to Habermas's statements of criticism against Jacques Derrida. See Jürgen Habermas, *The Philosophical Discourse of Modernity: Twelve Lectures*, trans. Frederick Lawrence (Cambridge, MA: MIT Press, 1987), 183–84, see also footnote 46, pages 406–407.
45. While it is neither necessary nor desirable that everyone who writes on contemporary philosophy write something that in one way or another faces up to the challenges of Habermas, it is indeed unfortunate that in otherwise superlative works like those of John D. Caputo and Hent de Vries no attempt was made to directly address Habermas's criticisms of Derrida's "athestic messianism and mysticism." See John D. Caputo, *The Prayers and Tears of Jacques Derrida: Religion without Religion* (Bloomington/Indianapolis: Indiana University Press, 1997), and Hent de Vries, *Philosophy and the Turn to Religion* (Baltimore/London: Johns Hopkins University Press, 1999).
46. Habermas, *The Philosophical Discourse of Modernity*, 406–407, note 46, last sentence.
47. Jürgen Habermas, *Postmetaphysical Thinking: Philosophical Essays*, trans. William Mark Hohengarten (Cambridge, MA: MIT Press, 1992), 15. Bold added, italics in original. Compare with what Habermas says in "The Unity of Reason in the Diversity of Voices" later in the same book, especially page 145.
48. See Robert C. Holub, *Jürgen Habermas: Critic in the Public Sphere* (London/New York: Routledge, 1991); Max Pensky, "Universalims and the Situated Critic" in Stephen K. White, ed., *The Cambridge Companion to Habermas* (Cambridge: Cambridge University Press, 1995), 67–94. Lewis Edwin Hann, ed., *Perspectives on Habermas* (Chicago/La Salle: Open Court, 2000). See also Martin J. Beck Matustik, *Jürgen Habermas: A Philosophical-Political Profile* (Lanham, MD: Rowman and Littlefield, 2001).
49. I have been aided in the following reconstruction by the outstanding study of José M. Mardones, *El Discurso religioso de la modernidad. Habermas y la religión* (Barcelona: Editorial Anthropos, 1998).
50. See Jürgen Habermas, "Concerning the Public Use of History," in *New German Critique* 44 (Spring/Summer 1988): 44. In German, see Jürgen Habermas, *Eine Art Schadensabwicklung* (Frankfurt am Main: Suhrkamp Verlag, 1987). See also "On the Public Use of History" in Jürgen Habermas, *The Postnational Constellation: Political Essays* (Cambridge, MA: MIT Press, 2001), 26–37.
51. Jürgen Habermas, *Theory and Practice*, trans. John Viertel (Boston: Beacon, 1973), 142–69.
52. Jürgen Habermas, *Toward a Rational Society: Student Protest, Science, and Politics* (Boston: Beacon, 1970), 92.
53. Habermas, *Toward a Rational Society*, 97.
54. Ibid., 98.
55. Ibid., 99.
56. Ibid., 99.
57. See the excellent work by Juan Luis Segundo, *The Liberation of Dogma: Faith, Revelation, and Dogmatic Teaching Authority*, trans. Phillip Berryman (Maryknoll, NY: Orbis, 1992). The original title *El Dogma Que Libera* was lost in translation. But the entire book is precisely about a tradition that instigates criticism in its very process of transmission.

58. Jürgen Habermas, *Legitimation Crisis*, trans. Thomas McCarthy (Boston: Beacon, 1975).
59. Ibid., 118.
60. Ibid., 120.
61. Habermas mentions Pannenberg, Metz, Moltmann, and Sölle, but one should also add Bloch, and Benjamin, who directly and deeply influenced this first generation of political theologians, See *Legitimation Crisis*, 121. See also Habermas's discussions with some theologians transcribed in Dorothee Sölle et al., *Religionsgespräche. Zur gesellschaftlichen Rolle der Religion* (Darmstadt und Neuwied: Hermann Luchterhand Verlag, 1975). See also the references to political theology in *Theorie und Praxis: sozialphilosophische Studien* (Frankfurt am Main: Suhrkamp Verlag, 1993), 418ff.
62. Ibid., 121. Italics in original. Compare with the following statement from Habermas's 1974 speech on the occasion of his receiving the Hegel Prize that is granted by the city of Stuttgart. "Gott kennzeichnet fast nur noch eine Kommunikationsstruktur, die die Teilnehmer nötigt, sich auf der Grundlage der gegenseitigen Anerkennung iherer Identität über die Zufälligkeit einer bloß äußeren Existenz zu erheben." *Zur Rekonstruktion des Historischen Materialismus*, 101. This speech was partly translated as "On Social Identity," *Telos* 19 (Spring 1974): 91–103.
63. Frankfurt am Main: Suhrkamp Verlag, 1976.
64. Published in English in Jürgen Habermas, *Communication and the Evolution of Society*, trans. Thomas McCarthy (Boston: Beacon, 1979), 95–129.
65. Ibid., 99.
66. Habermas, *Communication and the Evolution of Society*, 105.
67. Ibid., 121.
68. This is Karl Jasper's term. See his *The Origin and Goal of History* (New Haven: Yale University Press, 1957). For Jaspers the Axial Age represented a radical transformation in the relationship between humans and the cosmos, and humans and their own self-consciousness. During the Axial Age, humans became conscious of Being qua Being, but also of human consciousness. At once, humanity recognized its ability to comprehend everything, while simultaneously recognizing its own limitations. The most important aspect of this dual recognition is that universality became a normative ideal, that is, a standard but also a goal.
69. See in particular Jürgen Habermas, *Zur Logik der Sozialwissenschaften. Erweiterte Ausgabe* (Frankfurt am Main: 1985). This book originally appeared in 1970 but was later expanded in 1982. The English translation omits much of this text and focuses only on the second section of the German version, namely the section on hermeneutics.
70. Jürgen Habermas, *The Theory of Communicative Action*, vol. 1, *Reason and the Reationalization of Society*, trans. Thomas McCarthy (Boston: Beacon, 1984), 140.
71. See Jürgen Habermas, *The Theory of Communicative Action*, vol. 2, *Lifeworld and System: A Critique of Functionalist Reason*, trans. Thomas McCarthy (Boston: Beacon, 1987), 54. Note that this conceptualization of the differentiation of religious outlooks in terms of a differentiation of linguistic and verbal modes was already elaborated by Döbert in the early seventies. What differs, now, in Habermas's treatment is that this "linguistic" understanding is backed by a fullfledged "universal pragmatics," that is, a theory that describes language and reason in terms of validity claims, domains of action, and forms of rationality.
72. Ibid., 56.

73. Ibid., 60.
74. Readers of Habermas might be unfamiliar with the voluminous literature that makes these claims plausible and credible. A point of entry to the idea that the religious linguistifies and it is linguistified, see John Dominic Crossan's numerous books, in particular *In Parables: The Challenge of the Historical Jesus* (New York: Harper and Row, 1973), *The Dark Interval: Towards a Theology of Story* (Niles, IL: Argus, 1975), *The Cross That Spoke: The Origins of the Passion Narrative* (San Francisco: Harper and Row, 1988). For a comprehensive and systematic overview of the impact of the "linguistic turn" on bible studies, and religion in general, see The Bible and Culture Collective, *The Postmodern Bible* (New Haven: Yale University Press, 1995).
75. Habermas, *The Theory of Communicative Action*, vol. 2, 61.
76. Ibid., 77. This is a paraphrasing of the original German. See Jürgen Habermas, *Theorie des kommunikativen Handels. Band 2. Zur Kritik der funktionalistischen Vernunft* (Frankfurt am Main: Suhrkamp Verlag, 1981), 119.
77. Ibid., 77. Translation slightly altered. The original reads: "Die Aura des Entzückens und Erschreckens, die vom Sakralen ausstrahlt, die *bannende* Kraft des Heiligen wird zum *bindenden* Kraft kritisierbaren Geltungsansprüchen zugleich sublimiert und veralltäglicht," 119.
78. Ibid., 92. Compare with Marcel Gauchet, *The Disenchantment of the World: A Political History of Religion*, trans. Oscar Burge (Princeton: Princeton University Press, 1997). For Gauchet, the departure of the gods from the world means the turn inward. The otherness of the gods is replaced by the otherness that the aesthetic experience grants us. Religion is replaced by Art, the prophet by the artist, the priest by the cultural critic.
79. See Jacques Derrida, "Faith and Knowledge: The Two Sources of 'Religion' at the Limits of Reason Alone" in Jacques Derrida and Gianni Vattimo, eds., *Religion* (Stanford: Stanford University Press, 1998), 1–78.
80. Habermas, *Postmetaphysical Thinking*, 145.
81. See my book *Adventures of Transcendental Philosophy: Karl-Otto Apel's Semiotics and Discourse Ethics* (Lanham, MD: Rowman and Littlefield, 2002).
82. Jürgen Habermas, *Atenas y Jerusalem: Ensayos sobre Religion, Modernidad y Razón*, edited and with an introduction by Eduardo Mendieta (Madrid: Trotta, 2001).
83. Now in *The Future of Human Nature* (Cambridge, UK: Polity, 2003), which has the long essay on eugenics and the liberal state.
84. *Zwischen Naturalismus und Religion: Philosophischen Aufsätze* (Frankfurt am Main: Suhrkamp Verlag, 2005), section 2, tellingly entitled "Religious Pluralism and Civic Solidarity." Although there are other essays throughout sections 3 and 4 that deal with religion explicitly as well.
85. Professor Habermas allowed me to translate and include this essay in the volume I was editing at the time: "On the Relation between the Secular Liberal State and Religion" in Eduardo Mendieta, ed., *The Frankfurt School on Religion* (New York: Routledge, 2004), 339–48.
86. See, for instance Habermas's review of Rorty's book *Achieving Our Country*, in Jürgen Habermas, *Time of Transitions* (Cambridge, UK: Polity, 2006), 136–41.
87. Habermas, *Time of Transitions*, 138.
88. Richard Rorty, "Conversation as a Conversation-Stopper" in Richard Rorty, *Philosophy and Social Hope* (New York: Penguin, 1999), 168–74. This essay is a review of Stephen L. Carter's *The Culture of Disbelief: How American Law and Politics Trivialize Religious Devotion* (New York: Basic, 1993).
89. Rorty, *Philosophy and Social Hope*, 173.

90. See Richard Rorty, *Take Care of Freedom and Truth Will Take Care of Itself: Interviews with Richard Rorty*, edited and with an introduction by Eduardo Mendieta (Stanford, CA: Stanford University Press, 2006), 118. This comes from an interview I conducted with Rorty shortly after September 11, 2001.
91. A translation of this chapter has already appeared: Jürgen Habermas, "Religion in the Public Sphere," *European Journal of Philosophy* 14.1 (2006): 1–25.
92. Habermas, "Religion in the Public Sphere," 5.
93. Ibid., 5.
94. Ibid., 10.
95. Ibid., 17.

Chapter 9. Which Pragmatism? Whose America?

1. See Morris Dickstein, ed., *The Revival of Pragmatism: New Essays on Social Thought, Law, and Culture* (Durham, NC: Duke University Press, 1998); John Patrick Diggins, *The Promise of Pragmatism: Modernism and the Crisis of Knowledge and Authority* (Chicago/London: The University of Chicago Press, 1994); James Livingston, *Pragmatism and the Political Economy of Cultural Revolution, 1850–1940* (Chapel Hill/London: University of North Carolina Press, 1994); see also Richard J. Berstein, "The Resurgence of Pragmatism," *Social Research* 59.4 (Winter 1992): 813–40; and James T. Kloppenberg, "Pragmatism: An Old Name for Some New Ways of Thinking," *Journal of American History* 83.1 (June 1996): 100–38.
2. See Richard Rorty's *Philosophical Papers*, 3 vols. (New York: Cambridge University Press, 1991–1998), and most recently the afterword to his collection of essays *Philosophy and Social Hope* (New York: Penguin, 1999); for Richard Berstein, see his *Philosophical Profiles* (Philadelphia: University of Pennsylvania Press, 1986), and *The New Constellation: The Ethical-Political Horizons of Modernity/Postmodernity* (Cambridge, MA: MIT Press, 1992); for Nancy Fraser, see *Unruly Practices: Power, Discourse, and Gender in Contemporary Social Theory* (Minneapolis: University of Minnesota Press, 1989). See also the excellent discussion in Chantal Mouffe, ed., *Deconstruction and Pragmatism* (New York: Routledge, 1996), with essays by Simon Critchley, Jacques Derrida, Ernesto Laclau, and Richard Rorty.
3. Gayatri Chakravorty Spivak's monumental *A Critique of Postcolonial Reason: Toward a History of the Vanishing of the Present* (Cambridge, MA: Harvard University Press, 1999) establishes once and for all, irrevocably and unequivocally, in almost a manifesto fashion, the family relationship between postmodernism and postcolonialism.
4. On different versions of pragmatism, see James T. Kloppenberg, "Pragmatism: An Old Name for Some New Ways of Thinking?"
5. For an overview of Cornel West's place within American cultural life, see the informative and thoughtful piece by Robert S. Boynton, "The New Intellectuals," *Atlantic Monthly* (March 1995): 53–69. See also the special symposium on West's *The American Evasion of Philosophy* in *Praxis International* 13.1 (April 1993), with essays by Robert B. Westbrook, Garry M. Brodsky, Lorenzo C. Simpson, and a response by Cornel West.
6. L. S. Klepp, "Every Man a Philosopher King," *New York Times*, late ed., final. Sunday, December 2, 1990, magazine section, page 57ff.
7. New York: *Monthly Review*, 1991.

8. A fairly recent text on DuBois by Cornel West is again indicative of this uncompromising and unflinching self-criticism: see Henry Louis Gates Jr. and Cornel West, *The Future of the Race* (New York: Knopf, 1996).
9. Trenton, NJ: Africa World Press, and Grand Rapids, MI: Eerdmans, 1988.
10. New York: Routledge, 1993.
11. Boston: South End, 1991.
12. Madison: University of Wisconsin Press, 1989.
13. West, *The American Evasion of Philosophy*, 6.
14. Ibid., 36.
15. Ibid., 85.
16. Ibid., 169.
17. Richard J. Bernstein, "American Pragmatism: The Conflict of Narrative" in Herman J. Saatkamp Jr. *Rorty and Pragmatism: The Philosopher Responds to His Critics* (Nashville, TN: Vanderbilt University Press, 1995), 54–67. See also Thomas Bender and Carl E. Schorske, eds., *American Academic Culture in Transformation: Fifty Years, Four Disciplines* (Princeton: Princeton University Press, 1998), especially the pieces by Hilary Putnam and Alexander Nehamas.
18. Bernstein, "American Pragmatism," 55.
19. See Immanuel Wallerstein, *The End of the World as We Know It: Social Science for the Twenty-first Century* (Minneapolis: University of Minnesota Press, 1999); and Walter Mignolo, *Local Histories/Global Designs: Coloniality, Subaltern Knowledges, and Border Thinking* (Princeton: Princeton University Press, 2000).
20. See Cornel West, *Beyond Eurocentrism and Multiculturalisms*, vol. 1: *Prophetic Thought in Postmodern Times* (Monroe: Common Courage, 1993), 31–58, and "Pragmatism and the Sense of the Tragic" in *Keeping the Faith: Philosophy and Race in America*, 107–18.
21. West, *The American Evasion of Philosophy*, 233; West, "Religion and the Left" in *Prophetic Fragments*, 13ff.
22. Cornel West, *Race Matters* (Boston: Beacon, 1993), 19.
23. On the relationship between memory and hope, see the discussion in the introduction to David Batstone, Eduardo Mendieta, Lois Ann Lorentzen, Dwight N. Hopkins, eds., *Liberation Theologies, Postmodernity, and the Americas* (New York: Routledge, 1997), 15.
24. Richard Rorty, *Achieving our Country: Leftist Thought in Twentieth-Century America* (Cambridge, MA: Harvard University Press, 1998), 31.
25. Richard Rorty, "The Prophesor and the Prophet," *Transition* 52 (1991): 70–78, at 73.
26. See Cornel West, "Introduction" in *The Cornel West Reader* (New York: Basic, 1999), xviii–xix in particular.

INDEX